INSIDERS' GUIDE®

OFF THE BEATEN PATH® SERIES

Off the
SIXTH EDITION
Beaten Path®

west virginia

A GUIDE TO UNIQUE P

SU CLAUSON-WICKER

foreword by Senator Jay Rockefeller

INSIDERS' GUIDE®

GUILFORD, CONNECTICUT
AN IMPRINT OF THE GLOBE PEQUOT PRESS

The prices, rates, and hours listed in this guidebook were confirmed at press time. We recommend, however, that you call establishments to obtain current information before traveling.

To buy books in quantity for corporate use or incentives, call **(800) 962–0973, ext. 4551,** or e-mail **premiums@GlobePequot.com.**

INSIDERS' GUIDE®

Text design by Linda Loiewski
Illustrations by Carole Drong
Illustrations drawn from photos by Larry Belcher (p. 79) and by David E. Fattaleh (p. 160), courtesy of West Virginia Division of Tourism
Illustration on page 77 drawn from photo by Arnout Hyde Jr.
Illustration on page 102 drawn from photo by Thomas R. Fletcher
Illustrations on pages 87, 93, 98, 143, and 160 drawn from photos by Su Clauson-Wicker
Maps by Equator Graphics © Morris Book Publishing, LLC
Spot photography throughout © James Lemass/Superstock

ISSN: 1539-5715
ISBN 13: 978-0-7627-4218-9
ISBN 10: 0-7627-4218-6

Manufactured in the United States of America
Sixth Edition/First Printing

Contents

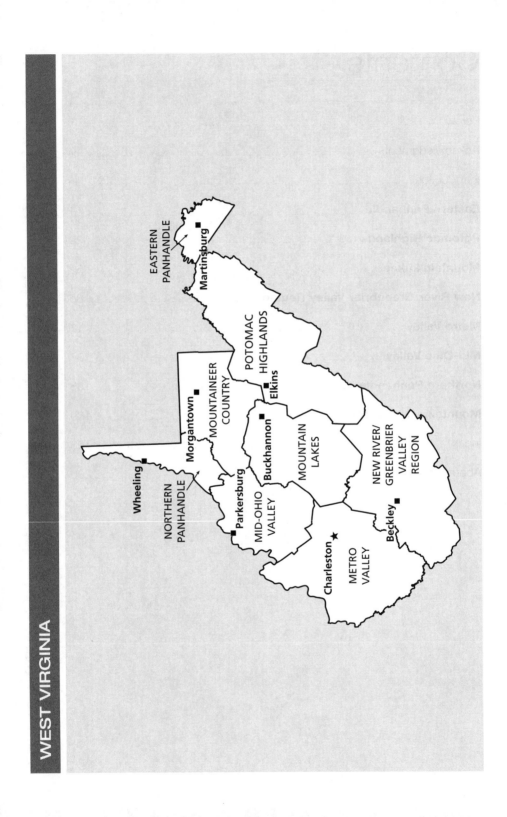

WEST VIRGINIA

EASTERN PANHANDLE
Martinsburg

POTOMAC HIGHLANDS

Morgantown
MOUNTAINEER COUNTRY

Elkins

Buckhannon

MOUNTAIN LAKES

NEW RIVER/ GREENBRIER VALLEY REGION

Wheeling

NORTHERN PANHANDLE

Parkersburg

MID-OHIO VALLEY

Charleston

METRO VALLEY

Beckley

Foreword

There is a definite magic, a sense of wonder and adventure and tradition, about traveling the hidden back roads of America. It is a soothing tonic for the daily stresses and distractions of our high-energy lifestyles. We seek relief and escape along these quiet country roads, while always seeking out an adventure around the next bend.

My home state of West Virginia has history and heritage almost guaranteed to provide travelers with the ultimate off-the-beaten-path experience. Our rugged mountains, wild rivers, lush valleys, and warm, welcoming people are a prescription for "getting away from it all." With fewer than 1.8 million people living in towns and communities spread across more than 24,000 square miles, the Mountain State has seemingly limitless places to explore and enjoy.

In the pages that follow, you'll be introduced to scores of overlooked sights, sounds, tastes, and personalities that collectively offer a glimpse into the West Virginia experience. You'll travel from the hauntingly beautiful hollows of the southern coalfields to the aristocratic colonial pathways of the Eastern Panhandle. You'll experience the powerful natural magnificence of the New River Gorge and the simple, easy charms of quiet country inns. You'll hike the backcountry of the pristine Cranberry Wilderness and stroll beneath the gaslight lamps of Victorian Wheeling.

My guess is that you will come away as struck by West Virginia's wondrous beauty and relaxing pace of life as I did some thirty years ago, when I first came to the state as a VISTA worker.

Naturally, West Virginia has changed a lot in that time. Modern interstate highways, a growing tourism industry, and new economic development attract millions of visitors to our state each year. While we may not be "undiscovered" any longer, there are more hidden natural and cultural gems woven into the Appalachians than you could get to in endless weekends.

I hope you will use *West Virginia Off the Beaten Path* to lead you to some of the truly rare American riches found within these borders. It will be time well spent and a travel experience far removed from everyday life, restful and soothing and thick with history, hospitality, natural beauty, and adventure.

—Senator Jay Rockefeller

Acknowledgments

I'd like to express my indebtedness to the first authors of *West Virginia Off the Beaten Path,* Stephen and Stacy Soltis, whose lively prose and vivacious spirits blazed an exhilarating path to follow in our mutual mining of the hidden and not-so-hidden treasures of the Mountain State. Thank you for the standards; thanks for the zest.

I'd also like to thank scores of friends and colleagues throughout West Virginia for their insight, knowledge, kindness, encouragement, and hospitality. I am especially indebted to: Jack Thompson of Morgantown/Preston Convention and Visitors Bureau, Tony O'Leary and Matt Turner of West Virginia Tourism, Todd Gillespie of Stonewall Resort, Catherine Miller, Chris and Mary Lou Harnett, Angela Harding, Myra Bonhage-Hale and Amy Kaczynski of Greenbrier Convention and Visitors Bureau, Kari Thompson of Parkersburg Convention and Visitors Bureau, Kay Fanok of Historic Morgan, Nan Morgan of General Lewis, and Senator Larry Rowe of Malden, who showed up with the key for the locked gate to the Booker T. Washington Homeplace just as I was preparing to climb the fence. And thanks to my husband Bruce Wicker and dear friend Susan Kwilecki for their great interest, patience, and assistance in identifying the good stories to tell. A heartfelt thanks to all.

Introduction

While the populace of some parts of the country wax poetic about the notion of "a sense of place," West Virginians, by comparison, seem to take theirs for granted. West Virginians may chafe to get back to the Mountain State should they take a job in the flatlands, but they are never ones to inflict their "West Virginianess" on others. Unenlightened outsiders may argue that West Virginians have to adopt this stance; after all, there isn't much to romanticize in this impenetrable land of "hillbillies, moonshiners, and bloodletting coal miners."

West Virginians know perfectly well—as do most visitors who actually get off the interstate—that the tiresome stereotypes are bunk. West Virginians are about the most friendly and most helpful people you'll find. They live in a state that can claim one of the lowest crime rates in the nation and the lowest cost of living. Their state is not only beautiful, but in many spots it's awe-inspiringly gorgeous.

In fact, West Virginia may have the most intense sense of place to be found anywhere in the United States. Wedged between the bustling megalopolis of the eastern seaboard and the industrial corridors of the Midwest, West Virginia—thanks to a rugged terrain—has remained lightly populated and overwhelmingly pastoral in character. Yes, it's more rustic than its neighbors, but it's also greener, more relaxed, and refreshingly more informal.

The late CBS television correspondent Charles Kuralt once said he could have spent all his time in West Virginia—there are that many interesting stories here. This book is an attempt to get travelers to those stories—to the little town that still burns Old Man Winter in the Swiss tradition, to the bejeweled Hare Krishna temple and the "haunted" state prison, to road bowling at the Irish Spring Festival, to bungee jumping at New River Bridge Day.

West Virginia is a small state with distinctive divisions: some historical, some geographical, some cultural, and some social. The Eastern Panhandle, which reaches east to within an hour's drive of the nation's capital—and is also closer to five other state capitals than its own—is more aligned with the urban lifestyle of Northern Virginia than it is with other parts of West Virginia. On the other hand, residents of the industrialized Northern Panhandle consider themselves northerners, while those in southern and central West Virginia are decidedly southern. In the Ohio Valley, many sound and think like midwesterners.

West Virginia Off the Beaten Path begins in the Eastern Panhandle. From here, we make a clockwise swirl around the state. Sometimes you have to backtrack to see everything, but it's well worth the effort.

A word of explanation is needed here about the dining and lodging pricing key used in this book. Prices in these mountains can seem ridiculously inexpensive to an urbanite. In West Virginia, you can still find respectable hotel rooms for $40 a night, bed-and-breakfast stays for under $70, and entrees for $7.00. Sure, you'll find higher prices in some of the cities and most of the Eastern Panhandle, but in general costs are a little lower than elsewhere.

Our pricing range reflects this. This guide will give you an indication of what you can expect to pay for the average main entree: under $7.00 is considered budget; $7.00–$15.00 is inexpensive; $15.00–$24.00 is moderate, and more than $24.00 is expensive.

When it comes to lodging (for a standard double, excluding room tax), anything under $50 is considered budget; $50–$74 is inexpensive; $75–$109 is moderate; $110–$175 is expensive, and anything over $175 is very expensive.

West Virginia at a Glance

- **Nickname:** the Mountain State
- **Admitted to the Union** in 1863 after breaking from Virginia in 1861
- **Capital:** Charleston
- **Principal cities:** Charleston, Huntington, Wheeling, Parkersburg, Morgantown
- **Population:** 1.8 million
- **Land area:** 24,181 square miles
- **Climate:** Average statewide daily minimum temperature: January—28° F; average daily maximum temperature July—85° F. Winters can be severe in the Potomac Highlands and Allegheny Plateau, but summers here are free of the humidity that occasionally oppresses the Eastern Panhandle and the Ohio Valley
- **Major newspapers:** *Charleston Daily Mail, Charleston Gazette, Huntington Herald Dispatch, Wheeling Intelligencer, Parkersburg News & Sentinel*
- **Motto:** Mountaineers Are Always Free
- **State bird:** cardinal
- **State fish:** brook trout
- **State flower:** rhododendron
- **State tree:** sugar maple
- **Famous natives:** novelist Pearl S. Buck; Confederate general Thomas "Stonewall" Jackson; actor Don Knotts; pilot Chuck Yeager; diplomat Cyrus Vance; Nobel Prize winner John Forbes Nash Jr.
- **State Division of Tourism:** (800) CALL–WVA; www.callwva.com

Eastern Panhandle

The Eastern Panhandle, shaped somewhat like the head of a perched eagle, is West Virginia's easternmost region, and as such bears close association with neighboring Maryland and Virginia and even suburban Washington, D.C.

The three-county region is defined by its historic sites, springs and spas, and the Potomac River, which provides the northern border for the area. The far-western portion of the Panhandle (Morgan County) is mountainous and relatively isolated, while the central and eastern sections (Berkeley and Jefferson Counties) roll alongside the gentle terminus of the Blue Ridge Mountains and are pocketed with numerous small towns and a wealth of historical and cultural attractions.

Despite the fact that it's the state's most widely visited region, the Eastern Panhandle still offers an exhaustive array of hidden and unsung treasures. For first-time visitors to West Virginia, this is a good primer trip and a logical starting point if you're coming from the east.

The Shenandoah Valley

The fabled Shenandoah Valley, imprinted on the American psyche through song, stage, and screen, is more synonymous with

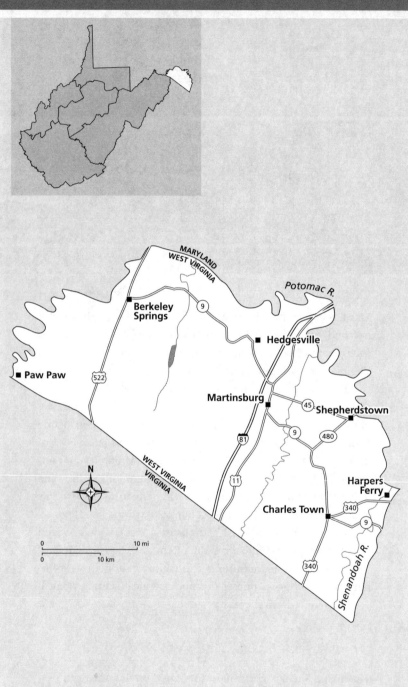

neighboring Virginia than West Virginia. There's no doubt about it, though, this historic and fertile valley rolls north into the Mountain State along with its namesake river, claiming all of Jefferson County and part of Berkeley County. Also known as the Valley of Virginia, the Shenandoah is one of several geographic entities that make up the Great Valley, a massive, erosion-carved trench stretching from south-central Pennsylvania to northeastern Tennessee. The Great Valley was a major southern migration route for Pennsylvania's Scots-Irish and German settlers, brave and industrious pioneers who lived close to the land, tapping its rich soil for crops and dense hardwood forests for shelter, furniture, and farm implements.

West Virginia's swath of the Shenandoah (a Native American term meaning "Daughter of the Skies") is an important agricultural region and a mecca for artisans, writers, cottage-industry entrepreneurs, retirees, and weekend retreaters from nearby urban areas.

This is a land deeply proud of its colonial history and colorful folklife, evidenced by such huge fetes as the Mountain Heritage Arts and Crafts Festival, held each spring and fall outside Harpers Ferry. The laid-back valley is conducive to relaxation, whether it is a lazy day of floating on the Shenandoah River or unwinding at the Charles Town Races, where thoroughbred horses have been going neck and neck since 1786.

BEST ANNUAL EVENTS IN THE EASTERN PANHANDLE

Winter Festival of the Waters
Berkeley Springs; January
through March
(304) 258–9147, (800) 447–8797
www.berkeleysprings.com

**Mountain Heritage Arts
and Crafts Festivals**
Charles Town; mid-June
and late September
(304) 725–2055, (800) 624–0577

**Contemporary American
Theater Festival**
Shepherdstown; last three weeks of July
(304) 876–3473, (800) 999–CATF

Apple Butter Festival
Berkeley Springs; second weekend
in October
(304) 258–3738, (800) 447–8797
www.berkeleysprings.com

**Mountain State Apple
Harvest Festival**
Martinsburg; mid-October
(304) 263–2500, (800) 498–2386

Christmas in Shepherdstown
Charles Town and Harpers Ferry;
late November through December
(800) 848–TOUR, (304) 876–2786

Above all this is a land of immense natural beauty. It was on the way back from a trip to Jefferson County that the late John Denver joined with songwriter Bill Danoff to pen the words to "Country Roads," an international recording hit that begins with the classic line "Almost heaven, West Virginia." These men knew the Mountain State.

At 247 feet above sea level, **Harpers Ferry** is the lowest point in the Mountain State. It's also West Virginia's easternmost city, wedged in the foothills of the Blue Ridge Mountains between Maryland and Virginia.

Harpers Ferry's 300 or so residents live less than an hour's drive from the suburbs of Washington, D.C., a blessing or a curse depending on to whom you talk. With urbanization slowly creeping westward, it seems fitting that this postcard village at the confluence of the Shenandoah and Potomac Rivers is the headquarters of the **Appalachian Trail Conservancy (ATC),** a more-than-eighty-year-old, nonprofit conservation group dedicated to maintaining and preserving the natural character of the 2,174-mile-long Appalachian National Scenic Trail. The celebrated foot trail, running from Springer Mountain, Georgia, to Mount Katahdin, Maine, was blazed by the ATC along the crests of the Appalachian Mountains in the 1930s, with help from several federal and state agencies and the Civilian Conservation Corps, the Depression-era organization responsible for developing many of our national parks.

eastern panhandle trivia

The town of Harpers Ferry consistently attracts the greatest number of visitors of any West Virginia attraction each year.

Today about two-thirds of the American population lives within 500 miles of this strip of mountain wildness. Harpers Ferry is situated near the halfway mark on the trail, and as such it is a natural gathering and refueling point for backpack-toting hikers. Much of the ATC's work is centered on ensuring that there is plenty of green buffer land for the tens of thousands of hikers who take to the trail each year, a mission that's backed by a major lobbying presence in the nation's capital. If you've ever stepped foot on the Appalachian Trail, or even just thought about it, make sure to pay homage at its headquarters in the cottagelike structure located on Washington Street. Inside you'll find interesting displays explaining the history and dynamics of the trail; a host of books, maps, posters, shirts, hats, and other hiking accessories; as well as information about volunteering and ATC programming. The headquarters, on 799 Washington Street, is open Monday through Friday from 9:00 A.M. to 5:00 P.M. It is open weekends mid-May through October from 9:00 A.M. to 4:00 P.M. Call (304) 535–6331 for more information.

BEST ATTRACTIONS IN THE EASTERN PANHANDLE

**Harpers Ferry National
Historical Park**
Harpers Ferry
(304) 535–6298
www.nps.gov/hafe

Cacapon Resort State Park
Berkeley Springs
(304) 258–1022 or (800) CALL–WVA
www.cacaponresort.com

**Coolfont Resort, Spa and
Conference Center**
Berkeley Springs
(304) 258–4500 or (800) 888–8768
www.coolfont.com

Charles Town Race Track
Charles Town
(304) 725–7001 or (800) 795–7001
www.clownraces.com

John Brown Wax Museum
Harpers Ferry
(304) 535–6342

O'Hurley's General Store
Shepherdstown
(304) 876–6907

A short walk up the hill from ATC headquarters (follow the signs on Washington Street) is *Hilltop House,* an old, unpretentious mountain inn that straddles a rocky bluff overlooking the shallow and fast-moving Potomac River. The place exudes charm, from the creaky wooden floors of the lobby to a partial fieldstone exterior dating from 1888. The Hilltop was built (and rebuilt) by Thomas Lovett, an African American with a great dream of owning a hotel in the town where John Brown was martyred. Lovett saw his first two hotels burn on the site before the 1920s, but he rebuilt each time. Over the years Hilltop has provided respite for Alexander Graham Bell, Mark Twain, Pearl S. Buck, and Woodrow Wilson, among others. The river and mountain vistas alone are worth a night's stay, but take at least a couple of days if for no other reason than to enjoy the inn's hearty regional fare, which includes famous Hilltop House fried chicken, jumbo lump crab cakes, smoked trout, and filet mignon. The dining-room menu, depending on the chef's temperament and the time of year, may also include such dishes as duck crepes with spicy plum sauce and veal piccata.

Hilltop's sixty-six rooms range from comfortable no-frills to an apartment-size top-floor suite with spectacular picture-window views and a Jacuzzi. Located across the street, but part of the property, is *The Old Stone Lodge,* a nineteenth-century landmark that doubles as a meeting room. A modern annex provides motel-style lodging. Room and dining rates are moderate for the metropolitan area. For reservations call (800) 338–8319.

From Hilltop you're maybe a five-minute walk to the center of the restored village, virtually all of which is contained in the *Harpers Ferry National Historical Park.* This is the single largest tourist draw in West Virginia. Although not exactly off the beaten path, a stroll through the National Park Service area is strongly advised for American history buffs, for it was here in 1859 that abolitionist John Brown raided the federal armory and arsenal in an attempt to seize guns and munitions needed for his planned slave rebellion. Although the raiders were ultimately apprehended by U.S. Marines under the command of a young Robert E. Lee, the action nevertheless was an important catalyst in the growing division over slavery—an issue that ultimately split open the nation with the advent of the Civil War. Here too are sights of special interest in African-American history. Storer College held the 1906 meeting of the Niagara Movement that led to the founding of the NAACP.

A good place to begin touring the town (named after an early settler who operated a ferry service) is at the park service's information center on Shenandoah Street. Rangers answer questions and distribute orientation maps that lead to such sites as the Harpers Ferry Armory fire-engine house, which is at the corner of High and Shenandoah Streets near the main-line tracks of the Baltimore & Ohio Railroad, and which served as the abolitionists' fort. Across the street the *John Brown Museum* chronicles Brown's raid, capture, trial, and hanging in neighboring Charles Town. Up yet another hill, this one overlooking the Shenandoah, stands *St. Peter's Catholic Church,* a gorgeous stone chapel built in 1830 and used continuously until its closing in 1994. A few steps away is the famous *Jefferson Rock,* a granite outcropping with a stunning, three-state view of the Blue Ridge Mountains and the merging rivers. Thomas Jefferson, who helped survey the area as a young man, sat upon the rock and wrote "the scene is worth a voyage across the Atlantic." The National Park Service facilities are open daily year-round (except Christmas) from 8:00 A.M. to 5:00 P.M. and from Memorial Day to Labor Day until 6:00 P.M. There are parking and walk-in fees, payable at the Cavalier Heights Visitor Center on U.S. Highway 340. A free shuttle bus service transports visitors to the park area. For more information, call (304) 535–6298.

Whether you're meandering through Harpers Ferry's peaceful hills or crowded streets and alleyways, it's impossible to escape the presence of the Shenandoah and Potomac Rivers. The Potomac, while on its 400-mile journey to the Chesapeake Bay from its source spring in Tucker County, West Virginia (see next chapter on the Potomac Highlands), takes on a wild-and-scenic demeanor as it flows through Harpers Ferry, churning up white water as it glides over limestone ridges and rocks. The same can be said of the Shenandoah, the northward-flowing river that ends its 150-mile path from Rockingham

County, Virginia, with a gentle white-water display that attracts anglers and rafters in droves. Harpers Ferry, you might remember, was the scene of devastating floods during the winter of 1996, when both the Shenandoah and Potomac crested at historically high levels. The flood damage, while extensive at the time, is now a mere memory. The Park Service Visitor Center, however, captures the catastrophe in great detail through a number of exhibits.

Fishing, tubing, canoeing, kayaking, and rafting trips can be organized on both rivers through **Blue Ridge Outfitters,** located about 2 miles south of Harpers Ferry off US 340 on Frontage Road. A best bet for an intermediate-level white-water experience is to canoe the Shenandoah Staircase, a 6-mile outing with several sets of Class I to III rapids (VI is the most advanced) and a few long stretches of flat water for fishing. The float ends with a dramatic entrance into the Potomac Watergap at Harpers Ferry. Most float trips, whether by raft, kayak, canoe, or ducky (an inflatable boat for two), embark daily from mid-May through October 31. Outfitting fees are moderate; phone reservations should be made by credit card. Call (304) 725–3444 or see www.broraft.com for more information.

West Virginia contains a treasure trove of offbeat museums, and one of the most unusual is **Harpers Ferry Toy Train Museum,** located 2 miles west of town on Bakerton Road just off US 340. Be prepared for a nostalgic trip back to childhood as you browse through the museum's large assortment of antique Lionel standard-gauge and O-gauge trains and accessories, most of them predating 1939. This was the personal collection of the late Robert E. Wallich, who in 1970 decided to share his sixty-year avocation with the public. The first Harpers Ferry Toy Train Museum was located in downtown Harpers Ferry and housed in a vintage Western Maryland Railroad baggage car. A few years later Wallich constructed an outdoor miniature railroad on his property in the outlying hills and

OTHER ATTRACTIONS WORTH SEEING IN THE EASTERN PANHANDLE

Berkeley Springs State Park
Berkeley Springs

DeFluri's Fine Chocolates Factory
Martinsburg

Homestead Farms Equestrian Center
Martinsburg

Opera House Theatre
Shepherdstown

**Shepherdstown Farmers'
Sunday Market**
Shepherdstown

Summit Point Speedway
Summit Point

eventually moved the museum to the same site. Wallich's son and grandson now run the museum and Joy Line Miniature Railroad, a train ride that's driven by a Cagney steam locomotive and appears to attract as many adults as kids. The museum is open April through October on Saturday, Sunday, and major holidays from 9:00 A.M. to 5:00 P.M. A small admission fee is charged. Special appointments for parties can be made any time of year. Call (304) 535–2291.

If you're spending the night in town, a Harpers Ferry Ghost Tour led by Shirley Dougherty or her granddaughter is a must-do. You'll gain a darker perspective on Harpers Ferry history as you wander the streets by lantern light, under the spell of a true storyteller. For reservations, call (304) 725–8019 May 30 through November 2.

As you leave Harpers Ferry en route to Charles Town on US 340, about a 5-mile trip, the landscape begins to open up, revealing rolling pastures and low, sloping mountains that form the outline of the Shenandoah Valley. *Charles Town,* the seat of Jefferson County, sits in the heart of the West Virginia portion of the valley. The city was incorporated in 1787 and named in honor of George Washington's youngest brother, Charles, a major landowner in the Eastern Panhandle. Charles Washington donated eighty acres to the burgeoning village and was charged with laying out its original streets—George, Samuel, Lawrence, Mildred, and Charles—dutifully named after Washington family members. Not surprisingly, Charles Town's main thoroughfare is Washington Street. The city's current population of just over 3,500 is projected to increase as it acclimates to its newfound status as an exurb of metro Washington, D.C.

While in town buy a postcard and have it mailed from the *Charles Town Post Office,* 101 West Washington Street. This is where the Honorary William L. Wilson, Charles Town native and U.S. postmaster general, started the nation's first rural free delivery, or RFD, in 1896. On this site also stood the town jail where John Brown was imprisoned while awaiting his treason trial. The post office is open Monday through Friday from 8:30 A.M. to 5:00 P.M., Saturday 9:00 A.M. to 12:30 P.M. Call (304) 725–2421.

To dig more into the turbulent history of Brown and Charles Town, stop by the *Jefferson County Museum* on the corner of Washington and Samuel Streets. Among the hundreds of fascinating curios here are old black-and-white photographs depicting the county's agrarian roots, surveying maps, equipment used by George Washington, and the wagon used to transport John Brown to his execution. The museum is open 10:00 A.M. to 4:00 P.M. Monday through Saturday, April through November. Admission is free. Call (304) 725–8628 for more information.

A sense of colonial elegance and gastronomic delight converge at the *Charles Washington Inn* at 210 West Liberty Street. The house was built of logs in 1787 by young Edward Tiffin and his family. When he reached manhood, Tiffin left for Ohio with a formal letter of introduction signed by George Washington and apparently impressed the frontier population, because he later became the state's first governor. In Tiffin's absence, the Charles Town house was fancied up with a brick facing, a spiral staircase, and carved mantelpieces. Today the establishment is a labyrinth of intimate dining areas serving smoked duck breast, scallops seviche, and prime rib. The inn's two chefs are also known for their crème brûlée and other rich desserts. Prices are moderate. The inn is open from 11:00 A.M. to 9:00 P.M. Monday through Saturday. Reservations are recommended. Call (304) 725–4020.

Although the Eastern Panhandle is one of the most densely populated regions of West Virginia, it still retains a strong rural character underscored by thousands of acres of cattle farms, productive croplands, and apple and peach orchards. The pastoral legacy of the Virginia gentleman farmer lives on in such places as **Hillbrook Inn,** a stunning English-style country manor house/hotel. Five miles southwest of Charles Town, off Summit Point Road (State Route 13), Hillbrook sits amid seventeen acres of gardens, lawns, woods, and ponds. Bullskin Run (in Virginia and West Virginia, large brooks and streams are known as "runs") dissects the property, enhancing its quiet elegance.

Inside the inn, guests might be greeted with the aroma of roasted pheasant from the kitchen or the sound of an oak-wood fire crackling in the tavern. A colorful mix of antiques and contemporary art fills the private rooms, giving the place an aristocratic aura that begs comparison to the manor homes of England's Cotswolds. Hillbrook's six guest rooms and four cottages all have private baths, sitting areas, queen-size beds, and air-conditioning. Two rooms have fireplaces. Lodging rates are equally aristocratic, but they typically include a seven-course meal with wine and a country breakfast. If you plan to come just for lunch, dinner, or an English high tea (Sunday), innkeeper Carissa Zanella suggests making reservations well in advance. A constituency of affluent—and loyal—Washingtonians apparently has already discovered this hidden gem. Hillbrook is open year-round, except Christmas. Check-in is after 3:00 P.M. and checkout is noon. Call (304) 725–4223 or (800) 304–4223.

Hillbrook's land, and some 2,200 acres surrounding it, once belonged to the Bullskin, or **Rock Hall Tract,** the first real estate owned by George Washington. The young man and future president actually surveyed the region in 1750 and took part of his salary to purchase Rock Hall Tract from a Captain Rutherford, an early settler. A state historical marker, located in front of South Jefferson Elementary School on Summit Point Road, signals the site of Washington's first farm.

Within earshot of the tiny hamlet of Summit Point, ***Summit Point Raceway*** unfolds a 2-mile-long course covering more than 375 acres. From early March to early December, the Sports Car Club of America (SCCA)–sanctioned track hosts a variety of professional and amateur auto, motorcycle, and go-kart races. Each May, for example, the Jefferson 500 Vintage Sports Car Race rolls the clock back a bit with a pair of 500-kilometer races—one for cars built before 1965 and another for 1965–1980 models. More for fun than competition, a vintage race might begin with an airplane sweeping down and leading the cars off the starting grid. In fall, the SVRA (Sports Car Vintage Racing)–sanctioned Blue/Gray Challenge is held (around the first weekend of October). You don't need a vintage car to take to the curvy track of Summit Point. The SCCA sponsors a series of race-car driving schools for wannabe Andrettis, no pit crew required. Or if you want to be prepared for the unexpected, take an accident-avoidance driver-training class—driving at high speeds on the 2-mile, 10-turn raceway is a thrill. If a seat in the grandstand is excitement enough, try revving up with a bowl of the track's famous "100 mph" chili and a cold beer. Admission to spectator events is moderate. Call (304) 725–8444 for event and driving-school information.

Before heading north on State Route 1 to Shepherdstown, duck down to the nearby ***Harewood*** estate, located on State Route 51 between Middleway

Burned Bridges

West Virginians faced conflicting loyalties during the Civil War; neighbor fought neighbor and sons faced off against fathers. In the Eastern Panhandle town of Shepherdstown, this was especially true.

If you look off the Rumsey Bridge on U.S. Highway 340 near Shepherdstown's Bavarian Inn, you can spot the piers of several bridges wiped out by flooding in the twentieth century. But you won't see any remains of the first bridge on the spot, a covered bridge burned by Confederate troops in June 1861.

One of the young Confederate soldiers, Henry Kyd Douglas, lived on Ferry Hill Plantation (now C&O Canal Park headquarters), the pillared house directly opposite on the Maryland side of the river. In his memoir, *I Rode with Stonewall*, Douglas described his turmoil as he gazed over at his home, knowing his father was an owner of the property he was destroying. "I knew I was severing all connection between me and my family and understood the sensation of one who, sitting aloft the limb of a tree, cuts it off between him and the trunk," he wrote.

Douglas later became the youngest member of General Thomas "Stonewall" Jackson's staff and rose to colonel. When his father died soon after the war ended, Douglas inherited Ferry Hill. He accepted the inheritance but chose never to live there again.

and Charles Town. The Georgian mansion was built in 1770 by Samuel Washington, the next oldest brother of George Washington and the first in the family to move to the Eastern Panhandle. Like all Washingtons, Samuel was active in public affairs, appointed to serve as both county lieutenant and justice of the peace. He died in 1781, and his unmarked grave lies in a family plot on the property. In 1794 Harewood hosted the wedding of James Madison and Dolley Payne Todd, whose sister, Lucy Payne Washington, was the mistress of the estate. The home has been continuously occupied and to this day is owned by a direct descendant. Unfortunately, Harewood is not open to the public, but its exterior and grounds can be viewed from the road.

eastern panhandle trivia

The eighteen-hole championship golf course located at Cacapon Resort State Park was created by the legendary golf-course designer Robert Trent Jones.

Claymont Court, just off Route 51, remains the only one of Jefferson County's Washington homes open to the public. In fact, it's possible to spend the night in this 1820 mansion built by George Washington's grandnephew Bushrod Washington. Claymont is a year-round retreat center run by followers of G. I. Gurdjieff and other self-awareness proponents. This estate, on the National Register of Historic Places, includes the magnificent main house, formal gardens, and massive brick stables, which have been adapted as a seminar center. Under the crystal chandeliers of what was always regarded as the grandest of the Washington homes, groups gather to learn more about yoga, tai chi, mindfulness, healing, spirituality, and sometimes scrap-booking. For information about upcoming events at Claymont Court, call (304) 725–4437 or visit www.claymont.org.

Shepherdstown lies up near the northern tip of Jefferson County, perched beautifully—and sometimes precariously—on the banks of the Potomac River. (The entire northern Potomac Basin is susceptible to dramatic flooding, and for folks living along the river roads, heavy spring rains can turn their homes into islands.)

Laid out by Thomas Shepherd in 1734, Shepherdstown is the oldest burgh in West Virginia, and its painstakingly preserved eighteenth-century homes and shops have rightfully been deemed a registered district on the National Register of Historic Places.

History seeps out of every nook and cranny here. When General Washington called for more support for the siege of Boston in 1775, Shepherdstown paid heed. The famous Bee Line March of southern volunteers to Massachusetts began at Morgan's Spring, now part of ***Morgan's Grove Park,*** 1 mile south of town on State Route 480. Shepherdstown went on to supply more troops to the Revolutionary War than any city its size in the colonies. At one point Washington even considered that the humble town should become the nation's new capital city.

During the Civil War, Shepherdstown was a strategic river crossing into Maryland. Immediately after 1862's tragic battle of Antietam (just 5 miles away), in which more than 22,000 Americans were casualties of a single day's fighting, Shepherdstown became one massive hospital. Perhaps because of its empathetic nature, the town was spared major damages during the war.

This is equally fortunate for modern-day residents and tourists, who are blessed with one of the most charming townscapes in West Virginia. Over the years Shepherdstown's quiet appeal has lured scores of artisans, writers, merchants, musicians, and scholars—folks who've helped stamp a distinctive impression on the place. Today about 800 full-time residents and some 5,000 Shepherd College students call the town home. One friend commented that Shepherdstown has become "West Virginia's answer to Stockbridge [Massachusetts]," a mixture of Rockwellian idyll and bohemian funkiness.

The lifeblood of Shepherdstown has always been **Town Run.** The spring-fed brook runs through the town's alleyways, backyards, and parks and is used as an auxiliary water supply. During the village's infancy, Town Run powered **Thomas Shepherd's gristmill** (midblock of Mill Street), the area's first industry. (Interestingly, the gristmill, now a private home, still contains its 40-foot-diameter, cast-iron waterwheel, one of the largest of its kind in the world.)

At the **Blue Moon Cafe,** corner of Princess and High Streets, Town Run brook flows directly through the restaurant on its way downhill to the river. The waterway is covered to keep out pollutants, but the deli is open to hearty eaters, many coming from the nearby campus of Shepherd College. For a delicious meal, you can't go wrong with a mesquite chicken breast sandwich—a plump, mesquite-smoked chicken breast covered in melted provolone cheese and generously doused with the Blue Moon's Tex-Mex sauce. Top it off with one of the delicious desserts. In warmer weather, take advantage of the outdoor, streamside seating. Prices are reasonable. The cafe is open Monday through Saturday from 11:00 A.M. to 9:00 P.M., Sunday from noon to 3:00 P.M. Phone (304) 876–1920.

Some twenty years before Robert Fulton's *Clermont* steamed up the Hudson River, Shepherdstown resident James Rumsey built and successfully demonstrated a working steamboat on the Potomac. A replica of that boat is located across the street from the Blue Moon Cafe at the **Rumsey Steamboat Museum** (located in the backyard of the Entler Hotel and Shepherdstown Museum). Inside the boathouse/museum you'll also find displays and sketches outlining

Rumsey's fascinating life and inventions. In the 1780s George Washington appointed the budding engineer and inventor to manage the development of a navigation company on the Potomac. Washington hoped the company would be a key asset in opening up the West through an elaborate canal system. Rumsey, however, was enchanted with the notion of mastering the river's strong currents by way of a steam-driven piston that created a water-jet propulsion system. On December 3, 1787, Rumsey and a crew of eight Shepherdstown ladies boarded a small test boat appropriately named the *Rumseian Experiment* and chugged up the Potomac at a formidable three knots. With Washington's encouragement, Rumsey took the knowledge of his technological breakthrough and went to London to secure financial aid to build a larger and commercially viable ship. Unfortunately, Rumsey died on the eve of completing the new improved steamboat, and the project was soon aborted. These and other tales await visitors to the museum.

If you're lucky enough to be in Shepherdstown in August, the Rumseian Society (the group that runs the museum), under the guidance of Captain Jay Hurley, takes the steamship replica out onto the river for live demonstrations. The museum, with its colorful outdoor mural depicting the Shepherdstown riverbank as seen through Rumsey's eyes, is open from April through October, Saturday and Sunday, 1:00 to 5:00 P.M. Captain Hurley says individual and group tours also can be arranged in advance any time of year. Call (304) 876–6907 for more information and demonstration schedules. No admission is charged. Hurley, incidentally, is the proprietor of **O'Hurley's General Store,** a popular stop on most day-trip circuits through Shepherdstown. Stop by on Thursday nights for a harmonic blend of dulcimer, harp, and clarinet music. This is the place to find your steam engines, crockery, dinner bells, and much more. While down near the water, be sure to visit the **James Rumsey Monument** at the end of Mill Street. The tall Ionic column supports a granite globe of the world, a reference to the international reach of Rumsey's invention.

At Princess and German Streets sits Shepherdstown's famous **Yellow Brick Bank Restaurant,** a Continental eatery inhabiting a former—you guessed it— yellow-brick bank. During the Reagan years in Washington, the First Lady and lunch pal George Will dined here frequently, thus putting the place on the social circuit and well onto the beaten path. Nevertheless, if you decide to brave the swarm of trendy tourist diners, the lunchtime menu features an incredible sweet corn and jalapeño chowder and an equally blissful Monte Cristo sandwich. Prices are moderate for the region. Lunch is served 11:30 A.M. to 2:30 P.M. daily. Dinner is served 5:00 to 9:00 P.M. weeknights, until 10:00 P.M. weekends. Call (304) 876–2208 for more information.

James Rumsey Monument

The *Opera House Theatre,* just down German Street, is popular for its foreign and independently produced American movies, as well as music from jive to jazz. Call (304) 876–3704 or visit www .operahousemovies.com for a schedule.

The post-and-beam chalets and stone manor of the *Bavarian Inn* promise true German fare, and you won't be disappointed. Located just across US 340 from Shepherd University in Shepherdstown, this establishment envelops you in the warm, winey scent of Bavarian food as soon as you enter the dining room. In the ambience of dark, rich hardwood paneling, you can choose among popular German staples such as red cabbage, potato dumplings, and *jaegerschnitzel* (veal smothered in mushrooms and wine sauce). The chef here uses good white wine—not vinegar—in the rich meat dishes, and you'll notice the subtle difference.

The Bavarian Inn is open daily from 7:00 A.M. to 9:00 P.M. For more information call (304) 876–2551 or visit www.bavarianinnwv.com.

Before leaving town, you'll want to stroll through the bucolic grounds of *Shepherd University,* founded in 1872 as one of the state's first liberal arts institutions. It was in the building that is now the campus's McMurran Hall, at the corner of Duke and German Streets, that thousands of wounded soldiers were treated in the aftermath of Antietam. The school is widely recognized for its progressive programs in the natural and social sciences and in the arts and humanities. For the past several years, the college has played host to the *Contemporary American Theater Festival,* a showcase of new works by some of the country's most important playwrights. Performances are staged by the state's only *Actors' Equity theater,* a talent pool drawn from Shepherdstown and across the country. Past productions have included such ambitious and poignant works as *Black* by Joyce Carol Oates and *Dream House* by Darrah Cloud. "We want to help renew the American theater by providing a haven for artists to collaborate and take risks," says Ed Herendeen, the festival's producing director. The nearly monthlong thespian festival is typically held during the last three weeks of July and also includes staged readings, improvisational comedy, and concerts. For more information about the Contemporary American Theater Festival, call (800) 999–2283, or contact the college at (304) 876–3473.

Crossroads

Crossroads is the name we've given to the region that sits in the heart of the Eastern Panhandle and contains the historic railroad town of Martinsburg and all of Berkeley County west of U.S. Highway 11, sometimes still referred to as the Valley Pike. In the early eighteenth century, the region became home to the first settlers in what is now West Virginia and later evolved into a bustling center of wagon, coach, and rail travel to the West. The Valley Pike, now paralleled by Interstate 81, once served as the major north-south artery linking Pennsylvania's Cumberland Valley to the Valley of Virginia.

The legacy of the earliest settlers lives on in Berkeley County's more than 2,000 National Register historic sites, the highest concentration in the state. Crossroads' vast fruit orchards, cattle ranches, and truck farms, meanwhile, continue to find steady markets in the growing urban corridors of the East, and in recent years they have become the focus of open-space preservation efforts. The gigantic **Mountain State Apple Harvest Festival,** held the third weekend in October in Martinsburg, salutes one of the region's most successful agribusinesses.

With a population of 16,000—and growing—Martinsburg has long been the Eastern Panhandle's principal city, an industrial, agricultural, and transportation center that is just beginning to tap its tourism attributes. Because of its strategic importance as the western gateway to the neighboring Shenandoah Valley, Martinsburg was in the thick of the Civil War, once serving as a command center for Confederate general Thomas "Stonewall" Jackson, a native West Virginian. Though badly bruised during the war, the city remarkably preserved many of its glorious eighteenth- and nineteenth-century buildings.

eastern panhandle trivia

During the Civil War, the Union army occupied Martinsburg for thirty-two months.

One such structure is **Tuscarora Church,** 2335 Tuscarora Pike, about 2 miles west of downtown. Built from native limestone in 1740 by Scots-Irish Presbyterians, the country church was refurbished in 1803 and is still going strong. In election years the church serves as a polling place. Here's one bit of evidence that even the farthest eastern reaches of West Virginia were once the "Wild West": On the back walls of the church are the two original gun racks worshippers used to hang their pistols during services. The state's second oldest Presbyterian church holds Sunday service at 11:00 A.M. Call (304) 263-4579.

Another Martinsburg historical gem is the **General Adam Stephen House,** 309 East John Street, a native limestone home built around 1778 by the town's founder. Construction was prolonged by the Revolutionary War, in which

General Stephen served as soldier and surgeon. Like most Virginia gentlemen, Stephen was more intent on creating a home with a natural aesthetic than a grandiose design. This simple, four-room rectangular house is perched on a hill overlooking Tuscarora Creek.

Next to the home on the same property is the *Triple Brick Building,* built in 1874 by Phillip Showers, who at the time owned the Stephen House. The three-story building supposedly got its name because it contained three apartment units used by workers rebuilding Martinsburg's Civil War–torn railroad yards. It's now used as a local history museum, complete with quilts, period clothes, Civil War memorabilia, and musical instruments. Both the General Adam Stephen House and the Triple Brick Building are open from 2:00 to 5:00 P.M. Saturday and Sunday, May through October. Special viewing appointments can be made by calling (304) 267–4434. No admission is charged.

Three blocks to the north (200 block of East Martin Street) and across the tracks of the Baltimore & Ohio Railroad stands the *Roundhouse,* one of the finest examples of nineteenth-century industrial railroad architecture. Unfortunately abandoned years ago, the unmistakably round building was the nerve center of passenger and freight activity along the B&O route connecting Martinsburg to Baltimore in 1842. Most of the rail yard was destroyed by Jackson's troops during the Civil War, but the Roundhouse was rebuilt in 1866, and eleven years later it was the scene of a major rail-worker strike. The Roundhouse is finishing renovations but is open for tours and special events, including a festival in mid-July. For information call the office at (304) 260-4141 to set up a weekday morning tour.

West Virginia Firsts

The nation's first rural free mail delivery was started in Charles Town on October 6, 1896.

West Virginia was the first state to have a sales tax, effective July 1, 1921.

Bailey Brown, the first Union soldier killed on the battlefield in the Civil War, died on May 22, 1861, at Fetterman in Taylor County, West Virginia.

The first public spa was opened at Berkeley Springs in 1756.

Mrs. Minnie Buckingham Harper became the first African-American woman to become a member of a state or federal legislative body in the United States when she was appointed to the West Virginia House of Delegates in 1928.

Parkersburg citizens founded the first free public school for African-American children south of the Mason-Dixon Line in January 1862.

If you're looking for a place to stay in Martinsburg, consider ***Aspen Hall Inn.*** George Washington may not have slept here (or he may), but records show he did attend a wedding here in 1761. The farmstead was known as Mendenhall's Fort then, during the French and Indian War, and the elegant limestone mansion was built in 1750. Innkeepers Becky Frye and Charlie Connolly are historical interpreters at nearby Fort Frederick State Park and have carefully preserved many of the home's original features, such as strap hinges. Aspen Hall's parklike acreage includes a trout stream, but the inn is within walking distance of downtown. Another good thing to know: Innkeeper Connolly is a licensed massage therapist who gives Swedish relaxation massages by appointment. Aspen Hall is located at 405 Boyd Avenue. Call (304) 260–1750 for reservations.

Situated less than a mile away in the rolling hills east of the railroad tracks is the ***Old Green Hill Cemetery*** on Burke Road. It's patterned on the Parisian mold with an impressive display of stone-carved art. The expansive views of Martinsburg and its environs from atop the cemetery's hills are spectacular. Among those buried here are President Lincoln's bodyguard, Ward Hill Lamon; writer-artist David Hunter Strother (aka Porte Crayon) of *Harpers Weekly* fame; at least thirty unknown Confederate soldiers; and the parents of Belle Boyd. The grounds are open dawn to dusk.

eastern panhandle trivia

Nineteenth-century Bunker Hill Mill, located near Martinsburg, is the only mill in the state featuring dual waterwheels.

Belle Boyd, you might remember, was a Confederate spy working in cahoots with Stonewall Jackson. She was arrested and imprisoned twice but both times released for lack of evidence. After the war the Martinsburg native married one of her Union captors, went on to become a stage actress in New York and London, and later lectured and wrote a book about her spying exploits. Boyd's father, Benjamin Reed Boyd, built a twenty-two-room Greek-revival mansion in the center of the city, and in recent years the Berkeley County Historical Society has restored the ***Belle Boyd House,*** 126 East Race Street, turning a portion of it into a Civil War museum and historical archive. The house contains original family heirlooms, journal entries, and wartime artifacts. Hours are 10:00 A.M. to 4:00 P.M., Monday, Tuesday, Thursday, Friday, and Saturday between April 15 and November 1. For more information, call (304) 267–4713.

As you wend your way back to I–81, detour to 330 Winchester Avenue and stop in at ***WSG Gallery.*** Proprietor Jody Wright displays her own dog- and cat-themed paintings, carvings, and gifts and donates a portion of her sales to a no-kill animal shelter. Her studio/shop is located in a hundred-year-old smokehouse tucked behind her Victorian home on the corner of Winchester and Stephen Streets. The shop and studio are open Saturday and Sunday from 10:00 A.M. to 4:00 P.M. For more information, call (304) 263–2391.

Another popular stop in Martinsburg is the **West Virginia Glass Outlet,** on 148 North Queen Street, where you can admire the variety of the Mountain State's functional and art glass. Truffle lovers will consider **DeFluri's Fine Chocolates** a must-see. Brenda and Charlie Casabona have won awards for the excellent chocolates they create at their family factory at 130 North Queen Street. For more information about tastings and tours, call (304) 264–3698 or visit www.defluris.com.

From Martinsburg jump on the interstate or the slower but more scenic US 11 and head 8 miles south to Bunker Hill, a village known for its apple orchards and antiques shops. Two miles west of town, on Old Mill Road (State Route 26), is the rustic cabin home of West Virginia's first white settler, Colonel Morgan Morgan, a Delaware native who moved his family to this lonely western outpost in the 1730s. **Morgan Cabin,** now a living-history museum of the Berkeley County Historical Society, was made from local hardwoods and stone in 1734, much of which remains in the restored version that is listed on the National Register of Historic Places. Save for a twentieth-century farmhouse across the road, little seems to have changed in the past 270 years in this rural corner of Berkeley County. Standing in front of the cabin, one can almost imagine a clandestine Indian meeting taking place beyond the hills a few hundred yards to the south. One of the most violent clashes at Morgan Cabin took place during the Revolutionary War when one of Colonel Morgan's grandsons, an American soldier, was captured by Tories and executed in front of his family. The pioneering Morgans nevertheless went on to become one of the Eastern Panhandle's most prominent families. Neighboring Morgan County and Morgantown, in northern West Virginia, were named after them. Morgan Cabin is open Sunday, June through August, from 2:00 to 4:00 P.M. Special tours can be arranged year-round by calling (304) 229–5631.

Heading back into Bunker Hill, you'll pass **Christ Church** on the left. Built in 1740 and frequented by the Morgan family, it is believed to be West Virginia's first house of worship, predating Tuscarora Church by a few months. The brick Greek-revival church has been restored three times. Behind the church is the cemetery where Colonel Morgan and his wife are buried. **Bunker Hill Antiques Associates,** a local landmark, is directly next door at the corner of US 11 and Old Mill Road. The nineteenth-century mill-turned-emporium houses more than 170 furniture, jewelry, glass, book, and art dealers. It's open daily from 10:00 A.M. to 5:00 P.M. For more information, call (304) 229–0709.

From Bunker Hill, head back to the I–81 ramp at Inwood, but instead of getting on the freeway, continue west along George Washington Heritage Trail Byway, via Route 51. For about 5 miles, you'll roll past country stores and green pastures dotted with rust-colored barns before arriving in tiny **Gerrardstown.** Once this sleepy, historic district town wasn't so sleepy. Not long after it was laid out in 1784, Gerrardstown became a booming supply center for wagon trains headed west—that is until the westward railroad chose Martinsburg instead. Many of the village's original buildings from the eighteenth century remain along the byway—Cool Spring Farm, Gerrard House, Prospect Hill, and Marshy Dell.

Scan a map of West Virginia and you're bound to find dozens of towns with intriguing names—places like Burnt House, Toll Gate, Hurricane, Mud, Crum, and Nancy Run. In this region, there's a **Shanghai,** about 10 miles northwest of Gerrardstown. The name probably came from a local furniture manufacturer, according to Don Wood, director of the Berkeley County Historical Society. Another theory, he suggests, is that several citizens of the village were locked up in jail during a crucial election so they couldn't vote and thus were "Shanghaied."

To reach Shanghai, take Route 51 west to Mills Gap and hang a right on State Route 45. Continue 3 miles to Glengary, where you'll take the first right onto the kind of country road John Denver immortalized. In 5 miles, you'll see Shanghai—a few houses, a store, and a post office. The sense of being in backcountry is the main attraction, a feeling that increases as you head over Sleepy Creek Mountain.

Hedgesville, about 10 miles north of Shanghai on Apple Pie Ridge (next to Potato Hill), has a strong agricultural past. To celebrate this disappearing way of life, farmer L. Norman Dillon left Berkeley County money to start a farm museum. The **L. Norman Dillon Farm Museum** preserves some of the tools and practices of the trade, including apple graders, horse harnesses, milking machines, and hand plows. A quick look around the grounds reveals larger pieces of machinery, including sawmills, tractors, huskers, and harrows. All of this gear is put into action during the museum's fall and spring shows. On those occasions, sulfurous smoke and the ringing of metal on metal summons crowds to the blacksmith shop, where a smithy hammers cherry-red scraps of steel into hooks, knives, and latches. Eventually the farmstead will include a farmhouse, authentic West Virginia barn, and milking parlor. The museum, at the intersection of State Route 9 and Ridge Road across from Hedgesville High School, is open Saturday and Sunday afternoons April 1 to October 31. Call (304) 754–3845 for more information.

A Walk on the Dark Side of Harpers Ferry

Shirley Dougherty has been telling tales on Harpers Ferry since 1977. She's written a book, but the elderly storyteller is better known for the ghostly walking tours of town she started giving two decades ago.

"It's a violent place, and some mighty strange people have lived here," Dougherty says as she lights the red-oil lantern to lead her popular ghost tour. "In fact, they still do."

In Dougherty's own home on Potomac Street, the ghost of a Confederate spy fleeing guards has tumbled down the stairsteps night after night. A Union soldier standing at an upstairs window witnessed the spy dashing through his front door in the room below. As the Confederate spy tried to hide upstairs, the Union witness shot him. The young Confederate pitched down the stairs, hitting every step.

"It was his last fall, and folks are still hearing it," Dougherty says.

All the stories on Dougherty's tours and in her book *A Ghostly Tour of Harpers Ferry* have been carefully researched to determine that they correspond with documented deaths. Sudden, violent deaths seem most likely to produce ghostly phenomena, she says.

Dangerfield Newby, for instance. Newby had joined abolitionist John Brown on his notorious raid on the Harpers Ferry arsenal on October 16, 1859. A freed slave, Newby was angry and frustrated because his wife's masters hedged on a deal to free her. Newby was shot in the throat by angry townspeople, who decided to further vent their anger on his body by mutilating it and leaving it in the alley for the hogs to devour.

Dougherty takes her tour up Hog Alley, sharing the grisly story. Should you meet a middle-aged black man wearing an old slouch hat and an awful scar across his throat, you should know you have met Dangerfield Newby, come back to free his wife and children, Dougherty tells you.

There are others—a silent priest, a dying soldier on the threshold of St. Peter's Church, a flaming woman, and a flying lamp chimney. Although Dougherty, who is past seventy, can't spring up the stone steps with her former vigor, she still leads tours night after night, April through early November. Dougherty's granddaughter, Ann, assists with tours, and is gradually taking over Harpers Ferry Ghost Tours.

Tours meet at 8:00 p.m. Saturday nights in April and May and Friday and Saturday nights from June through October 31. For reservations, call (304) 725–8019.

Once you've admired the orchards from Apple Pie Ridge, turn west. The landscape takes a definite turn for the vertical as you head into the Springs and Valley Region, toward Berkeley Springs.

Springs and Spas

There's always been a certain mystique, a certain magical attraction, to the western edge of the Eastern Panhandle. Maybe it has to do with the legends left behind by the Tuscarora and Shawnee Indians who, along with other warring Appalachian tribes, regularly visited the region's "healing waters" in peace. Maybe it stems from the colonial tradition set by George Washington and Thomas Jefferson of "taking to the baths," the plentiful warm springs that cleansed, soothed, and revitalized the body.

Whatever it is, this land of springs and spas is evolving into one of the East's leading health resorts, art and antiques centers, and outdoor recreation areas. Its 231 square miles encompass all of Morgan County. The northern and western borders are formed by the winding Potomac River, and its rugged spine is shaped by the uplift of the Shenandoah Mountains. The scenic beauty of the landscape and the diversity of residents, from white-collar urban transplants to seventh-generation farmers, make for an unforgettable blend of sights and attractions.

Berkeley Springs, the area's largest town, bills itself as "the country's first spa." It's not a hollow claim. Shortly after George Washington's family and friends drew up a "plat" of 134 lots, named the streets, and incorporated the town of Bath, the community emerged as a haven for seekers of respite from a young and troubled nation. President George and First Lady Martha were such regular visitors during the presidency that historians dubbed Berkeley Springs the first "summer White House." Today massage therapists outnumber lawyers three to one in the little town. Visitors may soak in the mineral springs and sample more than twenty different bodywork treatments in six full-service spas.

The focal point of Bath (still its official name) has always been the warm mineral springs found in the center of town on Washington Street at what is now *Berkeley Springs State Park,* a seven-acre spring and bathhouse compound that is also the nation's oldest state park. The outdoor springs flow from the base of Warm Springs Ridge at a rate of 1,500 gallons a minute, surfacing at a constant 74° F. The park's Lord Fairfax public tap is a gathering point for locals and tourists who come to fill their jugs with the sweet-tasting mineral water. But the star attraction is the 1815 *Roman Bath House* and its private bathing chambers with water heated to a relaxing 102° F. The two-story bathhouse is the oldest public building in Morgan County. On the second floor is the *Museum of the Berkeley Springs,* which chronicles the development of the town and its springs through old photographs, sketches, exhibits, and water-bottling memorabilia. You'll also learn about the geology of the springs and the history of bathing wear. On the opposite side of the park is the Main

Bath House, offering water, steam, and therapeutic massage treatments; showers; and an exercise room. The park's baths are open from 10:00 A.M. to 6:00 P.M. daily, except Christmas and New Year's Day. Water treatments are inexpensive and popular, so it's best to reserve a private bath at least two weeks in advance. The museum is open weekends March to mid-November. Hours are 10:00 A.M. to 4:00 P.M. on Saturday and noon to 4:00 P.M. on Sunday. The park's number is (304) 258–2711.

Next door to the springs, the stately *Country Inn & Spa,* One Market Street, triples as a hotel, spa, and restaurant. The inn's signature white-columned facade is draped by the flags of Maryland, the District of Columbia, West Virginia, Virginia, Tennessee, and Kentucky, all of which are home to some family connection of the Barker family, which owns the inn. Comfortable rooms, many with brass beds, are available in the main house (more like a mansion), while an adjoining modern brick addition houses more contemporary-style digs. No matter where you bunk, you're but a few steps to the Renaissance Spa, where a certified staff will lead you through a choice of whirlpool baths, deep-muscle massages, European-style facials, manicures, and pedicures. If you're looking for a little lifestyle adjustment, the inn's diet center offers personal counseling and courses in nutrition and heart-healthy cooking. You may want to hold off on the diet center until after you've had a chance to sample the fare in the two dining rooms. A good choice is the steak Diane, prepared next to your table, and a glass of West Virginia wine. The Country Inn is open year-round. Lodging, spa, and dining rates are moderate. Call (304) 258–2210 or (800) 822–6630; www.countryinnwv.com.

There was a time when small-town America had real movie houses—theaters that were destinations in themselves, not just places where films were screened. Berkeley Springs has such a venue in the *Star Theatre* on Washington Street. Besides first-run films, the vintage 1930s movie house features 5-cent candies, popcorn from a 1940s hot-oil popping machine, fresh-pressed apple cider, and overstuffed couches in the back. Owners Jeanne Mozier and Jack Soronen restored the old theater (formerly a car dealership) in 1979 and have since brought more than 1,300 movies to town. Jeanne handles the booking, selecting films she believes represent the small community's taste, including kids' movies, adventures, comedies, and the occasional Merchant Ivory–type production. Jeanne also presides over a preshow lecture on polite theater behavior. Projectionist Jack shows films from a 1940s carbon-arc projector. Show time is 8:00 P.M. Friday through Sunday. A Thursday evening show is added from June through September. For feature information or to reserve a couch, call (304) 258–1404.

After the show, head down to ***Tari's Cafe & Inn,*** 123 North Washington, where you can sample outstanding seafood and pastas, enjoy laid-back conversation (this is a local watering hole), and hear some great live blues, rock, folk, and mountain music. The linguini here is heavenly and is served with a rich, creamy, white clam sauce. Another favorite is the Carbonara Supreme, a beautifully presented mix of bacon, fresh tomatoes, and blue cheese, all tossed with homemade fettuccine. Wild Woman Wings with blue cheese and Two Sisters Tilapia are other big favorites.

If you're planning to spend a couple of nights in the area, reserve a private room at the inn, which sits above the restaurant in this double town-house building. Tari's "sleep and dine" special for two ($179) covers any two nights and includes a lunch and a dinner. The cozy, loftlike rooms have private baths but no phones and are within close walking distance to all Berkeley Springs attractions. Single-night stays start as low as $59. The restaurant opens daily at 11:30 A.M. (noon on Sunday), with lunch lasting until 5:00 P.M. and dinner until 9:00 P.M. The bar typically stays open until 2:00 A.M. Call (304) 258–1196 for dining and room reservations.

Berkeley Springs is a veritable gold mine for antiques and craft collectors, with more than a dozen shops, studios, and consignment centers located within the central business district. In fact, *American Style* magazine voted Berkeley Springs one of the top art destinations in America for its galleries, concerts, theater, and artists' community. These and other outlying boutiques offer summer studio tours that let you see firsthand how local artisans create jewelry, pottery, stained glass, and furniture. The tours are headquartered at the ***Ice House Gallery,*** home of the Morgan Arts Council. For more information call (800) 447–8797.

The Old Factory Antique Mall, 112 Williams Street, feels more like a hands-on museum than a store. Old records, postcards, furniture, toys, jewelry, and books are spread throughout the expansive former factory building, filling every possible nook and cranny. It's a stop that requires at least an hour's worth of browsing and perhaps more if you're doing serious shopping or getting helplessly drawn in by an old baseball-card collection or a set of 1950s road maps. The Old Factory is open daily from 10:00 A.M. to 5:00 P.M. Call (304) 258–1788 for more information.

Bottling water may not be all that new a concept—after all, the Egyptians were doing it on the Nile back in the days of the great pharaohs—but it's an idea that's taking off in this country, much to the delight of Berkeley Springs' ***West Virginia Spring House Natural Water.*** Just a short walk from the Old Factory, at 106 Howard Street, this more than twenty-five-year-old bottling company has seen its home and office business balloon in recent years, with a market that saturates the mid-Atlantic states and extends all the way down to south Florida. Spring House gathers its water from the nearby springs at Berkeley Springs State Park, filling two tanker cars a day.

Tari's may have the best linguini in the Eastern Panhandle, but my choice for the best spaghetti and chicken cacciatore goes hands down to *Maria's Garden and Inn,* 201 Independence Street. Tucked away in a historic home (and an adjoining building that used to be a mechanic's garage), Maria's now operates as a full, nine-room bed-and-breakfast and is run by Peg and Jim Perry. The Perrys made their mark in Berkeley Springs by running a popular family restaurant, Perry's Pizza, from 1971 to 1982. Today their inn and restaurant is somewhat of a local institution and is fast gaining the attention of discerning diners and lodgers from the Washington-Baltimore area. Complementing the pasta dishes is a range of delicious regional favorites such as homemade crab cakes and stuffed manicotti.

Eating here can be a somewhat spiritual experience—one that extends beyond the food. All three dining rooms are decorated with replicas and paintings of apparitions of the Virgin Mary from around the world. Embedded in the restaurant's stone-wall entranceway, for example, is a reproduction of the Miraculous Cloth of Our Lady of Guadalupe portrait, which has hung in the Basilica in Mexico City for more than 450 years. For those too stuffed to leave, Maria's has several guest rooms done up in a country chic decor. A first-floor suite comes with a second bedroom and kitchenette. Room rates start at $75 for a single and $150 for the suite (summer rates May 1 through November 1). The inn is open year-round, but be sure to make advance reservations for the busy spring and fall months. A two-night minimum is required on weekends in May through October. Travelers should also note that the restaurant is closed on Wednesday. For more information, call (888) 629–2253 or (304) 258–2021; www.mariasgarden.com.

On your way out of Berkeley Springs on Route 9 west, you might elect to pay a visit to another famous landmark, *Coolfont Resort* (800–888–8768). On the way over the mountain, you'll glimpse the stone Berkeley Castle jutting from Warm Springs Ridge. The castle was built in 1885 by Colonel Samuel Suit for his young bride.

Coolfont, located 5 miles off Route 9 on Cold Valley Road, is the spa of choice among the Washington stress set. Former drug czar William Bennett kicked his cigarette habit here, and former vice president Al Gore has been a loyal customer for years, even once setting off a mini panic by getting lost in the woods with Tipper. Washington dignitaries find many appealing reasons to drop out of public view at the 1,300-acre resort. Coolfont seems to be sheltered in a bubble of serenity, with its warm pool, meditation room, massage therapy rooms, and spa facilities. An outdoor sunbathing deck overlooks the tennis courts, and there's also a snowtubing park for thrilling winter rides. A Robert Trent Jones golf course lies just down the road. If you're of the female persuasion, you may be tempted to try the Wild Women Weekend, a melange of yoga, massage, belly dancing, drumming, and aerobic exercise. Coolfont is one of the region's leading proponents of ecological innovations, growing its own organic vegetables for the dining room and using wetland plants to help purify its waste water. For reservations or more information, call (800) 888–8768 or (304) 258–4500.

Back on Route 9, the road winds up to the 1,000-foot summit of **Prospect Peak.** A scenic overlook affords a three-state view of the Cacapon and Potomac River Valleys. The vista was described by *National Geographic* magazine as one of America's "outstanding beauty spots."

In Praise of Pawpaws

The last official days of summer in mid-September are the best time for making a pilgrimage down to the pawpaw patch. In Paw Paw, West Virginia, you may have to get down to the riverside a few days early to beat out the raccoons for a taste of this incredibly sweet wild fruit known here as the West Virginia banana.

If you've never sampled a pawpaw *(Asimina triloba),* you should. It tastes like its tropical cousins, the banana and mango, served up in a custard-like pulp popping with vitamins A and C. It has no shelf life, but North America's largest native fruit is credited with being a lifesaver for Indians and frontiersmen traveling the river valleys of the Southeast and Midwest in the fall.

The pawpaw made the news in 1992 when a Purdue University researcher reported he had isolated a powerful anticancer drug as well as a natural pesticide from the pawpaw tree. Those substances are found primarily in the twigs and smaller branches.

West Virginian Neal Peterson has known the pawpaw was special all along. About 27 years ago, he founded the PawPaw Foundation and has been engaged in pawpaw research to genetically perfect a marketable fruit. For the past ten years, he's been evaluating fruit from the carefully selected 600 trees he's planted at a University of Maryland experiment station.

Peterson's PawPaw Foundation distributes information on nurseries, pawpaw propagation, recipes, and a seed exchange. The pawpaw Web site is www.paw paw.kysu.edu. In West Virginia, native pawpaw saplings are sold at Enchanter's Garden nursery in Talcott; call (304) 466–3154.

That delicious aroma in the air is coming from directly across the road at **Panorama at the Peak,** formerly a private club that now serves some rather intimidating beef dishes and other West Virginia favorites. If you have an aversion to red meat, don't fret: the Panorama trout is outstanding, as is the vegetarian pasta. The meal is only half the treat, though. The sunset views from here are breathtaking, and the restaurant has a fascinating history.

The original stone-and-wood building was constructed in 1929, and its interior wooden beams, booths, and wall decor were made from all seventeen different hardwoods found in West Virginia. The fireplace, which is kept burning most of the year, is made from local Oriskany sandstone. Don't worry if you walk up and find the front door locked. Simply ring the buzzer and they'll let you in. It's all part of a tradition that goes back to the days when the Panorama was a private drinking establishment, kind of like a speakeasy, and you had to buzz to get in. Meals are priced moderately. The restaurant is open from 4:00 to 8:00 P.M. Wednesday through Friday and 3:00 to 9:00 P.M. Saturday and Sunday. For reservations call (304) 258–9847.

A fitting final detour in the Eastern Panhandle is to trek west over Great Cacapon Mountain to the little town of **Paw Paw,** the region's westernmost point. Like so many towns in the Eastern Panhandle, Paw Paw lies along the Potomac River and was once a vital rail center. It's named for a tree with a banana-like fruit common to this area. Most of the current 550 residents are direct descendants of the town's original settlers—folks who tamed the river and harvested timber from the surrounding virgin forests. There's not a lot of tourism here, save for outstanding river fishing and exploring the **Paw Paw Tunnel,** a ½-mile-long mountain tunnel carved by engineers in the mid-1800s during the construction of the Chesapeake & Ohio Canal connecting Washington, D.C., to Cumberland, Maryland. Although named after the West Virginia village, the tunnel is actually across the river in Maryland. It's open year-round to hikers and bikers.

Paw Paw is home to the Mountain State's only nudist resort. At the **Avalon nudist camp,** it's normal to see naked folks riding golf carts, swimming, playing tennis, dancing, batting around a volleyball, even attending camp church services. But no one here has to be unclothed, except in the pools, sauna, and spa. "We let people get undressed at their own pace," says owner Phyllis Gaffney. "We tell people the sooner they try it, the more comfortable they'll be. It's a step toward being more authentic, we think."

But for all the freedom that prevails, some traditional values remain. The Gaffneys have canceled memberships and asked men to leave for making harassing comments to women. (No women have menaced men yet, they say.) Avalon is a membership club, but visitors are welcome. Call (304) 947–5600, or check www.avalon-resort.com.

The West Virginia Department of Transportation designated the **George Washington Heritage Trail** as a West Virginia Scenic Byway in February 1998. The year 1999 saw the marking and full implementation of the trail's 137 miles. The trail presents an excellent opportunity to visit some of the more important historic sites and points of interest in the three counties of the Eastern Panhandle. The trail makes a 112-mile loop through the counties, with a 25-mile branch off to the town of Paw Paw. The trail was established to commemorate the life and legacy of our first president and his connection to the Eastern Panhandle. The well-marked trail may be covered in about four hours—but why? It is better to linger along the way and make a day of it. Visitors are never far from gas, food, and lodging at any point on the trail. For a map and more information, call the Martinsburg–Berkeley County Convention and Visitors Bureau at (304) 264–8801 or (800) 498–2386.

Places to Stay in the Eastern Panhandle

BERKELEY SPRINGS

Aaron's Acre Bed and Breakfast
501 Johnson Mill Road
(304) 258–4079
www.aaronsacrebandb.com
Moderate

Cacapon Resort State Park
U.S. Highway 522 (south of Berkeley Springs)
(304) 258–1022
www.cacaponresort.com
Inexpensive

Coolfont Resort
State Route 9 (west of Berkeley Springs)
(304) 258–4500
(800) 888–8768
www.coolfont.com
Moderate to expensive

CHARLES TOWN

The Carriage Inn Bed and Breakfast
417 East Washington Street
(304) 728–8003
(800) 867–9830
www.carriageinn.com
Expensive to very expensive

Towne House Motor Lodge
549 East Washington Street
(304) 725–8441
Inexpensive

FOR MORE INFORMATION

Jefferson County Convention and Visitors Bureau
(304) 535–2627 or (866) 435–5698

Martinsburg/Berkeley County Convention and Visitors Bureau
(304) 264–8801 or (800) 498–2386

Travel Berkeley Springs
(800) 447–8797
www.berkeleysprings.com

HARPERS FERRY

Angler's Inn
846 Washington Street
(304) 535–1239
www.theanglersinn.com
Moderate to expensive

Hilltop House
400 East Ridge Street
(800) 338–8319
www.hilltophousehotel.com
Moderate

HEDGESVILLE

Woods Resort
Mountain Lake Road
(304) 754–7222
www.thewoodsresort.com
Moderate to expensive

MARTINSBURG

Aspen Hall Inn
405 Boyd Avenue
(304) 260–1750
www.wvbnbs.com/inns/
44.html
Moderate

Days Inn
209 Viking Way
(304) 263–1800
www.travelwv.com
Moderate

Hampton Inn
975 Foxcroft Avenue
(304) 267–2900
Moderate

SHEPHERDSTOWN

Bavarian Inn and Lodge
State Route 480 (adjacent to
the Potomac River Bridge)
(304) 876–2551
www.bavarianinnwv.com
Moderate to very expensive

Thomas Shepherd Inn
Duke Street
(888) 889–8925
(304) 876–3715
www.thomasshepherdinn.com
Moderate to expensive

Places to Eat in the Eastern Panhandle

BERKELEY SPRINGS

Highlawn Inn
Market Street
(304) 258–5700
www.highlawninn.com
Expensive

Inspirations
174 North Washington Street
(304) 258–2292
Budget

Lot 12 Public House
117 Warren Street
(304) 258–6264
www.lot12.com
Moderate

Maria's Garden
42 Independence Street
(304) 258–2021
www.mariasgarden.com
Inexpensive to moderate

HARPERS FERRY

The Anvil Restaurant
1270 Washington Street
(304) 535–2582
www.anvilrestaurant.com
Moderate to expensive

Hilltop House
400 Ridge Street
(304) 535–2132
(800) 338–8319
Moderate

MARTINSBURG

**Asian Garden Japanese
Restaurant**
748 Foxcroft Avenue
(304) 263–8678
Inexpensive

**Heatherfields Restaurant
(Holiday Inn)**
301 Foxcroft Avenue
(304) 267–5500
Moderate

**Historic Market
House Grill**
100 North Queen Street
(304) 263–7615
Moderate

Rebecca's
220 North Queen Street
(304) 267–2600
Moderate

SHEPHERDSTOWN

Bavarian Inn and Lodge
Route 480 (adjacent to
Potomac River Bridge)
(304) 876–2551
www.bavarianinnwv.com
Inexpensive to moderate

Potomac Highlands

West Virginia's grand Potomac Highlands region is the state's premier natural area, with a stunning landscape of rugged mountains, pristine rivers, secluded canyons, unusual ecosystems, and seemingly endless forests.

Sparsely populated and largely unspoiled, the Highlands stretch from north to south along the dramatic uplift of the Allegheny Mountains and Plateau, encompassing the counties of Hampshire, Mineral, Hardy, Grant, Tucker, Randolph, Pendleton, and Pocahontas. Despite the imposing terrain, the mountain roads here, if a little narrow, are well maintained and safe (assuming that you watch your speed) and perfect for relaxed and scenic touring.

Before venturing off the beaten path, be sure to check your fuel tank, because gas stations aren't nearly as plentiful here as they are in the Eastern Panhandle and other portions of the state. When in the backcountry, especially at dusk, keep a watchful eye out for deer and bear on the road.

The Allegheny Foothills

The Allegheny Foothills region is located directly west of the Eastern Panhandle. It contains Hampshire, Mineral, Grant, and

POTOMAC HIGHLANDS

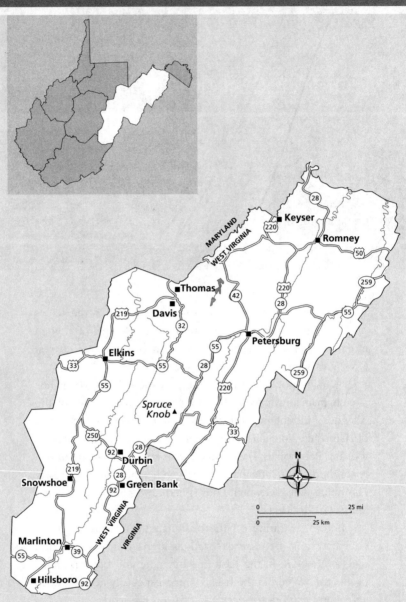

Hardy Counties, among the prettiest jurisdictions in West Virginia. Although decidedly mountainous, the landscape here is still gentler than other parts of the Potomac Highlands.

A good place to begin a tour of the Allegheny Foothills is in the Hampshire County community of Romney, the oldest incorporated city in West Virginia (1762). From Paw Paw, in the Eastern Panhandle, allow about a forty-minute drive down the winding Cacapon and North River Valleys and then another fifteen minutes west on U.S Highway 50. On your way you may want to make a stop in North River Valley, home to one of West Virginia's most unusual natural phenomena—*Ice Mountain.* As the state marker proclaims, this peak acts as "nature's icebox." Ice remains most of the year up on Ice Mountain, in crevices that exhale cold air all year. Formed from rock debris tumbling from the mountain's 200-foot cliffs, known as Raven Rocks, the holes and crevices collect ice 50 feet deep in places. The ice remains into summer, expelling cold air from about sixty pockets.

Because of this strange effect, Ice Mountain's rock talus is dotted with plants associated with subarctic regions or high elevations, such as twinflower, dwarf dogwood, and bristly rose. The preserve, protected by The Nature Conservancy, is open to visitors through guided tours April through November,

BEST ANNUAL EVENTS IN THE POTOMAC HIGHLANDS

Fasnacht
Helvetia; Saturday before Ash
Wednesday
(304) 924–9019

International Ramp Cook-Off
Elkins; late April
(800) 422–3304 or (304) 636–2717

**Potomac Eagle Fall Scenic
Rail Excursions**
Romney; May through October
(304) 424–0736 or (800) 22–EAGLE
www.potomaceagle.info

Fire on the Mountain Chili Cook-off
Snowshoe; second weekend in July
(877) 441–4FUN

Strawberry Festival
Hampshire County Fairgrounds
Augusta; mid-June
(304) 492–5128 or (304) 892–5013

Augusta Festival
Elkins; early August
(304) 637–1209
www.augustaheritage.com

**Autumn Harvest and
Roadkill Cook-off**
Marlinton; last weekend in September
(800) 336–7009

Mountain State Forest Festival
Elkins; late September through
early October
(304) 636–1824
www.randolphcountywv.com

usually on the second Saturday and third Thursday. To minimize impact upon the fragile environment, groups are limited to fifteen. There is no charge. To schedule a tour, call (304) 496–7359 or visit the volunteer guides' Web site at http://geocities.com/bailessteve.

At the base of Ice Mountain is the small village of North River Mills, which contains the remains of three mills. Each year the community holds North River Mills–Ice Mountain Day on a Saturday in June. The event features homemade ice cream, homegrown music, and tours of Ice Mountain. Call (304) 496–7359 for information.

Romney is said to have changed hands fifty-six times in the Civil War. On September 26, 1867, local citizens erected one of the earliest Confederate memorials in the United States. It still stands in Indian Mound Cemetery. Romney is also home to the graceful Hampshire County Courthouse and the *Taggart Hall Civil War History Museum.* Call (304) 463–4040 for information.

Foodies will love visiting *Gourmet Central* for tours and samples at one of West Virginia's leading herbal condiment producers. Owned by Chef Harv and Christy Christie, Gourmet Central was named among the top 205 places to visit by *Southern Living* magazine. Specialties include hot pepper jelly, salsa, and apple-pie jelly.

Just west of Romney on Fox Hollow Road is the *Freestyle Country Club,* where modern warriors battle on the paintball course, BMX track, and mountain biking trails. Although this is a membership club, racing events are open to the public. For further information call (301) 759–1010.

Romney's graceful colonial and Federal-style architecture, with homes and commercial buildings dating from the mid-1700s, stands in stark contrast to the rugged surrounding terrain of mountains and rocky pastures. This becomes quite evident as you head 4 miles north of town on State Route 28 to *Crystal Valley Ranch,* a 460-acre horse farm.

Here you're back in the wilderness, and there's no better way to savor the solitude than on the back of one of the ranch's trail horses. Crystal Valley's attentive staff will arrange trips according to your needs, whether it's an hour-long solo journey (with guide) or an all-day group outing up in the hills. The ranch also will arrange for a variety of camping, hiking, and backpacking trips. Fees tend to vary with the activity, but for less than $50 a day you can certainly rid yourself of the city-slicker blues. Crystal Valley Ranch is open year-round, weather permitting. A dinner theater similar to Dixie Stampede is in the works. For more information call (304) 822–7444.

If you've got children in tow, you may want to book a night at the *Almost Heaven Alpacas & Guest House,* where alpaca sweaters, scarves, and teddy bears can be purchased and alpacas can be petted.

After a night or two in the West Virginia woods, you're bound to feel like a frontiersman (or frontierswoman). To get a feel for the real McCoy, head north on Route 28 to **Fort Ashby,** the only French and Indian War fort still standing in West Virginia. This eighteenth-century relic of frontier life gives visitors an all-too-real look at how vulnerable settlers were to Indian attack. In fact, the fort is named for Colonel John Ashby, who barely escaped a raid here during the French and Indian War.

The large log structure was erected in 1755 on the order of George Washington as one of a chain of sixty-nine forts built to defend the Virginia frontier. Made from hand-hewn logs, it includes a massive chimney that is 14 feet wide and 4 feet thick. Much of the original interior woodwork and wrought iron, including the hinges on the doors, is still intact. After the French and Indian War, Fort Ashby was turned into a schoolhouse. It was restored and opened to the public on July 4, 1939.

The fort, owned by the Daughters of the American Revolution, is located on State Route 46, just inside the town limits of Fort Ashby. Visitors must call ahead to arrange tours. Admission is free, but donations are accepted and appreciated. Call (304) 298–3319 or 298–3318 for more information.

About 12 miles southwest of Fort Ashby on Route 46 sits the quiet riverside town of Keyser. Built along a hillside that slopes down to the Potomac River (which is very turbulent here), the Victorian-tinged town makes for a good stopping-off point for tired and hungry travelers. A great spot to unwind is the lovely **Candlewyck Inn,** 65 South Mineral Street, which is perched in the

BEST ATTRACTIONS IN THE POTOMAC HIGHLANDS

Blackwater Outdoor Adventures
St. George
(304) 478–3775
www.raftboc.com

Elk River Touring Center
Slatyfork
(304) 572–3771 or (866) 572–3771
www.ertc.com

Canaan Valley Resort State Park
Davis
(304) 866–4121 or (800) 622–4121
www.canaanresort.com

Snowshoe Mountain Resort
Snowshoe
(304) 572–1000 or (877) 441–4FUN
www.snowshoemtn.com

Blackwater Falls State Park
Davis
(304) 259–5216
www.blackwaterfalls.com

Seneca Rocks National Recreation Area
Seneca Rocks
(304) 567–2827

middle of Keyser's historic district a few blocks up the river. With its inviting Victorian facade and comfortable modern rooms, the Candlewyck offers a bit of luxury amid the rugged surroundings of the North Branch Valley. The dining room, which is open daily from 4:00 to 10:00 P.M., tempts travelers with hearty charbroiled steaks and fresh Maryland seafood delicacies such as Chesapeake Bay crab cakes and oysters. Each guest room comes with a private bath, two telephones, and color television. Rates begin at $59 and include a continental breakfast. Call (304) 788–6594 for reservations. Colorful antiques and curio shops along Mineral and Main Streets are just a short stroll away.

The area west of Fort Ashby and Keyser, along the banks of the North Branch of the Potomac River, was once one of intense surface coal mining, or, in the uglier vernacular, "strip mining." Although mining has kept the region somewhat economically viable, it has laid a heavy hand on its ecosystem. During heavy rains and river flooding—an all-too-common occurrence here—the abandoned coal mines fill with water and then ultimately release a toxic acidic runoff into the fragile Potomac, killing fish and plant life in its wake.

During the early 1970s visionaries from the U.S. Army Corps of Engineers decided to construct a special lake to control flooding and environmental degradation. The result is *Jennings Randolph Lake,* a 1,000-acre impoundment on the Potomac River bordering Maryland and West Virginia. It's located about 26 miles west of Keyser on Route 46. The lake acts as a receptacle for acid runoff and stabilizes the water downstream by periodically releasing pure water from the dam. The result is cleaner water in the lake and the river. The project has become so successful that brown trout, all but depleted during the 1970s, are now spawning in the tailwaters below the dam.

Aside from the environmental good stewardship, the lake has become a major recreational mecca for boaters, anglers, and campers. An interesting geological feature found near the lake's visitor center is *Waffle Rock,* a sandstone structure with a geometrical pattern resembling that of a waffle, the result of nearly 300 million years of folding, fracturing, and weathering. The lake facilities are open year-round. For more information call (301) 359–3861.

South of the lake, on the eastern slope of Saddle Mountain in Mineral County, sits a small, unassuming cabin that was the birthplace of Nancy Hanks, mother of Abraham Lincoln. The spare wooden structure was built in the late 1700s from native hardwoods the Hanks family cleared to farm the hollow. The cabin and surrounding hardscrabble pastures and woodlands are now part of the *Nancy Hanks Memorial,* a state park facility open to the public year-round from dawn to dusk. It is yet another reminder that seeds of greatness are often sown in the most humble of places. There is no admission charge for the area, but getting there can be tricky. From US 50, your best bet is to head south on Maysville Road toward the small farming community of Antioch. About 3 miles beyond Antioch, look for a brown state historic site sign on the right-hand side of the road. Head west about 2 miles to the cabin.

If you're still feeling adventurous, continue on Maysville Road about 10 miles and turn west onto Greenland Gap Road. This short but spectacular 4-mile stretch of road is home to the ***Greenland Gap Nature Preserve,*** part of The Nature Conservancy's effort to save unspoiled wilderness. In season you'll see spectacular rhododendron blooms, and any time of the year you can catch glimpses of the mountain gap's huge limestone walls, pristine creeks and waterfalls, and perhaps a bobcat or a black bear and her cub. Hundreds of turkey vultures and ravens glide in the gap's warm updrafts in the summer. In the warm months park your car alongside the creek and go for a wade in these gin-clear waters. Chances are you can spend an hour up on the gap and not see or hear another soul pass by. Two trails, one on each side of the gap, provide challenging, rocky climbs for the physically fit. The Mineral County preserve is open year-round from dawn to dusk, and there is no admission charge.

In neighboring Hardy County, down in the bucolic South Branch Valley, be sure to stop by ***Old Fields Church,*** one of the oldest houses of worship in the state. It's located just off U.S. Highway 220, about 3 miles north of Moorefield. The church was built in 1812 and was known at that time as the Fort Pleasant Meeting House. The small redbrick and tin-roof building was used by both Methodists and Presbyterians for more than a century. It also was reported to be the first schoolhouse in West Virginia. A few years ago the church was headed for the wrecker's ball before a local preservation group stepped in and began renovations. It's now owned by the Duffey Memorial United Methodist Church. Occasional services and social gatherings are still held here. Call (304) 538–6560 for more information.

When it comes to water quality, scenery, and isolation, few parts of the country can claim as many ideal canoeing waters as the Mountain State. ***Eagle's***

OTHER ATTRACTIONS WORTH SEEING IN THE POTOMAC HIGHLANDS

Seneca Caverns Riverton	**Beartown State Park** Droop
Greenbrier River Trail Cass to Caldwell	**Timberline Ski Resort and Mountain Biking Center** Davis
National Radio Astronomy Observatory Green Bank	**Durbin & Greenbrier Valley Railroad** Durbin

Nest Outfitters is the premier canoe rental and river vacation–planning company on the South Branch of the Potomac. It's located outside of Petersburg on US 220. Here, in the shadows of some of the highest peaks in West Virginia, anglers, campers, and canoeists from all over the United States come to experience more than 80 miles of virtually untouched rivers. Eagle's Nest experts can arrange group outings or tailor trips to individual tastes. There are eight different single-day trips of varying length and difficulty, and several two- to five-day trips also are available. For more details call (304) 257–2393.

For those in search of exciting white water, try rafting through the isolated *Smoke Hole Canyon.* The Lower Smoke Hole Canyon trip begins with breath-taking views of Cave Mountain and Eagle Rock, giant granite and limestone outcroppings that tower more than 100 feet above the river. Milder waters can be found by planning a trip through the Trough, a 3-mile-long canyon featuring a stunning 1,000-foot wall along one section. The majestic setting is made even more dramatic by the dozen or so American bald eagles that inhabit the area and are regularly sighted from the river.

If you're more interested in baiting a hook than paddling, Eagle's Nest also plans fishing trips. Hundreds of trophy-size small- and largemouth bass, catfish, and trout are landed each year on the productive South Branch. Canoeing and fishing trip reservations must be made by phone or by mail three weeks in advance for holidays and weekends. Prices start as low as $25 a day per canoe. That includes canoe, paddles, life jackets, shuttle service, safety lectures, and instructions. Eagle's Nest is open daily from April 1 through October 31. Call (304) 257–2393 for information.

As you wend your way south on US 220 from Petersburg, you'll pass a small white country store in the hamlet of Pansy about 6 miles down the road. Throughout your ramblings in West Virginia, you'll pass hundreds like this, but this one has had an international reputation as a weekly venue for classical country music, the kind played by George Jones, Patsy Cline, and Loretta Lynn. This is the *Country Store Opry,* a former grocery that doubles as a live bluegrass and old-time music venue. Although the bimonthly hoedowns have moved to Pendleton County High School in Franklin and McCoy's Grand Theater in Moorefield, an occasional summer reunion kicks up the spirits here in Pansy. These unpretentious gatherings often showcase some of the best mountain music ever made and are an integral part of the cultural fabric of Appalachia.

potomac highlands trivia

Roughly one-half the land mass of the Potomac Highlands is contained in the Monongahela National Forest.

The Wild Allegheny Trail

The **Allegheny Trail** winds the length of West Virginia along 330 miles of backbone ridges, hollows, and high bogs, through some of the Mountain State's wildest, prettiest territory. It purposely avoids civilization, so you can walk for hours without seeing a road. It doesn't lend itself to convenient shuttle points for the day hiker.

Greedy for a large helping of natural beauty one September Saturday, my husband, Bruce, and I embarked on a 15-mile segment of the Allegheny—a lot of footwork for occasional, 3-mile-a-day walkers. As soon as we entered the eastern Pocahontas County forest, we stumbled upon signs of nature—the skeleton of a 5-foot snake coiled in our path, a blueberry patch raked by giant paws, and the steaming scat of a large animal that had obviously eaten a mammal for breakfast. "Is this a warning?" I asked.

We saw dozens of specimens of bear scat over the next eleven hours, but no bear. Charleston resident Mike Maxwell, our hiking companion in the last hours of the day, had encountered a large cub falling out of a tree the day before. "It squalled when it fell," he said. "That can put the goose bumps on you. Then it looked at me and ran the other way."

We were glad he was with us.

Although we saw abundant signs of wildlife, the woods seemed unnaturally quiet. We had the sensation of being the strangers in neon spandex who bumbled into a country store and brought all conversation to a halt. Everything ceased breathing while the woodland waited for us to pass.

As the forest road dwindled to a single-track path, then to a random passage marked only by gold blazes on the oaks and hickories, we ascended Thorny Creek Mountain into Seneca State Park. The Allegheny Trail passes through four state parks as well as four state forests and the Monongahela and Jefferson National Forests. It stretches uninterrupted from the Mason-Dixon Line at Bruceton Mills to just south of exit 1 off Interstate 64 (Jerry's Run) east of White Sulphur Springs. There the trail disappears like an underground stream, to resurface near Laurel Branch in Monroe County and join the Appalachian Trail atop Peters Mountain. The right-of-way for the 20-mile missing link is still being negotiated.

Hiking the entire length of the Allegheny takes a month. Although we spent only eleven hours on the trail, we weren't spared the plodding weariness of through-hikers. As we ascended to what had to be the summits of Little, Thomas, and Thorny Creek Mountains, we watched the crests flatten out to reveal new heights above us. After six or seven hours on the trail, we stopped thinking, stopped observing, and just stepped, stepped, stepped.

We walked hard all morning, hard enough to hear our pulses thudding in our throats, and when we sat down for lunch, we realized we'd gone only 4.3 miles and had 10.7 more to reach our pickup point. Allegheny Trail miles feel twice as long as road miles.

When we reached the last mountain, the scrubby, wind-beaten vegetation seemed a mirror for our stoicism. Like the rest of the forest, which was preparing to go dormant until spring, we were ready to lie still for a long, long time.

Admission to the Country Store Opry at any location is $3.00 for adults, free for children under twelve. Music begin at 7:00 P.M. For more information, see www.pendletoncounty.net/cso/index.htm.

Seneca Rocks

Named after the imposing sandstone spires that tower high above the South Branch Valley, the Seneca Rocks region encompasses Pendleton and parts of Grant and Randolph Counties. The deep gorges, jutting rock formations, wild rivers, and arching mountains (including the highest point in the state—4,861-foot Spruce Knob) make for perhaps the most spectacular natural scenery in all West Virginia.

Born of Mother Earth's violent upheaval 185 million years ago, **Smoke Hole Gorge,** running mostly parallel with US 220 in Grant and Pendleton Counties, is one of the most remote and beautiful areas in the United States. Most people don't know that, because it's nearly impossible to get to. But it can be done.

Smoke Hole is where the South Branch of the Potomac River squeezes between North Fork Mountain and Cave Mountain, creating spectacular waterfalls, sluices, and white-water conditions. These raging waters have formed caves, carved canyons, and shaped the wild landscape in an extraordinary fashion. An ever-present fog through the "hole" makes visitors feel like they're in a bygone era. It's easy to believe the old myths here. Earliest settlers said the "smoke" came from a moonshiner's still. Some claimed it came from Indian fires.

potomac highlands trivia

The Mountain State Forest Festival, held each October in Elkins, is West Virginia's oldest and largest festival.

Smoke Hole is managed by the **Monongahela National Forest** as part of the Spruce Knob–Seneca Rocks National Recreation Area. It's a hunting, fishing, hiking, canoeing, and camping paradise. The easiest access into the gorge is via Route 2, near Upper Tract, a tiny town 18 miles southwest of Petersburg along US 220. Route 2 parallels the river into the canyon for about 8 miles. On the way in you might see a few fishermen and perhaps a canoeist or two.

After 8 miles the paved road ends at a junction featuring an old country store and a log church. One fork of the road continues along the river; the other rises to the north of the shoulder of North Fork Mountain and down to State Route 28. If you take the "high road," notice the small farms nestled in the hollows and the abandoned log cabins decorating the clearings. Traffic is almost nonexistent, so you might want to stop along the photogenic route for an impromptu picnic.

If you decide to spend the night, there are some outstanding places to sleep under the stars. The largest is the **Big Bend Campground,** with forty-six sites managed by the USDA Forest Service. It's open April 15 to October 31. As the name implies, the campground is situated along a huge bend of the river.

Primitive camping sites are scattered along Smoke Hole Road (Routes 28/11) on North Fork Mountain and throughout the backcountry except at trail-heads. For camping and other recreation information within the gorge, call the Forest Service at (304) 257–4488.

Just to the west of the Smoke Hole Gorge, off Route 28, about 10 miles south of Petersburg, lies another fascinating natural area, **Dolly Sods.** This 10,215-acre National Wilderness and Scenic Area is characterized by rugged boulder-strewn plains, windswept spruce trees, cool mountain air, and 50-mile vistas.

Dolly Sods was once a forest of giant red spruces and hemlocks, most claiming diameters in excess of 4 feet. These incredible trees were logged in the 1800s, and the hot fires that burned during the logging destroyed the under-lying fertile humus layer. About the same time local farmers burned the plains to create grazing land, or sods. One such group of pioneers that cleared the area was the Dahle family. Over the years Dahle somehow became Dolly, as in the present Dolly Sods.

The Sods' plant life and climate are what make it so unusual. It's actually more akin to the boreal forest of northern Canada than it is to any other part of the United States. In the summer azaleas, mountain laurels, rhododendrons, and blueberries thrive despite the infertile soil. Cranberries and insect-eating sundew plants are adjacent to more arid, boulder-strewn, open areas. Northern hard-woods are found in the coves and drainages, and red pines grow in several areas.

Save a little energy and appetite for some **berry picking,** a favorite pas-time among visitors and native bears. Blueberries, huckleberries, teaberries, and cranberries blanket the area. Ramps (a very strong wild leek) can be found in moist wooded areas. Take your fare to the shady Dolly Sods picnic area to eat, and enjoy the natural surroundings. The picnic area is on Forest Road 19 just south of the scenic area. Picnic tables, grills, and portable toilets are provided.

Dolly Sods has several hiking trails, all marked only by ax blazes or rock cairns (mounds). Distances are not indicated. When

potomac highlands trivia

Pendleton County claims more than 240 noncommercial caves, most of which are located on private land.

you're ready to pull off your hiking boots, you can bed down overnight in the area's only campground, Red Creek. It has twelve campsites (two walk-in and ten suitable for trailers). Portable toilets and a water well are provided.

A visit to Dolly Sods, rated one of the top ten backpacking trails in the nation by Trails.com, is well worth your time, but you should observe a few cautions. Because it sits directly atop the Allegheny Plateau, at elevations ranging from 2,600 to 4,000 feet, weather can change suddenly. Storms can be severe and life-threatening, and dense fog can confuse even the most experienced outdoorsperson. The area is noted for its fierce westerly winds (note the one-sided red spruce trees), snow in the fall, winter, and spring, and low temperatures during any month of the year. Also be watchful of poisonous snakes. And if that's not enough, be on the lookout for old mortar shells. Yes, mortar shells. The area was used for military exercises during World War II, and some live shells remain. If you come to a shell, don't touch it!

For more information about Dolly Sods, call the USDA Forest Service at (304) 636–1800, (304) 257–4488, or (304) 567–2827.

Straight down the road (literally) from Dolly Sods are the fabled **Seneca Rocks.** Named for one of the Indian tribes that passed through the area, these sandstone rock formations rise more than 900 feet above the North Fork Valley and Route 28 and U.S. Highway 33. This is one of the most popular rock-climbing areas in the East, and on any given weekend—or weekday for that matter—you'll see cars with license plates from as far away as Vermont, Florida, and Illinois.

If you're brave (or crazy) enough to scale these narrow spires, look for the words D.B., SEPTEMBER 16, 1908 carved into the top of the south peak. No one is quite sure who D.B. was, although one theory claims he may have been D. Bittenger, a civil engineer who surveyed the area for the Forest Service. Whoever

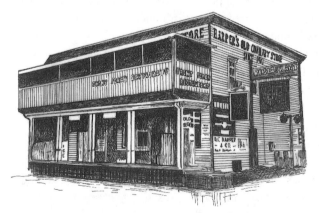

Harper's Old Country Store

he or she was, D.B. beat Paul Brandt, Don Hubbard, and Sam Moore to the top, a trio credited with being the first recorded climbers to master the rocks and reach the summit in 1938.

Since that time thousands of thrill seekers have climbed Seneca Rocks, including members of the Tenth Mountain Division, who trained here during World War II. For those who yearn to see the view from the top but don't want to risk life and limb in the process, there is another way. A steep and relatively safe 1.3-mile, self-guided, interpretive trail ascends the north edge of the rocks to a viewing platform.

If you'd rather keep your feet firmly planted on the ground, there's still plenty to do in the area, starting with a visit to the Seneca Rocks Discovery Center. Inside you'll find exhibits and a video explaining the history and geology of the area. In the adjacent picnic area, you can watch the brave climbers cling precariously to the rocks, or you can stroll down to the South Branch for a bit of catch-and-release trout fishing.

Seneca Rocks is open year-round. For more information, call the visitor center at (304) 567–2827.

The wild beauty of Seneca Rocks serves as a spectacular backdrop for **Harper's Old Country Store,** a thriving early-twentieth-century retailer that shows no signs of slowing down. It's one of the oldest continuously operated businesses in the state, still run by members of the Harper family. The wood-frame store was built in 1902 and originally operated under the name of D.C. Harper and Co. Its interior today is much the same as it was then. Inside you'll find groceries, hardware, clothing, snacks, gifts, and hunting and fishing equipment. While you're stocking up, take a look at the store's original board floor, the antique ceiling, and the original shelving and counters. You can't miss the mounted West Virginia black bear, which stands guard over the store's ground floor.

If you're in the mood to eat, step up to **The Front Porch** restaurant, located on the second floor of Harper's. It's nothing fancy, just simple, tasty, and well-prepared food in a casual atmosphere. The view isn't bad either. Try a slice of fresh dough pizza, or sample one of the wheat pita pocket sandwiches. They're good enough to lure you down from the rocks.

Harper's Old Country Store is located at the intersection of US 33 and State Route 55 in Seneca Rocks. Store hours are 7:00 A.M. to 8:30 P.M. weekdays and Saturday, and 8:00 A.M. to 8:00 P.M. Sunday. The restaurant is open April 15 to October 15 Saturday from 11:00 A.M. to 10:00 P.M., and Sunday through Friday from 11:00 A.M. to 9:00 P.M. Call (304) 567–2555 for more information.

Kids getting car claustrophia? Or maybe you're ready to climb the walls? **Mountaineer Wall,** at the junction in Seneca Rocks, is the perfect place to take bored, squirmy people. Let them expend excess energy climbing a real wall all day for just $10. There's no age limit, and full-body harnesses are available for the smallest children as well as adults. Every climber is supervised by a certified instructor. Tom Cecil, owner of the Seneca Rocks Mountain Guides Climbing Center, also invites experienced rock climbers to stop by and test their skills. Open 10:00 A.M. to 4:00 P.M. daily in June, July, and August and on weekends in May, September, and October. Call (800) 451–5108 or (304) 567–2115.

Now that you're loaded with provisions from Harper's, it's time to explore the state's highest mountain, *Spruce Knob,* and take in what's probably the finest vista in West Virginia. From Seneca Rocks, drive 10 miles south on US 33 before taking a right on County Road 33/4 (look for the sign to Spruce Knob National Recreation Area). After a mile or so, the paved mountain road will give way to gravel for the next 8 miles until you reach the summit of the 4,861-foot mountain. Budget one-half hour to get up the mountain (if you make it quicker than that, you're probably driving too fast), and keep your eyes posted for wildlife that will frequently dart onto the road. This isn't a place where you want to apply the brakes quickly; skidding on gravel on a narrow mountain road without guardrails isn't exactly conducive to relaxation.

Once you reach the summit of this gorgeous mountain, you'll be glad you made the trip. Near the top of the mountain, the gravel returns to blacktop and winds around to a parking lot. An easy ½-mile foot trail takes you along the summit ridge, which is sprinkled with massive limestone and granite boulders; windblown, one-sided, red spruce trees; and dense pockets of blueberry, huckleberry, and mountain ash. The trail ends at a two-story observation deck that affords views of more than 75 miles in any direction, including an eastern vista extending all the way to Virginia's Shenandoah Valley.

potomac highlands trivia

Spruce Knob, the tallest mountain in West Virginia (over 4,800 feet), marks the geographic center of the Potomac Highlands region.

Like the Dolly Sods Wilderness Area, the Spruce Knob region was once farmed by hearty Scots-Irish and German settlers, and traces of the pastures they forged by clearing timber can still be seen more than a hundred years later. If you plan to camp out, the USDA Forest Service maintains the forty-three-site Spruce Knob Campground about 3 miles down from the summit, next to Spruce Knob Lake, a twenty-five-acre pond that provides some good trout fishing. Backcountry camping also is allowed throughout Spruce Knob, and the same types of precautions you would take on Dolly Sods should be applied here (see page 40).

The recreation area is open year-round, except during snowy and icy periods when the roads can be life-threatening. For more information stop by the Seneca Rocks Visitor Center, or call (304) 567–2827.

The High Valley

The High Valley region is the area in and around Tucker County's Canaan Valley, pronounced "keh-NANE" by locals. It's the highest valley in the East and one of the most peculiar, geologically and geographically speaking, in the United States.

Canaan Valley is a place of quiet beauty where the deer will eat out of your hand—though allowing them to do so is illegal, unhealthy for the deer, and not allowed under any circumstances. The oranges, reds, and yellows of October are incomparable, and the lush springs, mild summers, and deep winter snows make the mountain vistas breathtaking. The 3,200-foot-high, 14-mile-long valley is located in Tucker County, near the Maryland border, and is bisected by State Route 32.

Portions of Canaan have been designated a National Wildlife Refuge because of the unusual Canadian forest plant life and the 8,400 acres of fragile upcountry wetlands—the largest wetland area in the central and southern Appalachians. Here more than 580 plant and 290 animal species thrive. For more information on the refuge, call (304) 866–3858.

The high Allegheny Mountains that rim the valley seem to act as magnets for snow. In fact, Canaan receives 150 to 200 inches of the white stuff each year. Late spring snows aren't uncommon. As you might guess, the valley has become one of the best ski areas in the Mid-Atlantic, boasting two downhill ski resorts, *Canaan Valley Resort State Park* (800–622–4121) and *Timberline Resort* (800–SNOWING), and the *White Grass* cross-country ski resort (304–866–4114). With a drop of 1,000 vertical feet, these resorts give you some of the longest ski runs in the East—up to 2 miles. The terrain and weather are conducive to Nordic skiing, and lessons are offered on the forest trails of all three resorts.

Looking for a downhill rush? In the 2005–6 ski season, Canaan Valley Resort introduced the East Coast to the latest extreme trend in winter sports—the airboard. Some call it a snow bodyboard; some call it "sled zeppelin," but everybody who zips down Canaan's slopes on the inflatable airboard says it's a thrill.

The airboard is a distant cousin of the traditional sled: In both cases, riders lie on their chests and glide downhill. But the resemblance stops there. Extreme riders have been known to reach speeds in excess of seventy mph on

To Canaan's Land, I'm on My Way

You can get a feeling for eternity sitting on the slope behind Canaan Valley Resort's lodge watching the light fade over miles of high marsh and forest. Life appears to go on forever in some form in nature's endless cycle. Could any small, petty thinking exist against sweeping perspectives like this?

I hear a distant "Who, who for you?" A barred owl? A little later, a woodcock circles with a high "chee." A doe saunters within feet of me, pausing to gracefully rub the top of her head with her back hoof.

Canaan Valley is a place of quiet loveliness where summers are mild and the winter snows deep (an average of 175 inches annually). Frosts have been recorded every month of the year, and cool night air slides down the mountains, leaving a dreamy fog over the valley most mornings between May and November.

Underneath its apparent tranquillity, Canaan Valley is still in recovery mode. In the earlier part of the twentieth century, this country was logged out of its spruce and hemlock forests. Even earlier, when Lord Fairfax's surveyors reached Canaan in 1746, there was hardly room to walk for the growth sprouting from the fertile, 8-foot duff layer of decomposing vegetation. Surveyor Thomas Lewis wrote: "Ye laurels and spruce grow so thick one cannot have the least prospect of seeing light except they look upwards."

But a century and a half later, fires kindled by logging detritus swept over the land, burning the deep, peaty soil that had taken thousands of years to develop. Through some rash will for survival, the vegetation we see today has managed to migrate back into this cool, humid climate. Many of these plants—including red spruce, balsam fir, high-bush cranberry, swamp saxifrage, and Jacob's ladder—are considered boreal species, two vegetation zones below tundra. They persist in portions of Canaan Valley now designated a National Natural Landmark.

For more information about lodging and nature programs at Canaan Valley Resort State Park, call (304) 866–4121.

the airboard, which is constructed like a white-water raft with side handgrips and ribbed runners underneath. To steer and stop, riders shift their weight. The airboard's comfort, stopping ability, and control at any speed make it fairly easy to learn in a one-hour lesson.

Canaan is the first U.S. ski area to offer an airboard terrain park where these bodyboarders can safely satiate their quest for a new wintertime adrenaline rush. The park has jumps and berms that will allow brave souls to catch major air and maybe even do barrel rolls here.

When the weather warms up, hiking, golfing, mountain biking, and fishing take center stage. Hikers take to the Blackwater/Canaan Trail, an 8-mile moun-

Leaf Peepers' Special

When the autumn leaf watch is just beginning in the lower elevations, Pocahontas County's 4,800-foot ridgetops blaze orange, gold, and crimson. The Greenbrier, Elk River, and Deer Creek valleys, more than 2,000 feet below, reach their peak display of red maple, yellow beech, and rusty oaks two to three weeks later in mid-October. Starting just after summer officially ends, the Potomac Highlands color show slides a little farther down the mountains each day.

And when the mountaintops are bare, it's easier to spot the last hawks and eagles on their southern migration.

One great way to enjoy the colorful vistas—especially if you have children in tow—is from the open passenger cars of Cass Scenic Railroad. The restored village of Cass remains relatively unchanged since it began life as a company town for the West Virginia Pulp & Paper Company around 1900. For fifty-eight years, residents awoke to the mill whistle and lived to the rhythm of the comings and goings of the rowdy wood hicks from their logging camps up on Cheat Mountain.

Luckily for leaf peepers, the mixture of spruce and hardwoods has grown back; now the restored Shay locomotive pulls retrofitted logging cars full of passengers up the 11 percent grade to Whittaker Station and Bald Knob. With thick black smoke gushing from the stack, huff-huffing and clanking like a kitchen band, the Shay transports you back in time as it pulls you up the mountain.

Even at full speed, the steam locomotive reaches only about 4 miles per hour uphill and 6 miles per hour down, so there's plenty of time to admire the scenery and look for deer, turkey, and bear along the tracks.

The view from Whittaker (1½-hour round-trip) is lovely; above the spruce forest from Bald Knob (5-hour round-trip), it's stunning. But take a jacket for the chilling wind whipping around the observation tower at 4,842 feet.

The Division of Forestry will provide weekly leaf-color reports late September through the end of October. To hear the weekly report, updated each Wednesday, call (800) CALL–WVA.

tain path connecting Blackwater Falls State Park to Canaan Valley State Park. In early March trout fishing heats up on the tea-colored Blackwater River and stays hot through the summer months. For those who'd rather swing a club than a fly rod, the eighteen-hole championship golf course at Canaan Valley State Park (800–622–4121) offers a great summertime escape.

At the northern edge of Canaan Valley sits the eclectic little town of Davis. Looking a bit like the fictional Cicely, Alaska, of the old television series *Northern Exposure*, Davis is the highest incorporated town (elevation 3,200 feet) east of the Mississippi. Here you'll find a number of unusual attractions. The ***Art Company of Davis*** is at the top of the list.

This enterprising venture is actually a membership cooperative formed in 1990 by a small group of local artisans as a forum to exhibit work and stimulate creativity. Today that group has grown to more than one hundred artists who produce both contemporary and traditional arts and crafts. Their wares are housed in a turn-of-the-nineteenth-century, 3,000-square-foot frame building located right on Route 32 near the bridge. Interestingly enough, the blue wooden building was once the company store for the Babcock Lumber and Boom Company.

All of the artwork, including wood carvings, textiles, and oil paintings depicting outdoor life in the region, are juried for quality and originality. Visitors to the company can pick up paintings, toys, quilts, pottery, baskets, rugs, musical instruments, photographs, furniture, and books on West Virginia crafts and culture.

The Art Company is open 10:00 A.M. to 6:00 P.M. Tuesday through Saturday, and 11:00 A.M. to 5:00 P.M. Sunday. For more information call (304) 259–4218.

Almost directly across the street from the gallery is *Bright Morning Inn,* a bed-and-breakfast that was once a boardinghouse for itinerant lumberjacks. Proprietors Robert and Linda Darfus took over the restored wood-frame building in July 1999. The B&B includes seven bedrooms and one suite, all with private baths. Right next door you can find even roomier accommodations at *Doc's Guest House,* a three-bedroom Victorian home. Breakfast is provided to all guests. Reservations are suggested for lunch and dinner, which typically feature local fish, meats, and produce prepared in a "country gourmet" fashion. The inn is open year-round. Rates range from $65 to $109 for double occupancy. Call (304) 259–5119.

The Western Slope

The Western Slope of the Allegheny Mountains shows its face in Randolph County, where the hills tend to come down on top of one another, adding to the mythical spirit of the place. The remoteness of the land seems only to intensify the friendliness of the people who live here.

From Davis, follow U.S. Highway 219 south through the Monongahela National Forest to Elkins, the Randolph County seat. This is the home of the *Augusta Heritage Center,* a haven for traditional Appalachian music, crafts, dancing, and folklore.

The world-renowned musical performance and craft-learning center was founded in 1973 on the secluded, tree-lined campus of Davis and Elkins College. Its guiding mission is to keep the spirit of West Virginia's mountain culture alive by sharing it with natives and visitors alike. It's been a huge success. Each July and August hundreds of students of all ages from across North America descend on Elkins to take part in Augusta's intimate workshops taught by master artists and musicians. Courses range from fiddle and banjo instruction to log-house building, Celtic stone carving, and African-American storytelling.

August also ushers in the **Augusta Festival** in Elkins City Park, a weekend celebration of free concerts, juried craft fairs, children's art and music exhibitions, dancing, food, and storytelling. The Spring Dulcimer Festival in April and the Fiddler's Reunion and Old-Time Week in October are homecomings of sorts for mountain musicians from throughout the United States and from as far away as Nova Scotia, Ireland, and Scotland. Most Wednesday evenings you can enjoy old-time jam sessions from 7:00 to 10:00 P.M. at Davis and Elkins College's Hermanson Center, from October to May, and at Elkins City Park June to September.

For more information on courses and programs provided by the Augusta Heritage Center, call (304) 637–1209.

If your travels haven't yet taken you to Europe, you can at least get a glimpse of what one European country must be like with a visit to the Randolph County community of **Helvetia.** This hidden village, tucked into the folds of the Alleghenies about an hour south of Elkins off U.S. Highway 250, was settled by feisty German and Swiss immigrants in 1869 and today has all the flavor of a true Alpine community. It was the first town district in the state to be placed on the National Register of Historic Places.

Helvetia claims about 225 inhabitants, considerably fewer than the 1,200 or so who populated the village and surrounding hills and hollows around the turn of the twentieth century during the area's logging boom. As you stroll the tidy streets, don't be surprised to hear a few residents chatting in their ancestors' native tongue.

It is the native cuisine, however, that keeps many outsiders returning to Helvetia on a regular basis. Find the sign that says GRUSS GOTT, TRITT EIN, BRING GLUCK HEREIN ("Praise God, Step In, Bring Luck Herein"), and you've found **The Hutte** restaurant, known for its locally grown food prepared in Swiss style. It's the hub of activity in Helvetia. Owner Eleanor Mailloux is a descendant of one of Helvetia's original settlers, and she doesn't skimp on authenticity. Menu items include pfeffernuss, a ginger cookie; Stout Country Soup, a thick vegetable beef soup; and a locally made cheese. All of this and more is served at Bernerplatte, the Swiss version of Sunday brunch. Other menu items include sauerbraten, bratwurst, homemade sausage, homemade breads, pineapple, and pickled beets. The Hutte is open daily from noon to 7:00 P.M. Call (304) 924–6435.

If you arrive on a weekday and want to stay over for the brunch, ask Eleanor if she has room at the inn. She also owns *The Beekeeper Inn* (304–924–6435), a bed-and-breakfast. It's a cozy, three-room affair complete with private baths, a common room overstuffed with books, and a large deck shaded by huge pine trees. Also available is the Alpine Penthouse, two large rooms that sleep a total of ten, for $35 per person per night with breakfast included.

After a sumptuous repast or a long afternoon nap, take a walk around this fairy-tale-like village. Don't miss the flag-bedecked bridge leading to the pottery shop; the Cheese Haus, formerly a working cheese shop; the one-hundred-year-old church; and the town museum housed in an original settler's cabin. For tours of the museum, call (304) 924–6435. The latter is filled with interesting artifacts, including the original Swiss flag the settlers brought with them from the old country.

Helvetia is no theme park. It's an active community with deep pride in its roots. As such, it celebrates its heritage with several endearing customs and festivals. Hundreds come from far and wide to attend such events as Swiss Independence Day in August, the Helvetia Fair in September, and Fasnacht, a Mardi Gras–like fete in February that celebrates the coming of spring. Fasnacht participants hang Old Man Winter in effigy and don costumes to "scare away" winter. If visitors arrive without proper costumes, they're encouraged to rummage through local attics to find something fitting to wear. The celebration is usually held the Saturday before Ash Wednesday and is kicked off with a community-wide Swiss feast and an Appalachian music show.

Nearby, deep in the heart of the hardwood forest, along a fork of the Buckhannon River, lies the small town of *Pickens.* Founded in the 1890s, Pickens doesn't have a lot going on these days. The town's post office has to be one of the smallest in the nation, only slightly larger than outdoor storage sheds commonly seen in the yards of suburban homes. The town has the distinction of being the wettest place in West Virginia. It receives more annual precipitation than most any place in the eastern United States—an annual 66 inches—much of it in snowfall. The snows received by Pickens are comparable to the lake-effect snows experienced by Buffalo, New York. The high mountains, cool weather, and wet conditions have conspired to produce an abundance of sugar maple trees in the area—such as one would expect to find only in Vermont.

With such a wealth of maple trees, the production of maple syrup is a booming concern—and the reason for Pickens's annual *Maple Syrup Festival.* Each year on the third full weekend in March, people come down from the hills and hollows to socialize, feast on pancakes and maple syrup, listen to good mountain music, and sell a few crafts made during the long, cold mountain winter.

The festival features a pancake feed on Saturday and Sunday, a 5K run, a muzzle-loading competition, and wood chopping and ax-throwing demonstrations. Free musical entertainment is found at the town pavilion and in the Opera House. Visit the sugar house and watch the syrup-making process first-hand. Artisans are at work—the most interesting of which may be the chain-saw sculptor, who, in a short period of time, makes a piece of art from a chunk of wood using only his chain saw.

Tradition says that Native Americans discovered the sweetness of the sugar maple when a hatchet was thrown into a maple trunk. A taste of the oozing sap was found to be sweet. Figuring a way to concentrate that sweetness, they would gather the sap, place it in a trough, and drop heated rocks into it to cause evaporation. There is about a fifty-to-one ratio in the process: fifty gallons of sap, when processed, will produce one gallon of syrup, and evaporation is still at the heart of syrup production today.

Early settlers in the region used maple trees as their primary source of sugar, as imported white sugar was very expensive. They would boil the syrup down to dry brown chunks. Only in the mid-1800s, when white sugar produced in the Caribbean brought the price down, was maple sugar displaced.

The sap is gathered over a six- to eight-week period from February to mid-March and must be processed right away. A succession of freezing nights and temperatures reaching the mid-30s to mid-40s in the day starts the sap coming up into the tree. Gathering involves drilling a hole about 2½ inches into the tree trunk and driving a tap, which is nothing more than a spout, into the hole. Either a bucket is dangled from the tap for sap collection or plastic tubing is attached. The tubing connects many trees and drains into large collection tanks. Each tree may have up to three or four taps. For more information call the Pickens Improvement and Historical Society at (304) 924–5404 or (304) 924–6288.

Mountain Wilderness

The Mountain Wilderness region consists of Pocahontas and parts of Randolph Counties. As its name implies, this is one of the most mountainous parts of West Virginia, and it contains the largest swath of the Potomac Highlands.

Any place that's called a "most beautiful spot" by someone as noteworthy as American inventor Thomas Edison must be special. The New Jersey–born inventor was referring to West Virginia's *Cheat Mountain Club,* an 1899 lodge along the banks of the Shavers Fork River and high atop the namesake mountain that contains nine of the state's ten tallest peaks. Edison, Henry Ford, and Harvey Firestone journeyed to this mountain in a Model T to enjoy the hunting and rustic charm of the region. The club is now open only to large groups that rent the entire facility, but people still make pilgrimages from urban areas to see mountainsides tricked out in ice crystals or fiery foliage and to hunt, ski, snowshoe, or hike.

The shriek of a train whistle in the village of Durbin below Cheat Mountain is no fantasy. Durbin maintains its tradition as a key railroad stop, but now *Durbin & Greenbrier Valley Railroad* excursion trains carry passengers into pristine mountain valleys where no wood saws whine.

The Cheat Mountain Salamander, the Tygart Flyer, and the Durbin Rocket haul passengers up mountains and through hidden valleys accessible only by foot or rail. Trips run from May 15 through Halloween and range from a two-hour jaunt to an eight-hour, 88-mile expedition. If the children get restless, the friendly engineer may invite them to ride up front with him and take turns helping to operate the controls. Or to look out for bears; black bear sightings are a regular feature on several runs.

If you've ever wanted to be a hobo or experience wilderness miles from the nearest railroad, rail camping may be in your future. You can board the train with your tent only, disembark at one of several remote campsites near the tracks, or you may rent the railway's *Castaway Caboose* for an overnight at the end of the line. Campers are dropped off in the afternoon and don't hear another sound of civilization until the approaching train whistles almost twenty-four hours later. Caboose accommodations include refrigerator, liners, modern shower, and bathroom, for $200 a night.

Telescope of the National Radio Astronomy Observatory

Or you can go for the ride, imagine roughing it, and set up camp in Frank Proud's Greenbrier Inn bed-and-breakfast back in town. For train rides and overnight, call (877) MTN–RAIL or go to the Web site at www.mountainrail.com.

Tourists with an interest in the scientific must find time to visit an impressive and somewhat eerie facility in eastern Pocahontas County, about forty minutes south of the Cheat Mountain Club in the town of Green Bank. Established in 1956, the *National Radio Astronomy Observatory* was built to provide state-of-the-art communications equipment for exploring the universe. The sprawling campus looks like something from the set of the 1997 film *Contact.*

Radio astronomy is a branch of astronomy in which celestial objects are studied by examining their emission of radio-magnetic radiation. It is a fairly recent science, with its earliest roots dating only from the 1930s. It was then that a researcher for Bell Laboratories, Karl G. Jansky, discovered extraterrestrial radio waves coming from a source near the center of the Milky Way galaxy.

Grote Reber, an astronomer and radio engineer, is largely responsible for the development of radio astronomy. Prompted by Jansky's discovery, Reber built the world's first radio telescope in 1937. He did it right in his backyard in Wheaton, Illinois. Thirty-one feet in diameter, this bowl-shaped telescope must have presented an unusual specimen of lawn art. It certainly must have provoked some strange looks and speculation by his neighbors. Why did he choose a 31-foot diameter? His building project was limited by the length of the boards he could obtain at the local hardware store. Reber's invention served as the world's only radio telescope until after World War II. His telescope is now on display by the entrance to the Green Bank observatory.

Set back deep in Deer Creek Valley, the observatory is ideally situated because the remoteness of the area and the surrounding mountains protect the sensitive receivers used on the telescopes against any human-made radio interference.

As you approach the installation on Route 28, you'll see several giant satellite dishes dotting the quiet valley, a startling sight against the lush landscape. The observatory houses a 140-foot radio telescope used to discover new molecules in the spaces between the stars. "Molecules," explains one of the tour guides, "reveal the birth sites of stars." This huge telescope is linked electronically around the world with other similar devices, helping create some of the sharpest images possible in radio astronomy.

The new GBT (Green Bank Telescope, or Great Big Telescope, as locals call it) is the largest fully steerable radio telescope on the planet. This huge iron ear, which resembles a satellite dish, is the size of one and a half football fields and thirty stories tall. Weighing 16.7 million tons, GBT took nine years and 249 ironworkers to build. The telescope turns and tilts as it gathers information from outer space—radio wave data about the births of galaxies and the composition of interstellar dust. GBT sits at the center of a National Radio Quiet Zone, a restricted area off-limits to cell-phone towers, set up by the Federal Communications Commission to protect the purity of signals from outer space from competing cell-phone or radio signals.

In October 2002 the National Radio Astronomy Observatory opened a $6.1 million education and visitor center, featuring hands-on displays that explain the instruments and discoveries of radio astronomy. Full-time science educators answer questions and guide visitors through a real-world research environment as they try out the role of astronomer. Through a connection to the GBT, visitors can eavesdrop on scientists receiving data via the real telescope. Visitors can explore the effects of signal interference from radio stations, manipulate a laser beam, and learn about how NRAO scientists became interested in astronomy, all in the science center.

Free tours are offered at the visitor center daily from 9:00 A.M. to 6:00 P.M. Memorial Day through Halloween. In November through May the facility is open Wednesday through Sunday from 10:00 A.M. to 5:00 P.M. with tours at 11:00 A.M., 1:00 P.M., and 3:00 P.M. On a clear day in the summer, you can stick around for a telescopic solar viewing at 2:45 P.M., a star party on Saturday night, and a star lab on Thursday at 2:00 P.M. Free "spacey" movies are screened first Fridays at 7:00 P.M. The observatory has a gift shop and cafe for guests. Call (304) 456–2150 or see www.gb.nrao.edu/epo/aec.shtml for details.

All aboooaaarrrddd! No, it's not the Chattanooga Choo Choo, but it may inspire you to sing just the same. *Cass Scenic Railroad* is a delight any month of the year, but in the fall the locomotive's 11-mile winding journey through the area's breathtaking foliage is really a treat. It's all part of the state park system, and it's the nation's only authentic and operating museum of lumber railroading.

Tourists board the train in the small railroad town of Cass, on the eastern slope of Cheat Mountain and less than forty-five minutes from Green Bank. The village, located on State Route 66 at the Greenbrier River, has remained virtually unchanged since the early years of the 1900s, when it was a company lumber town. At that time West Virginia led the nation with more than 3,000 miles of logging railroad line. The renovated, state park–operated line was the same used to haul lumber from the mountaintop to the mill in Cass.

Steam- and coal-powered locomotives haul passengers up an 11 percent grade (a 2 percent grade is considered steep on conventional railroads) using several switchbacks, then wind through open fields to Whitaker Station, where passengers disembark long enough to enjoy lunch or a cup of coffee from a park-run snack bar. Round-trip to Whitaker is ninety minutes. A four-hour trip is offered to 4,800-foot Bald Knob, the second-highest point in the state. If you're going in the fall, be sure to have a warm sweatshirt or coat handy.

Before or after the ride, most visitors stop in at the Cass Country Store. It was once the world's largest company store but now exists as a gift shop and restaurant. It's located near the depot, along with a small wildlife museum, a Cass history museum, a Cass historical diorama, and a Main Street full of locally made crafts.

For those who really want a taste of how nineteenth-century railroaders lived, choose overnight lodging from among several completely furnished state park cabins. These restored cottages sleep six to eight people, include private bathrooms, and come fully equipped with utensils, tableware, towels, dish-cloths, and linens. Wood stoves and electric heaters provide heat. Open year-round, the cabins are rented by the day up to a maximum of two weeks. The rates are very reasonable—a six-person cabin goes for $530 per week and $76 a night June through February; $480 weekly and $69 daily March through May. The cottages are only available for one-night stays Sunday through Thursday.

Rail excursions are offered from Memorial Day through the end of Octo-ber. Cottage and train reservations can be made by calling (800) CALL–WVA or (304) 456–4300.

Snowshoe Mountain Resort may not seem off the beaten path in winter, when as many as 3,000 visitors hit the slopes, but on its 11,000 acres you'll find trails seldom trod by human feet. Some 120 miles of hiking and mountain biking trails wind through Cheat Mountain's spruce forests, and several of these paths lead to Snowshoe's Sunrise Backcountry Cabin, a lodge so off the beaten path it's not even on the power grid.

The first cottage in Snowshoe's planned hut-to-hut hiking system, Sunrise offers catered meals by lamplight, ghost stories in front of a roaring fire, and a noctur-nal silence so profound you can hear the scream of a bobcat 2 miles away.

potomac highlands trivia

West Virginia's Snowshoe Mountain has been named the top ski resort in the Mid-Atlantic and Southeast by *Ski Magazine*. The resort boasts fifty-seven downhill runs and usually the best ski conditions south of Vermont.

Snowshoe also sets up snowmobile and—of course—snowshoe expedi-tions, as well as skiing, snowboarding, and snow tubing in season. Split Rocks Pools is a great place to splash around any time of year. With a geyser, slides, and hot tubs, the pools is the place to unwind. Ballhooter lift, open year-round, offers one of the best vistas of autumn leaves in the Potomac Highlands.

Summer fun at Snowshoe often begins at their Raven Golf Course, ranked as the number one public course in West Virginia by *Golfweek* magazine three years running. Mountain biking clinics for women, men, and children are also extremely popular. But you can choose from activities as leisurely as wildflower walks up to rock climbing and kayaking. The mountaintop adventure center also offers railroad/horseback riding combos, guided fly-fishing trips topped off by trout cooking class, and bass float trips, sporting clays, caving, and canoe-ing. Call the Snowshoe's Outdoor Adventure Center at (304) 572–5982 for fur-ther details, pricing, and date of availability or check Snowshoe's Web site, www.snowshoemtn.com.

There's no better—or quicker—way to get off the beaten path in West Virginia than by jumping on a mountain bike (the nonpolluting variety) and heading into the distant backcountry of Pocahontas County. Granted, this is not for everyone, but if you're in decent shape and lean toward the adventurous, give the good folks at the *Elk River Touring Center* a call. This mecca for eastern mountain bikers, located in Slatyfork off US 219 (about forty-five minutes from Cass), can outfit you for day, weekend, and weeklong guided fishing, cycling, hiking, or ski trips through the Potomac Highlands. Elk River rents bikes and an assortment of camping gear, including tents and sleeping bags, and will arrange for your meals in the wilderness. For overnight treks, you can choose to bunk down in a remote backcountry campground, isolated cabin, or cozy bed-and-breakfast. The restaurant, run by Mary Willis, serves healthful gourmet fare Thursday to Sunday evenings and is worth a few hours' drive. Seasonal specialties include pistachio-encrusted salmon and cranberry-glazed beef tenderloin. Live acoustic music accompanies an international buffet every Thursday night.

Back at the base station, Elk River also has a ten-room B&B and a restaurant with fantastic American, Italian, and Mexican fare. If you're in pretty good shape, request a trip on the famous *Greenbrier River Trail,* at 77 miles one of the nation's longest and most scenic mountain biking trails. It follows the path of the abandoned Greenbrier River railroad line, with a 0.5 percent grade the entire trip. Along the way you'll see some incredible vistas of the river valley and the namesake river, one of the cleanest and clearest in the country. You can also pick at the remnants of old logging villages, including an abandoned (empty) bank vault that marks the ghost town of Watoga. For more information call Elk River at (304) 572–3771.

Virginia and North Carolina may have the Blue Ridge Parkway, but West Virginia has the equally spectacular and much-less traveled *Highland Scenic Highway* (State Route 39/55). The 46-mile two-lane highway gives motorists a look at some of the most scenic and unusual countryside in America. The road begins north of Marlinton, off US 219 (about twenty minutes south of Slatyfork), and leads you through the wilds of the Monongahela National Forest to an elevation of more than 4,500 feet, ending in the town of Richwood. This is extremely remote country, and the roads aren't taking you anywhere fast—but that's the point after all. Unless you're camping, it's a good idea to make advance gas, food, and lodging arrangements in Richwood, Webster Springs, or Marlinton.

There's much more to experience here than what you see from your car. For those who want to camp out, pitch a tent at one of three rustic campgrounds located a short drive from the highway. *Summit Lake Campground* is just 2 miles off Route 39/55, and it's near a beautiful forty-two-acre reservoir. Tea Creek Campground is 1 mile from the parkway portion of the highway, and Day

Run Camp is 4 miles away; both are located along the beautiful **Williams River.** Recreational vehicles are allowed, but no hookups are available. Backcountry camping also is available in selected sites along the Williams River.

More than 150 miles of nearby trails lead hikers, backpackers, mountain bikers, horseback riders, and even cross-country skiers through such memorable natural attractions as **Falls of Hills Creek,** one of the state's prettiest cascading waterfalls. Lower Falls of Hills Creek is the state's second-highest waterfall at 98 feet.

Three rivers in the area—the Cherry, Cranberry, and Williams—provide some of the best trout fishing in the nation. The West Virginia Department of Natural Resources stocks these waters year-round with rainbow, brown, and golden trout. Native brook trout are also abundant in these cold and clear waters.

The **Edray Trout Hatchery** near Marlinton is the place to see all species of the Mountain State's trout in one location. Operated by the West Virginia Department of Natural Resources, the hatchery raises brook, brown, rainbow, and golden trout. About 3 miles north of Marlinton, turn onto Woodrow Road for about 1 mile. You'll see the sign. Call (304) 799–6461 for more information.

The Highland Scenic Highway will wind you along the eastern boundary of the 35,864-acre **Cranberry Wilderness,** a protected natural area of cranberry bogs, rare orchids, ferns, lilies, and numerous wildflower species. Stop in at the Cranberry Mountain Visitor Center, located at the junction of State Route 150 and Route 55, and get oriented before going out and discovering the bogs, which a forest ranger will tell you are acidic wetlands typically found much farther north in Canada and the northern United States.

Also at the visitor center is a ½-mile barrier-free boardwalk designed to give tourists a closer look at this fragile area. Guided tours of the bogs are conducted at 2:00 P.M. on Saturday and Sunday throughout the summer months or can be specially arranged by contacting the Cranberry Mountain Visitor Center at (304) 636–1800. The same number will provide you with information on all the above camping and natural areas.

The **Cranberry Mountain Lodge** is an isolated retreat for outdoor enthusiasts in some of West Virginia's highest mountains. The lodge is in a remote location, 6 miles from Hillsboro on John Wimer Road, behind a locked gate. It presents a tranquil lodging experience for outdoor enthusiasts. Located at a 4,000-foot elevation on top of Cranberry Mountain, the lodge borders Monongahela National Forest. The deck views are spectacular, exceeding 40 miles. You can hike, bike, or ski right out the front door to a vast trail system through the national forest.

When you rent the lodge, you rent the entire seven-bedroom, four-bath facility, so you get the privacy you want. Bring plenty of food—you will be doing your own cooking. Rates are based on the number of guests and length of stay—six being the minimum number of guests listed in the rate structure, sixteen being the maximum. Completely surrounded by nature in one of the state's most remote regions, the lodge is a nature lover's dream. Nearby attractions include Cranberry Glades Botanical Area and Black Mountain Black Bear Sanctuary. For more information call (877) 653–4848 or (304) 242–6070.

Driving the Highland Scenic Highway, or in any part of West Virginia for that matter, brings you up close to an amazing variety of hardwood trees, still one of the state's most lucrative natural resources.

Lumberjacks and literary folk have always lived side by side in West Virginia. In Hillsboro, 8 miles south of Marlinton, travelers and literary enthusiasts can tour the restored home of one of America's greatest novelists, Pearl S. Buck. Buck, you might remember, won the Pulitzer Prize for literature in 1932 for *The Good Earth*. Six years later, she was awarded the Nobel Prize for literature for her lifetime achievements. The Pocahontas County native is the only American woman to ever receive both awards. In 1983 the Pearl S. Buck U.S. postal stamp was first issued at Hillsboro as a tribute to its most famous daughter.

The **Pearl S. Buck Homestead** was built by Buck's mother's family—the Stultings—who emigrated from Holland in 1847. Buck (her married name) was born here in 1892 as Pearl Comfort Sydenstricker. Her father's birthplace, the Sydenstricker House, was originally built in neighboring Greenbrier County but was dismantled and reconstructed on the museum grounds to serve as a cultural center.

The house and outbuildings sit on sixteen lowland acres. A tour of the homestead, her cars, and original family furnishings gives you insight about her life, from missionary child to celebrity author. You can purchase rare autographed first editions by Buck in the gift shop. If you're really interested in Buck, come back on the first Saturday in June for her birthday celebration. Festivities always include a dramatic performance based on her life. For regular tours the house and grounds are open from 9:00 A.M. to 4:30 P.M. Monday through Saturday, May through October. Admission is $4.00 for adults; $1.00 for children. Call (304) 653–4430 for information.

Covered bridges hold a fascination for many, especially those old enough to remember the romance of parking with a date in the shelter of an old "kissing bridge." **Locust Creek Covered Bridge,** built in 1988, rates placement on the National Register of Historic Places. From Hillsboro, drive 2.2 miles south on US 219, then turn onto Locust Creek Road and go 3 miles to the bridge.

Civil War history still figures prominently in this part of West Virginia, especially just down US 219 at **Droop Mountain Battlefield State Park.** If you hear shots on the second weekend in October, it's not your imagination—West

Virginia's largest and last significant Civil War battle is reenacted in even years (2006, 2008, etc.). It was actually on November 6, 1863, that Union troops pinned the Confederates in place by attacking them on the ridge from the right, left, and rear. Throughout the morning General John Echols's smaller Confederate army blocked the highway with artillery, but in the afternoon they were overwhelmed by the crushing advance of General William Averell's Federal infantry on his left flank. After much bloodshed Echols fled south into Virginia with the remnants of his command.

Long after the battles were over, veterans gathered on Droop Mountain to remember the fierce struggle and mourn their dead. They proposed a memorial, which became West Virginia's first state park in 1928. The site of the raging battle is now a peaceful 285-acre park with footpaths, picnic facilities, children's play areas, a lookout tower, and a small museum containing artifacts from the battle. Confederate earthworks are still visible in the forest. For more information call (304) 653–4254 or visit www.droopmountainbattlefield.com.

Places to Stay in the Potomac Highlands

DAVIS

Blackwater Falls State Park
State Route 32
(304) 259–5216
Moderate

Canaan Valley Resort State Park and Conference Center
State Route 32
(304) 866–4121
(800) 622–4121
Moderate

Meyer House B&B
Thomas Avenue
(304) 259–5451
www.meyerhousebandb.com
Moderate

ELKINS

Graceland Inn and Conference Center
on the campus of Davis and Elkins College
(800) 624–3157
www.gracelandinn.com
Expensive

Huntersville Carriage House Inn
U.S. Route 39
(304) 799–6706
www.carriagehousewv.com
Moderate

HILLSBORO

Current Bed & Breakfast
State Route 31
(304) 653–4722
www.currentbnb.com
Inexpensive to moderate

MARLINTON

Jerico Cabins and B&B
Jerico Road
(304) 799–6241
www.jericobb.com
Inexpensive

ROMNEY

Hampshire House Bed and Breakfast Country Inn
165 North Grafton Street
(304) 822–7171
www.hampshirehouse1884.net
Moderate

SENECA ROCKS–SMOKE HOLE

North Fork Mountain Inn
14 miles south of Petersburg in the Smoke Hole Gorge
Smoke Hole Road
(304) 257–1108
www.northforkmtninn.com
Moderate

Places to Eat in the Potomac Highlands

CANAAN VALLEY

Big John's Family Fixin's
State Route 32
(304) 866–4418
Budget

Deerfield Village Restaurant
State Route 32 and
Cortland Lane
(304) 866–4698
Moderate

Golden Anchor
State Route 32
(304) 866–CRAB
www.goldenanchorcabins
.com
Moderate

DAVIS

Sirianni's Cafe
William Avenue
(304) 259–5454
Inexpensive

ELKINS

Graceland Inn and Conference Center
100 Campus Drive
(304) 637–1600
Moderate

FROST

Mill Run Restaurant and Trout Farm
State Route 92
(304) 799–6247
Moderate

HILLSBORO

Country Roads Cafe
U.S. Highway 219
(304) 653–4697
Inexpensive

MINGO

Brazen Head Inn
U.S. Highway 219
(304) 339–6917
(866) 339–6917
www.brazenheadinn.com
Inexpensive

ROMNEY

Stray Cat Cafe (Mexican)
U.S. Highway 50
(1 mile east of town)
(304) 822–8226
Inexpensive

SENECA ROCKS

The Front Porch Restaurant
junction of State Routes 28,
55, and 33
(304) 567–2555
Inexpensive

SLATYFORK

Elk River Inn
State Route 219
(304) 572–3771
www.ertc.com
Moderate

SNOWSHOE

Snowshoe Mountain Resort, the Red Fox
State Route 66 and U.S.
Highway 219
(877) 441–4FUN
(304) 572–1111
www.snowshoemtn.com
Expensive

SPRINGFIELD

The Cottage
(dinners Tuesday to Friday,
benefits senior programs)
State Route 28
(304) 822–7627
Inexpensive

FOR MORE INFORMATION

Pocahontas County Convention and Visitors Bureau
(800) 336–7009 or (800) 336–4649
www.pocahontascountywv.com

Randolph County Convention and Visitors Bureau
(800) 422–3304
www.randolphcountywv.com

Tucker County Convention and Visitors Bureau
(800) 782–2775
www.canaanvalley.org

Mountain Lakes

The Mountain Lakes region covers seven counties near the center of the state: Gilmer, Lewis, Upshur, Braxton, Webster, Nicholas, and Clay. It is a gentle place of small towns, tidy farms, country roads, and rolling green woodlands. The region is dotted with communities whose names are as distinctive as the people who have lived there for centuries. Hominy Falls, Tallmansville, Stumptown, and Erbacon line the two-lane roads with little stores, a few houses, and some of the friendliest people to be found anywhere.

The region is a sportsman's paradise. Its landscape is dominated by five major lakes: Summersville Lake (the largest in the state) in Nicholas County, Sutton and Burnsville Lakes in Braxton County, Stonewall Jackson and Stonecoal Lakes in Lewis County, and the small Big Ditch Lake in Webster County. The heart of the Mountain State is also a land of rivers. Here the Elk, the Williams, the Cherry, the Buckhannon, the Cranberry, and the Little Kanawha snake through this land, providing great fishing and canoeing opportunities. In fact, this is one of the most abundant wildlife regions in West Virginia, with more than 8,400 acres for lake fishing and 60,000 acres of wildlife management area.

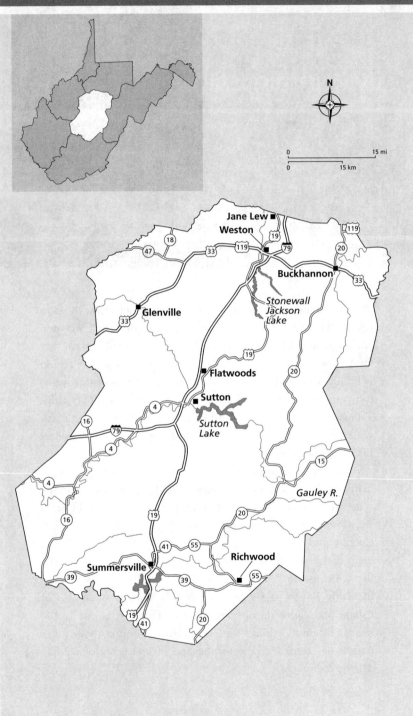

The area's low population density means there is plenty of space to get away and enjoy the natural surroundings. This is a remote land but one that's sprinkled with unusual attractions and festivals. Take your time and enjoy the scenery, for the pace of life here is relaxed and good for the soul.

The Mountain Lakes region is an area studded with sparkling though underutilized lakes and traversed by winding miles of lonely but scenic country roads. In far eastern Nicholas County, about a ninety-minute drive from the town of Clay, is **Richwood,** the gateway to the Monongahela National Forest and the Highland Scenic Highway (which we visited in the Potomac Highlands chapter). Each April, Richwood hosts the **Feast of the Ramson**—and, yes, that is the correct spelling—one of the state's largest ramp festivals, and for sure an event not for the gastronomically challenged. A ramp is a potently flavored wild scallion, a vegetable with staying power. It grows abundantly in rocky West Virginia hills and is often the first green vegetation to sprout on the hillsides in late March and early April. In pioneer times the ramp supposedly saved many a starving soul and helped prevent scurvy. Today the hearty leek-like vegetable is a local favorite and is often fried with ham and served with beans and potatoes. The Richwood festival, sponsored by the locally based National Ramp Association, is held at the local high school, at 1 Valley Way, where you're seated elbow to elbow with those who come back for more every year. Afterward, don't skimp on either the Alka-Seltzer or the breath mints.

BEST ANNUAL EVENTS IN THE MOUNTAIN LAKES REGION

Irish Spring Festival
Ireland; mid-March
(304) 452–8962

Feast of the Ramson
Richwood; mid-April
(304) 846–6790

West Virginia State Folk Festival
Glenville; mid-June
(304) 462–5065

Weston Gold Robbery Day
Weston; last weekend in June
(304) 269–7328
www.westongoldrobbery.com

West Virginia's Largest Yard Sale
Buckhannon and surroundings;
mid-August; (304) 472–1722 or
(304) 472–1757

Grape Stomping Wine Festival
Summersville; third weekend
in September
(304) 872–7332

Voices of the Mountains Storytelling Festival
Jackson's Mill; mid-October
(304) 269–7328 or (800) 287–8206
www.etc4u.com/folkfest/

Ramp up to Spring, West Virginia Style

When the tree frogs are announcing spring along tributaries of Nicholas County's Big Coal River, West Virginians know it's time to look for ramps. Ramps *(Allium tricoccum)* are wild leeks. For at least three centuries, the unfurling of ramps' pungent shoots in Appalachian valleys has signaled the end of winter and the time to eat spring greens.

Here in West Virginia, that time is celebrated with the Feast of the Ramson, using the folk name of ramps' relatives in the British Isles. In fact, Richwood claims the title of Ramp Capital of the World. It is true that the National Ramp Association began here eighty years ago and that Richwood's *West Virginia Hillbilly* newspaper once impregnated its newsprint with ramp oil and received a federal reprimand for fouling rural post offices with the odor.

Although early-twentieth-century schoolchildren who ate ramps may have been sent home from school to purge the stench from their systems, to the early settlers and Native Americans, the odor seemed trivial. Ramps were a nutritious change from their winter diet of game, dehydrated vegetables, nuts, and dried meats. The wild leeks are a good source of vitamin C as well as prostaglandin, a fatty acid useful in lowering blood pressure. Studies by Oregon State chemistry professor Phil Whanger, a native West Virginian, have indicated that women who eat ramp leaves increase their resistance to breast tumors.

The late wild foods evangelist Euell Gibbons considered ramps "the sweetest and best of the wild onions."

At festivals, ramps are served up with beans, corn bread, potatoes, trout, or in gourmet circles, with black beans, sole, or artichokes. Specialty vendors extend ramps' April through May season with offerings of pickled ramps, ramp vinegar, and ramp jelly.

For more information about Richwood's annual April Feast of the Ramson, call (304) 846–6790.

If you overindulge, you can walk off your discomfort on the Tri-Rivers Trail. The 16.5-mile course begins in Richwood and follows three rivers—the Cherry, Gauley, and Cranberry—to end at a tunnel.

From Richwood, you're also about equal distance from the attractions of nearby Summersville Lake and the high mountain country of the Cranberry Wilderness area (see "Potomac Highlands").

Summersville Area

At the heart of Nicholas County is the fast-growing town of Summersville—a virtually insignificant town thirty years ago. The expansion of U.S. Highway 19 changed all that. The road is part of a major north-south thruway, with Summersville being near the midway point for Canadian snowbirds headed to Florida.

Labor Day weekend marks the traditional end of summertime activities, but not in Summersville. The **Potato Festival** is held the following weekend, along with the reenactment of the Battle of Carnifex Ferry.

Events at the Potato Festival include a beauty pageant, a potato cook-off, a potato judging and auction, a parade, a classic car show, arts and crafts, and a 5K run. Nearby, the ***Carnifex Ferry Battlefield State Park*** has Civil War camps set up by reenactors. The camps open for public viewing at 9:00 A.M. on Saturday and Sunday. Throughout Saturday living-history events take place, while on Sunday morning there is an outdoor church service conducted by the reenactors. The reenacted Battle of Carnifex Ferry takes place on Sunday afternoon in odd-numbered years (2007, 2009, etc.). The weekend warriors demonstrate how on September 10, 1861, Union troops led by Brigadier General William Rosecrans forced the Confederates to abandon the ferry. The Confederate commander, Brigadier General John Floyd, retreated to Lewisburg, giving the Union control of the Kanawha Valley. As a result, the movement for West Virginia statehood proceeded without major resistance. Children and Civil War buffs alike find the booming volleys of cannon fire, drifting smoke, and uniformed soldiers quite appealing. This event seems to grow each year, pulling in participants from as far away as Canada and California.

Although the Potato Festival draws quite a number of people to the area, there is an even larger attraction that brings people from all across the United States and several foreign countries. It is the opening of the Gauley season.

The name ***Gauley River*** strikes fear into hearts of the white-water timid. The Gauley River is among the most challenging white-water rivers in the United States. Every year, for six consecutive weekends in September and October, during the annual draw-down of the Summersville Dam, people flock to the area to experience the white-water rafting thrill of a lifetime. During the draw-down the water is released at a constant rate of 2,800 cubic feet per second. The Gauley is a pounding, swirling, tumbling, fast-and-furious river.

Located in the heart of mountainous West Virginia, the Gauley flows through some of the most remote and gorgeous scenery in the eastern United States. It is channeled through a steep canyon that is an average of 500 feet deep. Recommended only for commercial rafting trips and expert kayakers, the river crashes in Class V rapids over and around boulders the size of homes. This high-velocity creek is one of the top ten white-water rivers in the world, offering more than one hundred major rapids in its course. Riding the Gauley is as pure an adrenaline rush as one could possibly hope for—or want. Just listen to the names of some of the rapids: Heaven Help You, Upper and Lower Mash, and Pure Screaming Hell.

Gauley season starts the Friday after Labor Day. Dam release days are Friday through Monday for five weeks, then Saturday and Sunday the last weekend. Saturdays and Sundays book up fairly quickly with the commercial rafting companies. Fridays and Mondays find fewer people on the river.

Don't think you will be doing the Upper Gauley your first time out. Rafting companies require a minimum age of fifteen or sixteen, depending upon the company. All recommend that rafters have white-water experience on either the New River or Lower Gauley. (Brochures make it sound like a requirement, but there is no way to fully enforce such a rule.) The Gauley is a mighty river, however, and it simply wouldn't make sense to attempt it with no white-water experience.

The Lower Gauley is quite thrilling, with rapids from Class III through Class V, with some easy flat water in between. The Upper Gauley is Class III to Class V+, with back-to-back rapids and almost no flat-water breaks.

Mountain River Tours was one of the first outfitters to regularly schedule excursions down the Gauley. Call (800) 822–1386 for more information or to schedule a rafting trip. For a complete listing of rafting companies in the state, phone (800) CALL–WVA. Call the Summersville Convention and Visitors Bureau at (304) 872–3722 for more information on the Battle of Carnifex Ferry Reenactment and the Potato Festival.

BEST ATTRACTIONS IN THE MOUNTAIN LAKES REGION

West Virginia Jackson's Mill and Historic District
Weston
(304) 269–5100

West Virginia State Wildlife Center
French Creek
(304) 924–6211
www.wvdnr.gov/wildlife/wildlifecenter
.shtm

Kirkwood Winery/Isaiah Morgan Distillery
Summersville
(888) 498–9463
www.kirkwood-wine.com

Mountain Air Balloons
Buckhannon
(304) 472–0792
www.mountainairballoons.com

Central West Virginia Farmers' Market
Weston
(304) 269–2667

West Virginia Museum of Glass
Weston
(304) 269–5006
http://hometown.aol.com
/wvmuseumofglass/

OTHER ATTRACTIONS WORTH SEEING IN THE MOUNTAIN LAKES REGION

Stonewall Jackson Resort
Roanoke

Lambert's Vintage Wines
Weston

Poplar Forest juried crafts
Flatwoods

Appalachian Glass
Weston

Holly River State Park
Hacker Valley

Catherine Miller Designs Glass Studio
Buckhannon

A good place to stay is the **Brock House** (304–872–4887), an 1890 twenty-one-room mansion up in Summersville located not far off US 19. The three-story Victorian with gingerbread trim was built to provide lodging for guests when the Nicholas County Court was in session. It has since been renovated to include six guest rooms. The enticing aroma of home-baked breads and muffins drifts up the stairs each morning, and after breakfast guests head off to see such local diversions as the Carnifex Ferry Civil War battlefield and crystal-clear Summersville Lake.

Probably the last place most people think of to go scuba diving is West Virginia, but few lakes in the United States have the extraordinary water clarity found in 2,800-acre **Summersville Lake,** which is actually a dammed section of the Gauley River in central Nicholas County. In some parts of the lake, underwater visibility exceeds 50 feet. **Sarge's Dive Shop** leverages this natural attribute by offering a host of dive charters and snorkel trips along the cliff-like shores of the lake. If you're new to scuba diving, owners Mark and Eric Allen offer certified courses, including private instruction, and have plenty of gear for rent. In addition, an underwater photography class is offered for those who want to take the scuba experience a bit further. Pontoon boat tours of the lake also are offered from here.

Sarge's is located at Long Point Marina, a mile south of Summersville off US 19. Diving reservations are preferred, but walk-ins are welcome, says Mark. Call (304) 872–1782 or see www.sarges.net for more information.

Along with Summersville's expansion came some fine dining, and two places of distinction are worth noting. **Cafe Acropolis**—a restored farm-house—sitting high on a hill overlooking US 19, serves outstanding Greek and Italian cuisine. Hours are 11:30 A.M. to 2:00 P.M. and 5:00 to 10:00 P.M. Tuesday through Friday. Saturday hours are 5:00 to 10:00 P.M. Closed Sunday and Monday. Call (304) 872–0254 for more information.

Up the Creek Smokehouse is located in a new building constructed in an old-fashioned way. The structure, built on a pattern similar to a barn, is made of locally cut rough-hewn hemlock with a huge "Rumford" cut-stone fireplace dominating the dining area. The fireplace is said to have been built following a design by Benjamin Franklin. Rocking chairs before the fireplace invite guests to sit a spell, relax, watch the fire burn, and take in the ambience. Antique farm implements hanging on the walls complement the rough lumber. Hours are 5:00 to 9:00 P.M. Tuesday through Thursday, 5:00 to 10:00 P.M. Friday, 11:00 A.M. to 10:00 P.M. Saturday, and noon to 9:00 P.M. Sunday. Call (304) 872–7335 for more information.

For some, the right beverage goes hand in glove with a fine meal. If you have any interest in the inside operations of spirited libations, you should stop by *Kirkwood Winery* and its new *Isaiah Morgan Distillery,* just off US 19 on Phillips Run Road north of Summersville. Rodney Facemire or one of his employees will be happy to explain the makings of a Kirkwood wine, whether it's a specialty ginseng or garlicky ramp wine or one of their award-winning Foch, chardonnay, or Seyval meads.

A newer operation, the Isaiah Morgan Distillery is housed in the tasting house. Forget your impressions of tarnished green stills; this West Virginia distillery is a gleaming stainless steel apparatus that converts bubbling corn, rye, or grape mash into 180-proof whiskey. (Of course it's watered down by more than half for market.)

You can purchase any one of Kirkwood's thirty-four wines here, but you may only taste the whiskey. By West Virginia law, the Southern Moon Whiskey is purchased by the state and resold through licensed outlets. Kirkwood/Isaiah Morgan is open for tours and tastings Monday through Saturday from 9:00 A.M. to 5:00 P.M. For a good time, visit during their *Grape Stomping Festival,* held each year on the third weekend of September. Call (304) 872–7332 or go to www.kirkwood-wine.com for more information.

After Summersville, you might also want to get off the main drag and do a little sightseeing on county roads as you head up to *Sutton.* Take State Route 41 to Route 55 to Muddlety, then take the county road through Enoch before catching Route 16 again near Clay. This time go north; then get on Interstate 79 briefly to Sutton. It may sound out of the way (what isn't in this part of the state?), but the drive through the countryside is interesting and serene.

In Sutton grab your wallet again, for here's another not-to-be-missed opportunity to own a handcrafted item or two. Head to Main Street's *Landmark Studio for the Arts,* housed in a beautiful nineteenth-century building that has been a Baptist, a Presbyterian, and a Methodist church. (Note the art nouveau stained-glass windows.) Folk art, however, is not all the studio has to offer. The studio's stage hosts the best local thespians and musicians in the state, including the West Virginia Symphony's Montani String Quartet and Melvin Wine, a Braxton County fiddler who received the National Endowment of the Humanities Heritage Fellowship, an award given to those with the finest folk traditions.

Artists from around the world exhibit their work in the studio's lobby. Here you'll find fine art and sophisticated designer crafts, such as hand-painted silk, hot-glass sculpture, and even contemporary Chinese soapstone pieces. Local resident Bill Hopen, an internationally known sculptor, often exhibits here as well. The studio is open to the public, and tours can be arranged, but hours tend to vary and change frequently. Call (304) 765–3766 for hours and more information.

While you're in Sutton, you'll have a good opportunity to get wet. **Sutton Lake** has 1,500 surface acres of water recreation, including a marina with boat rentals. The lake is located just off I–79, and anglers come from everywhere to hook into the excellent largemouth, small- mouth, and spotted bass. Even if you don't enjoy fishing, you can take a spin around the lake in a boat, enjoying the beautiful scenery of the **Elk River Wildlife Management Area,** which abuts the lake. The park is open year-round, dawn to dusk. Call (304) 587–7652.

mountain lakestrivia

The town of Sutton, located along the banks of the Elk River about 60 miles northeast of Charleston, is considered the geographic center of the state.

Just north on I–79 is the reputed center of West Virginia. An enterprising businessman decided this was reason enough to establish an outlet-store complex and conference center at **Flatwoods.** Among the array of factory outlets, you'll find Greenbrier shops (from the famous resort), tool stores, craft shops, and the **Lee Middleton Dolls** outlet, the only Lee Middleton baby-doll nursery outside Ohio. Here you can don a sterile gown and pick out the baby you want to adopt. A nurse will assist you in preparing the baby for travel and drawing up adoption papers.

Perhaps as many middle-aged women as little girls adopt the collectible dolls, complete with curled toes and pouty lips. Their warm, tinted vinyl skin and weighted bodies seem so realistic that they are used as baby stand-ins in the television drama *ER*. The less-expensive My Own Baby line recently earned the first-ever UL classification for safety with children two and under. The dolls are manufactured just a quarter mile from the West Virginia line in Belpre, Ohio.

Another unique shopping opportunity lies within the neighboring walls of **Poplar Forest,** a juried gallery of the **Central Appalachian Arts and Crafts**

Cooperative. The collection includes bold quilts, pottery, glass, furniture, hand-forged ironware, dulcimers, toys, music, books of regional interest, wine, and food. The outlet is open from 10:00 A.M. until 6:00 P.M. Monday through Wednesday, 10:00 A.M. until 9:00 P.M. Thursday through Saturday, and noon until 6:00 P.M. on Sunday. The phone number is (304) 765–3995.

But while some are shopping in the Mountain Lakes region, others are fishing. So glorious is this area for fishermen that some say it's where righteous anglers go when they die. You can also grab your fishing pole and splash over to nearby *Burnsville Lake.* Just north on I–79, this lake was formed when the U.S. Army Corps of Engineers dammed the Little Kanawha River. Bass, crappie, muskie, and channel catfish are abundant in these 968 acres of water. Surrounding the reservoir are 12,000 acres known as the *Burnsville Wildlife Management Area,* which at the right time of year is home to migrating waterfowl, grouse, quail, turkey, deer, and innumerable bow-hunters. Motel accommodations and camping are abundant, including the *Bulltown Campgrounds,* which is waterside. Operated by the Corps of Engineers, more than 200 sites are available from the first week in April to December 1. For reservations and information, call (304) 452–8006. Bulltown is named for Captain Bull, chief of the Delaware tribe that once lived in the area.

After you've done all the fishing you can stand (or all your spouse can stand for you to do), there's a lot to see around the lake on foot. Head over to the *Bulltown Historic Area,* where the U.S. Army Corps of Engineers moved several log structures to prevent their destruction when the dam was being built. Originally built between 1815 and 1870, the pioneer settlements were disassembled by the corps, moved, then reconstructed right near the campgrounds. Today, during the warm-weather months, living-history demonstrations show how quilting, clothes washing, gardening, cooking, and other household chores were accomplished by nineteenth-century pioneers of the backcountry. This site was also where the *Battle of Bulltown* raged, a twelve-hour skirmish between Union and Confederate soldiers fought on October 13, 1863. The Southerners, led by Stonewall Jackson's cousin, Colonel William L. Jackson, were attempting to capture the Union garrison stationed at Bulltown. They failed, and Union forces held their ground in West Virginia.

Also in Bulltown don't miss the early-nineteenth-century *Cunningham Farmhouse,* a dogtrot-style house seized by the Union forces during the war and which bears the bullet holes to prove it. Farther down the trail, which takes you along the *Weston and Gauley Bridge Turnpike*—used by both North and South to transport supplies—you'll find *Johnson House,* built in 1883 by a freedman, and *St. Michael's Church,* one of the first Catholic churches in the state. It rests on a hill, overlooking the battle site. During the second week of October in odd years (2007, 2009, etc.), reenactors restage the Battle of Bulltown.

In July, Bulltown offers a special treat for kids with an interest in what school was like more than a century ago—quite an eye-opener for our technologically sophisticated children today. For three hours kids attend school in rural Appalachia of the mid-1800s, with games, lessons, and homework from authentic period texts.

An interpretive center shows a six-minute show on the lake and its facilities and houses nineteenth-century memorabilia and Civil War battle artifacts. Follow the 1-mile interpretive trail around the grounds, or better yet, take the 2:00 P.M. tour of the houses, church, and battlefield. The center is open from mid-May through mid-October, 10:00 A.M. to 6:00 P.M., but closes two hours earlier from September 1 to October 30. It's closed from October 30 to May 1. Call (304) 452–8170 or (304) 853–2370 for more information.

Stonewall Country

Lewis, Gilmer, and Upshur Counties contain the largest towns in the region, most of which are close to I–79. But don't spend all your time on the interstate, because most of the goodies are way off the beaten path. This route will leave your car trunk filled with arts and crafts, your head swimming in history, your stomach filled with good food, and your toes tapping a happy beat.

From Burnsville Lake, veer slightly to the west on State Route 5 to **Glenville,** home of the Stonewall Jackson Jubilee, an annual Labor Day event for crafters (see details later in this chapter). If you're in town on the third weekend in June, follow your ears to the **West Virginia State Folk Festival** (304–462–8427). Fiddles, banjos, mandolins, autoharps, and hammer dulcimers ring through the streets. If you've ever wanted to learn how to mountain dance, the festival is the place to be. The festival opens on the third Thursday of June at the Country Store Museum and ends with a Sunday service at a historic church.

Now head north, either back on I–79 or on US 33, into **Weston,** a community planned by Stonewall Jackson's grandfather. This charming little city with Victorian mansions and gingerbread-bedecked homes is famous locally as the **Christmas Town** because of its spectacular light show during the holidays. Beginning the day after Thanksgiving and lasting through New Year's Day, a quarter of a mile of Main Street is illuminated with blue and white snowflake lights that dance along to a choreographed computer program. A lighted Santa and his reindeer fly overhead, above all the downtown storefronts, which also have been adorned with an incredible array of lights and designs. Across the street from the courthouse, on Center Avenue, sits a 37-foot blue spruce, glowing brilliantly with hundreds of colored lights.

Interesting landmarks abound in Weston, such as the **Old Weston State Hospital,** located on Second Street. This imposing structure is actually the largest hand-cut stone building in the United States and one of the largest in the world. Proud but vacant since the 1970s, the Gothic compound stands poised on the brink of adaptive re-use for some other purpose. Civil War reenactments are held periodically on the grounds, and plans are afoot to install a museum or possibly a casino. Another building of note is Lewis County's only public library. It is housed in the historic *Jonathan-Louis Bennett House,* 148 Court Avenue, once home to one of Weston's most prominent families. The seventeen-room high-Victorian Italianate mansion contains a few pieces of original furniture and other furnishings amid the book stacks. Visitors to the library are allowed into certain sections of the home, which offer a glimpse of life during the Victorian era. The entire house can be viewed by special tour arrangements. The Louis Bennett Library is open Monday through Friday from 10:00 A.M. to 6:00 P.M. and Saturday from 10:00 A.M. to 2:00 P.M. Call (304) 269–5151 for more information.

mountain lakestrivia

West Virginia native son and Confederate hero Thomas "Stonewall" Jackson died from wounds inflicted after being accidentally shot by one of his fellow soldiers in a battle near Fredericksburg, Virginia.

Just off US 33 at **Appalachian Glass & Gifts,** you can find Matt Turner and his son Chip blowing glass dipped from a red-hot kiln. Father and son honed their skills at nearby Princess House before the glass factory closed. "It's a dying art," says Chip, "and because we want people to appreciate it, we take our portable kiln out to festivals and fairs. We want to keep our heritage alive."

The Turners twirl and dip the hot gobs of glass until they have a bubble the size of a Red Delicious apple. Though the finished product looks like something to hang on your Christmas tree, they call it a friendship ball. "Folks didn't have much money, so they'd wrap up one of these for birthdays and give it with something homemade, like a pie or an apron. The one who got it would pass it on to somebody else with another homemade gift. It made its way around a community like that," Chip Turner says.

In the same long building, Donna Wilfong and her daughter make quilts to sell. A queen-size wedding ring pattern goes for $500. Appalachian Glass & Gifts also features a stained-glass artist, a candlemaker, a potter, a woodworker, and a candy maker. The studios are free and open for viewing six days a week. Call (304) 269–1030 for more details.

Downtown Weston is the home of the *West Virginia Glass Museum,* open noon to 4:00 P.M. daily except Sunday and Wednesday. Here you'll see fine representatives of many of the glass-making operations that used to produce glass in Ohio, Pennsylvania, and West Virginia in the twentieth century. Of the dozens of plants that produced marbles, window glass, tableware, and art, only about a half dozen remain. The museum's gems are its Tiffany decorated glass tiles and winners of its annual paperweight contest. It also boasts the largest collection of glass toilet bowl floats in the nation. No admission is charged, but donations are welcome. The museum is located on the corner of Main Avenue and Second Street in downtown Weston and can be reached at (304) 269–5006.

If you're in the mood for a picnic, Weston has a delightful *Farmers' Market* Monday through Saturday, bursting with fresh local produce, handcrafted furniture, and some very good West Virginia wines. It's on the right just as you come into town on US 33. Also, a few turns off US 33 is an unusual place to help fill up your picnic basket. *Smoke Camp Crafts* has homegrown table teas, Appalachian herbs, and almost fifty varieties of jams and jellies made with wild and organically cultivated fruits (you can also pick up a few cleansing lotions at the same time). Traditional and exotic herb blends here run the gamut: the Headache Blend, the Herbal Moth Repellent, the High-Blood-Pressure Blend, the Hot Flash Tea, Menopause Blend Tea, and PMS Capsules.

Owners Dot and Bob Montgillion are more than happy to share their insight and will even arrange for special garden tours and nature hikes. You might want to pick up a copy of Dot Montgillion's book, *Modern Uses of Traditional Herbs,* which details the history, cultivation, preparation, and use of seventy-six herbs. Smoke Camp Crafts is located on Smoke Camp Run Road, about 5 miles northwest of Weston. Call the Montgillions at (304) 269–6416 for more information and for directions.

Another herb shop, *La Paix Farm,* 15 miles west of Weston near Alum Bridge, produces balms, salves, and special fragrances distilled on the premises. La Paix's effervescent owner, Myra Bonhage-Hale, used grant money and her own savings to acquire an essential-oil distillery where she processes her own lavender, peppermint, and lemon balm, as well as the fragrant and medicinal herbs of other growers. At La Paix (which means "peace" in French) and through her Web site, www.lapaixherbfarm.com, Bonhage-Hale sells honey lip balm, passionate gardener hand cream, catnip, and assorted home-brewed fragrances. Lavender is her favorite. "Lavender has antibacterial, anti-inflammatory properties, and it's good for depression and anxiety," she says. "We should use it in hospitals."

The farm's original residence, a 200-year-old cabin reputed to have been a safe house on the Underground Railroad, is fragrant with lavender. So is the

West Virginia's Biggest Liar Takes to the Parks

Bil Lepp has just told 400 adults his hound dog hauled a 168-car CSX train loaded with West Virginia bituminous coal clear from Cowen to Grafton, West Virginia, and he hasn't cracked a grin. In fact, he's earnestly elaborating on the quality of the coal, that it's scrubbed, "so as not to pollute the great state of West Virginia," and not one of the highly educated, librarian types in the audience shows any sign of incredulity. No, they're totally with him in the tailwind of that train, howling with delight, tears of laughter streaking down their cheeks.

The spectators hang on as Lepp drops West Virginia-born test-pilot Chuck Yeager to the wheel of that engine and fastens himself by the tongue to an ice-steel boxcar "like scandal to Martha Stewart." They don't flinch when he pulls out a seventy-four-function Swiss Army knife ("What, yours doesn't have a sewing machine function?") to save his hide.

They leap to their feet, cheering. This bunch would follow Lepp anywhere. Boyish-looking Lepp shrugs, hands in the pockets of his faded jeans. Should an ordained Methodist minister be getting away with this? Lepp's life is as good as an Appalachian Jack Tale, and he is crafty Jack.

Lepp, who left the pulpit in 2003 to become a full-time storyteller, has won the **West Virginia Liar's Contest** at the Vandalia Festival so many times he's no longer allowed to enter; he's the emcee these days. He's also pushed credibility several notches above believable in performances at the Smithsonian Folklife Festival, Timpanogos (Utah) Storytelling Festival, Washington Storytellers Theatre, and many other venues across the nation.

You can hear Lepp tell his outrageous lies in West Virginia's state parks from May through September. His stories usually take place among West Virginia landmarks, especially in the Mountain Lakes region where he spent his youth, and they almost always involve his dog, his fishing rod, a bear, and a train.

Lepp describes his original yarns as Appalachian stories. "Not traditional stories, maybe—everything I tell I wrote or my brother Paul did. The stories we tell come out of the culture and people of Appalachia, hill people from West Virginia to mid-Ohio."

To see Lepp's schedule, check his Web site, www.buck-dog.com, or that of West Virginia state parks: www.wvstateparks.com/sumperf.html.

green and lavender Victorian two-story adjoining it. But in a resourceful modern touch, La Paix puts a discarded satellite dish to use as the roof of a Japanese tea house in the sprawling herb garden.

From April until October, Bonhage-Hale and fellow West Virginia herbalists sponsor workshops on such topics as herb propagation, culinary herbs, essential oil distillation, making cosmetics, and building sanctuaries. Tours of her herb gardens, heritage vegetable patch, feng shui garden, and silver labyrinth are always included. La Paix's main event is the annual mid-June *Lavender Fair,* featuring diverse culinary and gardening workshops, a lavender cooking contest, Celtic music, Irish dancing, and catering by award-winning Stonewall Resort chef Dale Hawkins. For directions and more information, call Bonhage-Hale at (304) 269–7681 or see www.lapaixherbfarm.com.

Stonewall Jackson Lake meanders close to the interstate at the Roanoke exit south of Weston. Before the Stonewall Jackson Dam was built in 1986, there really was a small town called Roanoke here. Now Roanoke lies underwater, and a Roanoke plaza at *Stonewall Jackson Lake State Park* headquarters commemorates the vanished village. It has been replaced with the 198-room *Stonewall Jackson Resort* and its ten furnished cottages. And thirty-six campsites offer direct contact with the surrounding natural beauty. On a pretty weekend when the Arnold Palmer signature golf course is in full swing, the place is livelier than bygone Roanoke during harvest season.

Stonewall Jackson Lake's clear waters and 82 miles of shoreline make the state's second-largest lake extremely popular with anyone who likes to boat and fish. Largemouth bass, muskie, crappie, catfish, and bluegills are more likely to take your bait here than at any other West Virginia lake. The bass fishing rates among the best in the nation. The lake's tailwaters are stocked with trout.

For a way-off-the-beaten-path overnight, Stonewall Resort rents houseboats. You can spend days exploring the 26-mile lake and nights being lulled to sleep by the light swaying motion of a large boat on a nearly currentless lake. The 45-foot crafts contain all the comforts of home—fully equipped kitchens, TVs, DVDs, CD players with external speakers, and bedding for up to eight people. After a two-hour training session, you're good to go. Houseboats are rented for a two-night minimum at $200 a night or $900 a week, plus gasoline. Call (888) 278–8150.

If you're more of an indoor person, you could conceivably spend your whole vacation in the grand, Adirondack-style Stonewall Resort lodge. When you tire of ogling the lake and mountains, you could swim in the indoor/outdoor pool, mellow out in the hot tub, check out the game room, or try any of two dozen services at Mountain Laurel Spa—from a gentleman's facial to an artsy nail polish to the Golfer's Advantage massage. The Girlfriend's Getaway pampers two with massages, facials, manicures, pedicures, and champagne.

Chef Dale Hawkins's *Stillwaters* restaurant continues the lodge's tradition of pampering with favorites such as corn-crusted rainbow trout, grilled rib-eye, crawfish-stuffed chicken, and Appalachian egg rolls. The upholstered twig furniture is surprisingly comfy, so you can blame it if you have a hard time pushing away from the table.

Of course you should get outside. The 3,800-acre park offers dinner cruises, miles of hiking and biking trails, a wildlife exhibit, a 374-slip marina with boat rentals, and an outstanding golf course. The cart-only golf course reputedly is not for the faint of heart. However, six sets of tees give golfers of various abilities a chance to score.

The golf course, cottages, and resort are operated by Benchmark Hospitality, which also developed the $42 million project within the state park. In thirty years or so, ownership of the resort will return to the state of West Virginia.

Admission to the park is $2.00 per vehicle. The park and resort are open year-round. Call (304) 269–0523 or check out www.stonewallresort.com for more information.

If you want to know more about the Stonewall Jackson Lake Dam, visit the U.S. Army Corps of Engineers' visitor information center with its walks for viewing the dam and fishing access to the tailwaters. You reach this area by heading north on I–79 to exit 96 (first Weston exit).

About 15 miles east of Stonewall Jackson Lake is the community of **Buckhannon,** named one of the Top 100 Small Towns in America by Random House books. It's a college town with a surprising number of unusual attractions, including an underground theater where foreign films are screened each Friday evening. The **Lascaux Micro-Theater** is located at 33 East Main Street (304–473–1818). Another nearby attraction is **West Virginia Wesleyan College,** the largest private institution of higher learning in the state. Founded in 1890 by the Methodist Church, West Virginia Wesleyan is a learning community of more than 1,600 students from thirty countries. Take a stroll around the beautiful, century-old, Georgian-style campus near the Buckhannon River and recall your school days. Be sure to duck into the gorgeous **Wesley Chapel,** a classic Greek-revival structure that seats 1,600 worshippers, making it the largest church in the state. The chapel, with its signature white steeple and Casavant organ with 1,500 pipes, holds regular religious services as well as special performing arts events, lectures, and community activities. The adjacent rhododendron garden blooms spectacularly in the late spring and early summer. During the tour you may also notice the modern Rockefeller Athletic Center, named for WVWC's former president Jay Rockefeller, also once the governor of West Virginia and now a U.S. senator. Campus tours are available, and reservations are requested. To make arrangements, call (304) 473–8510.

The history of this area has been linked with its manufacture of fine glassware. Although most of the glass factories have closed, two Buckhannon artisans are following their hearts to continue the craft. Ron **Hinkle's Dying Art**

Glassworks is open for demonstrations of the old art of glassblowing, Monday through Friday, 9:00 A.M. to 2:30 P.M. You can visit his gallery between 9:00 A.M. and 4:00 P.M. daily, except Sunday. To get there, take State Route 20 south from Buckhannon 5 miles to Sago Road and follow the signs.

Buckhannon glass engraver Catherine Miller is one of a tiny number of Americans who still earn a living cutting glass with stone wheels. Her engravings of birds, flowers, animals, and angels are elegantly detailed, with a translucence that plays games with light. Visiting her **Catherine Miller Designs** shop on a sunny day is an incomparable experience. Light streams through the crystal and colored vessels, dancing in sync with the Celtic music that accompanies Miller as she works in the adjacent studio.

Miller's shop glitters with the work of other fine glass artists as well, including Pilgrim Glass's cameo collection, former Steuben artist Steve Fenstermacher, Scott Bayless, Zellique, Willow Creek Glass, and Douglas Replogle and Jennings Bonnell paperweights—a collection worthy of a contemporary museum— only this is for sale.

Miller learned basic cutting techniques on her lunch hour while working in local glass shops but developed her own style with intaglio engraving. She has been invited to design ornaments for the White House Christmas tree and created ceremonial glassware for the last three presidents, as well as Fabian, Mel Gibson, Rosie O'Donnell, Arnold Palmer, several governors, and various foreign diplomats. In 2003 her graceful engraved vase was pictured worldwide in an ad for Teleflora's Mother's Day bouquet. She has engraved rosebuds on the windows of antique cars and created Florida's national bocce awards, as well as personalizing countless stemware for weddings worldwide. Prices range from $30 to $3,000.

Catherine Miller Designs, off US 33 behind the Buckhannon Hampton Inn, is open from 9:00 A.M. to 5:00 P.M. Tuesday through Saturday. Call (304) 472–6664 or visit her Web site www.catherinemillerdesigns.com for more information.

If you're in Buckhannon in the middle of May, you're in luck—the city's most anticipated event is forthcoming. The **Strawberry Festival** promotes the harvesting of the local crop of strawberries. This weeklong event includes three days of parades with bands from all over the United States, dozens of floats, and even a Strawberry Queen and her court that float down Strawberry Lane. Tons of strawberries are served every imaginable way—and then some. You'll also find the usual festival food fare along with music and scores of craft exhibits, antique cars, and sports competitions. For more information on the citywide festival, call the West Virginia Strawberry Festival at (304) 472–9036.

Two miles north of town is another unusual attraction—a tree with a great story. At the spot where Turkey Run Creek enters the Buckhannon River (just off U.S. Highway 119), look for the ***Pringle Tree.*** This large, hollow sycamore tree is the third generation of one that provided shelter for two brothers, John and Samuel Pringle, who had deserted from the British army. The brothers ran from Fort Pitt (now Pittsburgh) in 1761 and, on finding the tree in 1764, lived in its cavernous base for more than three years before venturing away from the area for ammunition. When they discovered the war was over, they returned to civilization but soon came back to the area to show others where they had lived in the wild. As legend goes, the party was so impressed by the bounty of the land, they decided to settle the area, making the spot the first permanent settlement west of the Alleghenies in Virginia. The tree is symbolic of the movement into the western frontier.

Pringle Tree Park is open from May 1 to November 1 during daylight hours. The park has picnic grounds, a playground, bathroom facilities, and a boat launch. Call the Upshur County Chamber of Commerce at (304) 472–1722 for more information.

Just south of Buckhannon on Route 20 is the community of ***French Creek*** and the ***West Virginia State Wildlife Center.*** The center has roots in a game farm established on this 329-acre tract during the 1920s. The original facilities were beyond renovation, so an entirely new exhibit area was designed and built beginning in 1984.

Today visitors to the center can see elk, bison, mountain lions, timber wolves, white-tailed deer, black bears, coyotes, river otters, and many species of birds, all native to the state, in their natural habitat. A 1½-mile loop walkway through the habitat is lined with interpretive signs to help you learn more about the animals and their impact on West Virginia history. The spacious enclosure allows animals to interact naturally with their environment.

Enjoy the picnic area, then take a walk to the stocked pond to see trout, bass, catfish, and bluegill. The park is still growing, too. Already plans have been made for an educational and interpretive center, auditorium, nocturnal animal exhibit, reptile exhibit, and aquarium. The park is open April 1 through October. Hours are 9:00 A.M. to 5:00 P.M. daily. Admission is $2.00 for adults, $1.00 for children three to fifteen. Younger children are free. For information call (304) 924–6211.

If you're fortunate enough to be in the Mountain Lakes region in mid-March, then by all means head over to the aptly named Lewis County town of ***Ireland,*** about 10 miles west of Rock Cave. By the second week of March, most West Virginia fields are beginning to green—a rich, dark green, reminiscent of the rolling hills of the Emerald Isle itself. In the town of Ireland, the locals are celebrating their Celtic roots with one of the state's most festive Irish celebrations. The weeklong ***Irish Spring Festival,*** usually starting around

The Pringle Tree

the fifteenth of the month and always including St. Patrick's Day, is alive with so-called pot o' luck dinners, Mulligan stew cook-offs, Irish gospel choirs, leprechaun contests, Irish jig contests, harp concerts, road bowling, a parade, a kite-flying contest, and many more distinctively Irish pastimes.

The region around Ireland, like most of West Virginia and the southern Appalachians, was settled by Irish and Scottish pioneers, many of whom were ostracized by the British gentry who owned the sprawling plantations of the flatter and infinitely more fertile lowlands of Virginia, the Carolinas, and Georgia. Irelanders claim their community was first settled by an Irishman named Andrew Wilson, a gentleman who in his later years was known affectionately as "Old Ireland." According to local legend Wilson "lived to see 114 springtimes." When folks from around the countryside learned of this long life, many were convinced that there was something about the quality of life in Ireland—West Virginia—that was conducive to long life. Hence the town grew in numbers and prestige. Today it's home to 200 souls, but the population more than doubles during the festival. The town also receives a deluge of cards and letters from around the country to be postmarked "Ireland" for St. Patrick's Day. For more information on the festival, contact the Lewis County Convention and Visitors Bureau at (304) 269–7328.

Lodging is somewhat scarce along the back roads of the Mountain Lakes region, so you might want to take a spin over to **Holly River State Park,** located just off Route 20 on the northern tip of Webster County. The park is the state's second largest in area; ten fully equipped modern cabins are interspersed among the lushly forested hills and along the namesake river, which

Playing in the Road

Brush up on your underhand throw. There's a new old sport catching on in central West Virginia. The West Virginia Irish road-bowling season goes into swing in March with the Irish Spring Festival in—of course—Ireland, West Virginia.

Like their Irish counterparts who started the game 350 years ago, these strong-armed bowlers hurl an iron ball down a 1.2- to 2-mile country-road course. The player or team reaching the finish line in the fewest shots wins. A good shot, not counting the 15-foot running start, is 150 yards. The Mountain State record is 422 yards, but it was downhill—well, it's hard to find a flat place in West Virginia.

Veteran bowlers compete side by side with newcomers and giggling sixth-grade girls at these friendly events. Eleven years ago David Powell saw a televised Irish road-bowling game and brought the sport back to West Virginia, where it has been gaining popularity on back roads.

"We've had record numbers for most of our matches lately," says Powell, who has been coordinating Irish road bowling throughout West Virginia for the past decade.

The West Virginia road-bowling circuit holds nearly twenty events on fourteen stretches of road throughout the state. The season opens annually with Lewis County's Irish Spring Festival and ends with the Yankee Skedaddle at nearby Stonewall Resort in November. In between, bowlers keep their arms in shape through competitions at the West Virginia Strawberry Festival, West Virginia Carp Festival, Preston County Buckwheat Festival, Barbour County Fair, and other West Virginia events. For more information, contact the West Virginia Road Bowling Association at (202) 387–1680 or www.wvirishroadbowling.com.

offers tremendous trout fishing in the spring and fall. The park also has a restaurant, visitor center, pool, and game courts. If you're looking for a more primitive experience, Holly River has eighty-eight campsites, all wooded and private with outdoor fireplaces and grills. Don't leave the park without hiking over to the two scenic waterfalls, Tecumseh and Tenskwatawa. Call (304) 493–6353, or check the Web site at www.hollyriver.com.

About 20 miles northwest of Buckhannon, and maybe a ten-minute drive north of Weston, is another charmingly named community in Lewis County, *Jane Lew.* The town is named after Jane Lewis, mother of Lewis Maxwell, one of the founders of Weston and a man who bought most of the land where this present-day burgh sits. In town, off Main Street on Trolley (follow the signs for glass factory tour), you'll find *Masterpiece Crystal.* Known for its high-quality, lead-free crystal, Masterpiece employs twenty craftspeople in its small factory. Arrive on a weekday before 3:00 P.M. and you'll be able to view the glassblowers working with stemware on the open floor. Look for Masterpiece crafts-man Douglas Replogle, who's earned a national reputation for his colorful paperweights. Although most Masterpiece crystal is sold to restaurants, you can buy handmade stemware, decanters, vases, candlesticks, bells, and marbles at the gift shop, which is open 9:00 A.M. to 5:00 P.M. seven days a week. Call (304) 884–7841 for more information.

Also in Jane Lew, on US 19 North, is **Astolat Garden Perennials,** the place to go for local ornamental grasses, ferns, and flowers. You can browse the half-acre display gardens and cut your own bouquet. The staff here is happy to provide visitors with advice on plant selection and culture, garden design, and maintenance. The gardens are open April 15 through September 30, seven days a week. Call (304) 884–6770 for more information.

Three miles west of Jane Lew is *Jackson's Mill Historic Area,* the boy-hood home of Confederate legend General Thomas "Stonewall" Jackson. His grandparents settled the land and built the area's first gristmill along the banks of the West Fork River. Their son Cummins, Thomas's uncle, took pos-session of the property at the death of his father and ran the lucrative busi-ness, which included two mills, carpenter and blacksmith shops, and a store. Thomas came to live with Cummins and his family in 1830 after the death of his parents, Jonathan and Julia. He left in 1842 for West Point and a brilliant military career.

The Jackson compound was also an important part of life for the entire surrounding area. Because of the Jackson family's interest in politics and the importance of their mill to the area economy, the homestead became a gathering place for area settlers.

Today the 523-acre park is open for tours and features *Jackson's Mill Museum,* a gristmill dating from 1841. The structure itself is amazing: The two-and-a-half-story wooden building, sitting on a stone foundation, is made out of lumber produced from that on the original foundation.

Don't miss the half-hour film on the life of Stonewall Jackson; then feel free to wander amid the

Jackson's Mill

artifacts, tools, and other items remaining from another era. See the apple butter kettle, the chicken watering jug, the varmint trap, and cheese press, among other authentic curios.

Also of interest on the property are **Blaker Mill** and the **McWhorter Cabin.** The mill, disassembled stone by stone from another part of the county and moved to its new location at Jackson's Mill, is a fully operating gristmill. Today you can see nineteenth-century technology at work as locally grown grains, actually used in the conference center's kitchen (see later), are ground and even sold to the public.

The 200-year-old, hand-hewn, log McWhorter cabin, also relocated here, was the handiwork of Henry McWhorter, a New Yorker who had served in the Revolutionary War before moving south. He and his family lived in the one-room cabin for thirty-seven years. It is located on the original site where the Jackson home once stood. Admission is $4.00 for adults, $2.00 for children under twelve. Jackson's Mill is open Memorial Day through Labor Day from 10:00 A.M. to 5:00 P.M. and on weekends in May, September, and October. Closed Monday. For further information and specific times, call (304) 269–5100.

If you're near Jackson's Mill in the summer, stay around for one of the best festivals anywhere in the United States. Usually around Labor Day weekend, hundreds of artisans gather here for the **Stonewall Jackson Heritage Arts and Crafts Jubilee** to exhibit traditional Appalachian handicrafts. Blown and stained glass, pottery, quilts and dolls, handmade lace, and dozens of other items are displayed here.

Crafters aren't the only ones who show up. This is one of the state's premier mountain music showcases. Singers and musicians from around the region put on quite a show with mountain dulcimers, guitars, banjos, and fiddles echoing through the hills deep into the night, along with the stomping of cloggers. History buffs, meanwhile, will enjoy the eerily realistic Civil and Revolutionary War battle reenactments, while rugged outdoorsmen will be in awe of the wood-chopping demonstration, in which hardy men and women slice through native hardwoods as if they were butter. The West Virginia University team puts on a particularly impressive show of how much wood a woodchuck can chuck. Past turkey-calling champions compete in turkey- and owl-calling contests. With all that gawking you'll be doing, you'll need sustenance. Mouthwatering vittles are everywhere, including pork barbecue sandwiches, catfish platters, cobblers, corn bread and beans, pancakes, barbecued chicken, and ice cream made on the spot. Call (800) 296–1863 or (304) 269–7328 Monday through Friday, 9:00 A.M. to 4:00 P.M., for admission prices and further information.

When you're through enjoying the historic area at Jackson's Mill, it's time to take in the park's more modern amenities. Today it has a beautiful stone

Conference Center providing year-round activities for those seeking to get away from the office or simply to take a vacation. Originally a youth camp (this was the site of the nation's first state 4-H camp, established in 1921), it now has a contemporary twenty-three-room stone lodge and fourteen cottages to house guests. Various private rooms also are scattered around the campus. More than twenty meeting facilities are available for groups as large as 400 or as few as 10. Accessibility isn't a problem, either; the center has an airstrip, built in 1935 and improved later when the Navy trained pilots here.

Rates are very reasonable and in the off-season are offered at 70 percent off for Sunday through Friday morning stays. For information, call (304) 269–6140.

The Mountain Park

The rugged lifestyle and athletic prowess of the lumberjacks—those responsible for timber harvesting—are brought to life every spring at the *Webster County Woodchopping Festival* in Webster Springs. The backbreaking competition is held here in late May, with special events taking place the entire preceding week. The choppers hail from as far away as Australia and New Zealand for the Southern World title.

For the past several years, the finals of the competition have been televised on ESPN. It's a fascinating event that corresponds with the peak spring plant and flower bloom in the mountains. Webster Springs, located on the banks of the Elk River, is a natural attraction in itself. For more information on the festival, contact the Webster County Development Authority at (304) 847–7666.

Another Webster County event not to be missed is the annual *Webster County Nature Tour* at Camp Caesar near Cowen. Spring arrives a little later than marked on the calendar in the mountains of Webster County, but you can count on it by the first weekend in May. There is a briskness to the air, but the sun's warmth is soothing. As far as the eye can see, mountain ridge is stacked against mountain ridge. It is not for nothing that Webster County is called the Mountain Park. The Elk Mountain hike is steep but revitalizing, with no signs of civilization when you reach the summit. The Elk River snakes over the valley floor far below.

mountain lakestrivia

The Elk River, which bisects central West Virginia, is widely regarded as one of the best trout fisheries in the state.

Elk Mountain is just one beautiful area covered by the annual Webster County Nature Tour. Another area covered in this annual event is the *Leatherwood Tour.* This tour follows an old railroad grade along Leatherwood Creek

The Golden Apples of Clay County

Anderson Mullins of Clay County was mighty fond of apples, enough so that he traded a larger farm for his brother Bewell's thirty-six acres of bottomland and hillside orchards on Porters Creek.

A. H., as he was called, experimented with some stock from Stark Brothers Nursery, but he knew the golden apples that won him first prize at the Clay County Fair every year didn't come from any tree he'd planted. In September 1914, Mullins sent samples of the miraculous golden apples to Stark Brothers Nursery in Missouri. Paul Stark knew red apples dominated the market, so he wasn't impressed with the freckled yellow apples—until he took a bite.

"With one in hand, you can't be sure whether you're eating an apple or drinking champagne," Stark later wrote in his catalog. He hopped on a train, traveled over 1,000 miles, then rode a horse another 25 miles to a remote farm near the Clay/Kanawha County line. The tree was everything he'd hoped for—vigorous, prolific, and able to produce large golden apples that stayed crisp until spring.

Although no one knows for sure how much he offered the Mullins family—some say $5,000; others say $10,000—when Stark left the tree was enclosed in a wire cage and Stark Brothers had a deed for the 900-square-foot plot it stood on.

The Golden Delicious, as Stark named it, came about by accident. The result of natural pollination, the apple was literally created by the birds and the bees. Within two years the grafts he took back to Missouri were producing apples, and word of the "great, glowing, glorious apple" spread across the nation.

The great horticulturist Luther Burbank wrote, "After observing the Golden Delicious in my experimental gardens . . . I have no hesitation in stating that it is the greatest apple in all the world."

Although the original Mullins Golden Delicious tree died in the 1950s, a roadside plaque marks the spot where it once sprouted. In 1973 Clay County baked up a 6-foot apple pie and began the annual tradition of a *Golden Delicious Festival.* To find it, go to downtown Clay on the third weekend of September and follow the scent of baked apples, or call (304) 587–7652.

for about 2½ miles to beautiful Leatherwood Falls. The constant roar of Leatherwood Creek making its steep descent has one peering around each turn, expecting to see a huge waterfall. Leatherwood Falls is a special treat; aqua-green water plunges 30 feet over a rock ledge to a beautiful pool below. It is at the falls that many of the hikers choose to eat lunch. All that can be heard is the soothing roar of the falls; conversation is muted.

The tour is put on by the Webster Springs Garden Club in conjunction with the West Virginia Department of Natural Resources and the West Virginia

Department of Agriculture. The weekend activity is centered on **Camp Caesar's** 300 wooded acres. The camp has been open since 1922 and offers ten rustic cabins. Sleeping arrangements for the weekend are dormitory style, and guests need to bring pillows and sleeping bags.

The cost for the weekend event is under $100 per person. The fee covers accommodations, tours, refreshments, five meals served over the three days, and entertainment for two days. This is certainly a down-home country experience in the beautiful mountains of Webster County.

Be sure to bring sturdy hiking shoes and comfortable clothing. Dress in layers, because the weather frequently goes from cool mornings to very warm afternoons. Don't forget sleeping bags, pillows, towels, and washcloths. Call Stella Riffle, Garden Club member, for more information at (304) 847–2735, or call Camp Caesar at (304) 226–3888 or 847–2145.

While in the Cowen area, it would be a shame to pass up **Betty's Hilltop Diner.** Located at the top of the hill leaving Cowen on Route 20 north, the diner provides some of the best home-cooked meals you will find anywhere. Open daily from 7:00 A.M. to 9:00 P.M., the popular eatery takes great care in providing sumptuous meals. Daily lunch and dinner specials are to be had for less than $5.00. Call (304) 226–3800 for more information.

Perhaps more than any other Mountain State county, Webster County lays claim to world-class fishing in numerous crystalline mountain streams and rivers. Truly outstanding trout fishing can be experienced in the Williams River, Cranberry River, and Elk River above Webster Springs. Special regulation areas, such as the fly-fishing-only section on the Dogway Fork of the Cranberry River and the catch-and-release trout fishing areas on the Back Fork of Elk, Cranberry, Williams, and upper Elk Rivers may appeal to the Orvis crowd. If you're seeking the West Virginia golden trout, try the Little Kanawha River, Holly River, Sugar Creek, Fall Run, and Desert Fork. The West Virginia Department of Natural Resources lists the Elk and Little Kanawha Rivers as among the state's best smallmouth bass streams. What aren't listed are the best native trout streams—small, cold tributaries with shaded pools deep in the forest. After a day of wandering along the rivers, it's time to relax in the pool or picnic grounds at **Baker's Island Recreation Area,** in the Elk River right in downtown Webster Springs.

Places to Stay in the Mountain Lakes Region

BUCKHANNON

Deer Park Inn and Lodge
Heavener Grove Road
(304) 472-8400
Expensive

Governor's Inn B&B
76 East Main Street
(304) 472-2516
(866) 246-8466
Moderate

Post Mansion Inn
8 Island Avenue
(304) 472-8959
Moderate to expensive

Riverside Bed & Breakfast
113 Island Avenue
(304) 472-0796
www.riversidewv.com
Moderate

SUMMERSVILLE

Comfort Inn
U.S. Highway 19 North
(304) 872-6500
Moderate

Sleep Inn
U.S. Highway 19 North
(304) 872-4500
Moderate

WEBSTER SPRINGS

Mineral Springs Motel
1 Spring Street
(304) 847-5305
Inexpensive

WESTON

Ingeberg Acres
712 Left Millstone Road
(304) 269-2834
Inexpensive

Places to Eat in the Mountain Lakes Region

BUCKHANNON

Aesop Cafe
15 East Main Street
(304) 472-3758
Inexpensive

CJ Maggies American Grill
16 East Main Street
(304) 472-2490
Inexpensive

COWEN

Betty's Hilltop Diner
State Route 20
(304) 226-3800
Budget

SUMMERSVILLE

Cafe Acropolis
331 McMillion Drive
(304) 872-0254
Inexpensive

La Carreta Mexican Restaurant
Merchants Walk
Shopping Center
(304) 872-6570
www.lacarreta-mr.gpg.com
Inexpensive

Shoney's
U.S. Highway 19 North
(304) 872-6785
Inexpensive

Up the Creek Smokehouse
State Route 41
near U.S. Highway 19
interchange
(304) 872-7335
Inexpensive

SUTTON

Cafe Cimino
400 Fourth Street
(304) 765-2913
Moderate

FOR MORE INFORMATION

Buckhannon/Upshur County
Convention and Visitors Bureau
(304) 472-1722 or (888) 707-1722

Lewis County Convention and
Visitors Bureau
(304) 269-7328

Summersville Convention
and Visitors Bureau
(304) 872-3722

Webster County Development
Authority
(304) 847-2145

New River/Greenbrier Valley Region

The New River/Greenbrier River region offers the most diversity in land, character, and attractions of any area of the state. These eight counties in southeastern West Virginia make up a land of extremes—stupendous wealth in the millionaires' homes in historic Bramwell and the grinding poverty of played-out mining towns several miles away; the pristine Greenbrier River as well as creeks choked with mining runoff or buried by mountaintop removal operations. It's a region of piercing beauty and glaring neglect, of comely horse farms and crumbling coal camps, of ATVs, llamas, and hickory-club golf. That's what makes it such an interesting place to visit. Take your time on the back roads (don't try to do otherwise on the notorious county one-laners); stop at the country stores, diners, and roadside attractions. This is a fascinating corner of America.

The Greenbrier and Bluestone Valleys

This scenic stretch in southeastern West Virginia runs roughly from White Sulphur Springs in the north to the Bluestone River Gorge in the south and contains virtually all of Greenbrier and

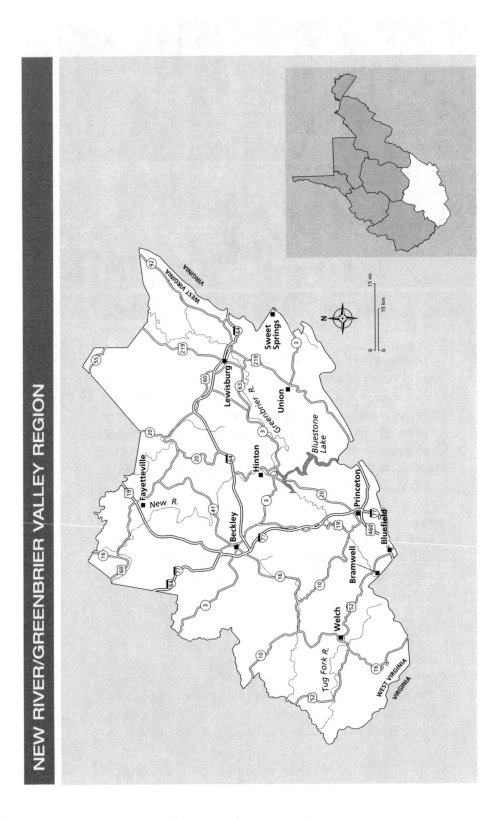

Summers Counties. It's a region of verdant rolling farmland, inviting old inns, and remote getaways.

The luxurious ***Greenbrier Resort*** is perhaps the most on-the-beaten-path attraction in West Virginia. (You know you're on the beaten path when your past clientele has included Prince Rainier and President Bill Clinton.) There are, however, some off-the-beaten-path features here, such as the ***Greenbrier Bunker.*** This secret hideaway—at least it was until the *Washington Post* blew its cover in 1992—is a 112,000-square-foot maze of barracks and storage areas reserved for congressmen and other government officials in case of a nuclear attack. The two-story underground structure was designed to accommodate 1,500 people at a time. The site was selected because the Greenbrier has always been a popular vacation spot for politicians and other members of Washington officialdom. It is also far from any large population center, yet accessible by interstate, Amtrak, and an airport boasting the Mountain State's longest runway. The outside entrance to the bunker no longer remains a well-kept secret, even though Washington is trying to distance itself from this embarrassing relic of the cold war. The renovated bunker is open for tours several times each week. Call (304) 536–1110.

While those not spending the night at the Greenbrier have only three options for visiting the famed four-star resort—golf, dinners in the main hall (with reservations), and the bunker tours—guests have a myriad of options for filling their day. The sportsman or -woman will want to head up Kate's Mountain to the Greenbrier Gun Club for sporting clays, skeet, and trap. Quail hunting excursions are also available. The facilities are open to beginners and advanced marksmen alike.

For those more inclined to watch wild creatures, a falconry academy is offered in the ancient art of working with raptors. Now add a roster of other

The Greenbrier Resort

BEST ANNUAL EVENTS IN THE NEW RIVER/GREENBRIER VALLEY REGION

Historic Bramwell's Tour of Homes
Bramwell; second Saturday in
May and December
(304) 248–8381 or (800) 221–3206

**Appalachian String Band
Music Festival**
Clifftop; early August
(304) 558–0220

State Fair of West Virginia
Lewisburg/Ronceverte
second week of August
(304) 645–1090
www.wvstatefair.com

Hinton Railroad Days
Hinton; mid-October
(304) 466–5420

New River Gorge Bridge Day
Fayetteville; mid-October
(304) 574–3834 or (800) 927–0263
www.officialbridgeday.com

October Sky Festival
Coalwood; early October
(304) 297–4960 or 5102
www.homerhickam.com

**Battle of Lewisburg Living History &
Reenactment**
Lewisburg; third weekend in May
(800) 833–2068
www.battleoflewisburg.org

activities, including shooting the white water down West Virginia's Gauley or New Rivers, honing Land Rover driving skills, hitting the trails on a mountain bike, swimming in the infinity-edge pool, achieving outdoor chef skills at Steven Raichlen's Barbecue University, taking the spa treatment, or playing a round on one of the famed golf courses.

While you're in the mood for golf, why not vary your experience—at *Oakhurst Links.* At this nine-hole course in White Sulphur Springs, the Montague family founded the first golf course and organized golf club in America in 1884. Oakhurst Links also boasts having the first known golf tournament in the States, in 1888.

Golfers played on a rough Scottish green, made their own tees, used hickory clubs, and played with a gutta-percha ball.

You still play this way at Oakhurst Links. You tee up your rubber ball on a dollop of sand and strike it with a replica hickory club from Scotland. Watch out for the roaming sheep—they keep the place mowed. Participants in the National Hickory Championship the last weekend in July play in knickers.

So leave your clubs and tees at home. All replica equipment is included with your greens fees. Call (304) 536–1884 or visit www.oakhurstlinks.com for tee times.

Tours galore are available in historic **Lewisburg,** the Greenbrier County seat. The 200-year-old community, located about 10 miles west of White Sulphur Springs on U.S. Highway 60, has more than seventy eighteenth- and nineteenth-century historic sites (for public tours call North House Museum at 304–645–3398), not to mention Civil War battle reenactments, dozens of antiques and specialty shops, eight art galleries, a fall ghost tour, and a taste of the town festival.

Antiques shops in Lewisburg come in many forms—you'll see antiques and crafts, antiques in art galleries, even antiques and fabrics, as well as **Robert's Antiques,** touted as "Lewisburg's finest antiques and wine shop." Besides holding wine tastings, Robert's displays a gorgeous collection of hand-carved bars, confessionals, and cabinets. Other not-to-miss stops on the 5-block tour of Lewisburg are **Peddler's Alley Antiques,** the contemporary **Harmony Ridge Gallery,** the zany **New Horizon Gallery,** and **Wolf Creek Gallery** and **High Country Gallery,** two upscale clothiers, both featuring a Filenes-style bargain room. This wonderfully pedestrian-friendly town also offers two great bakeries and several of the Mountain State's best eateries.

One of the best walking tours begins at 105 Church Street in the **Carnegie Hall** building. Yes, there is another Carnegie Hall, and most locals refer to the New York cultural institution as "the other one." Just like its Big Apple counterpart, Lewisburg's Carnegie Hall was funded entirely by the iconoclastic business tycoon Andrew Carnegie. Interestingly, it was the first electrically lighted public building in town and in this corner of West Virginia. Built in 1902, the ornate four-story building is the artistic nerve center of Lewisburg. It houses eleven classrooms and three art galleries. The centerpiece 500-seat auditorium stages drama, musical, and performance-art productions throughout the year and is now supported by local contributions. The building is open year-round Monday through Saturday, 9:00 A.M. to 5:00 P.M. Sunday hours are from May through October, 1:00 to 5:00 P.M. Call (304) 645–7917, or visit www.carnegie hallwv.com.

Carnegie's neighbor across Church Street is the **Old Stone Presbyterian Church,** the oldest Protestant church building in continuous use west of the Alleghenies. On any weekday between 9:00 A.M. and 4:00 P.M., you can sit in one of the boxed pews or climb up to the balcony where slaves sat in ladderback chairs. Except for electricity and cushioned seats, the old church looks much the same as it did in 1796, when some parishioners walked 20 miles from places like Renick's Valley, Irish Corner, and Big Clear Creek for services. Guests are always welcome to join the congregation for the 11:00 A.M. service each Sunday.

North House Museum sits on the opposite side of a wide, green lawn from Carnegie Hall. A wing removed in the twentieth century was recently restored to the 1820 hotel, giving ample accommodations for the Greenbrier Historical Society's genealogical archives. These documents date from 1778 to the present and contain the signatures of Thomas Jefferson, George Washington, and James Monroe. The museum also houses a fabulous collection of wedding gowns from 1820 to the mid-1900s, a Conestoga wagon, and an 1896 buggy used to deliver mail to the first RFD (Rural Free Delivery) postal customers in the nation. The postmaster general at that time hailed from the Mountain State, so his first three pilot routes were in West Virginia—in Charles Town. The second-oldest quilt in the nation—a 1795 broderie perse design—shares museum space with Confederate general Robert E. Lee's saddle and a chair he willed to his servant. But the artifacts of the everyday life of the common citizen are most evident here—the tools, weapons, and kitchen implements of people who worked the soil and fought off marauding Shawnees. Hoop skirts, string ties, and teacups are part of the education here at North House. Children are encouraged to dress up in 1850 costumes supplied by the museum as they learn the customs and manners of the day while sipping afternoon tea. To participate, call ahead for reservations at (304) 654–3398. This is also the number to arrange for a stimulating guided tour of the museum—one that will explain the torture device in the nursery as well as the true story of the Greenbrier Ghost.

Around May 23, the town reenacts the **Battle of Lewisburg,** complete with a camp dance, a ladies' tea, historical impersonators, a fife and drum corps, and a funeral cortege ending in the Confederate cemetery. Reenactors give a realistic portrayal of the 1862 defeat of Confederate troops under General Henry Heth by General George Crook's Union forces, but no bridges will burn this time around.

No matter what weekend you visit, you can still pay your respects at the cross-shaped mass grave of ninety-five unknown soldiers at the **Confederate Cemetery** on McElhenny Street and view the cannonball that is still stuck in the southwest corner of John Wesley Methodist Church.

Given all there is to do, you'll probably want to spend at least one night in Lewisburg. Try the 1834 **General Lewis Inn**—from there you can walk to almost any place in this safe little town—and a night with the General is like stepping into your own friendly little museum. The inn is chock-full of antique glass, china, household utensils, firearms, and curios. It even has a Memory Hall museum and a front desk that Thomas Jefferson leaned over when he registered at Sweet Chalybeate Springs Hotel. An old stagecoach used on the mineral springs circuit is parked out front. You can wander through the open guest rooms and pick out the room you want for the night—there are twenty-six from which to choose, each furnished with a bed more than a hundred years old and other period antiques. An occasional ghost is rumored to haunt Room 208 in the east wing, but most folks say the scent of sumptuous country cooking is the only thing wafting through these halls. Butterscotch, the inn cat, confines herself to hostess duty in the sitting room and front hall these days. The dining room serves country classics like fried chicken and baked ham with a chef's touch.

For a jaunt that's really off the beaten path, go underground at **Lost World Caverns** on one of Steve Silverberg's wild cave expeditions. You'll be outfitted with a lantern on your helmet, kneepads, and gloves because you'll be doing a bit of crawling through subterranean chambers few others behold. You're guaranteed to see a few sleeping little brown bats and maybe a salamander or cricket, but mostly it's just your group and the formations. You'll hear water dripping off the walls and the echo of your footsteps on stone. This cave harbors the oldest known stalagmite in the world (500,000 years) and the nation's largest stalactite, a thirty-ton chandelier of pure white calcite. If you prefer light and open spaces, you can opt for the standard ½-mile self-guided tour. **Lost World Natural History Museum** contains castings of almost a dozen dinosaurs, as well as petrified dinosaur eggs and dung. Rocks and artifacts in the gift shop will tempt junior (and senior) geologists.

Dick Pointer: Enslaved Hero

One of Lewisburg's most celebrated war heroes is buried in an African-American cemetery beside Carnegie Hall. On May 29, 1778, in the last significant Indian raid on the Greenbrier region, Dick Pointer almost single-handedly fought off a band of Shawnees attempting to storm Fort Donnally while the militia slept upstairs.

As the Shawnees battered the door with tomahawks and began to force it open, Pointer seized a musket. He fired through the cracked door into the crowd of Native Americans. They fell back, and Pointer was able to secure the log door with help from a white comrade.

Troops from Camp Union commanded by Captain William Johnston drove the Shawnees out of the Greenbrier region the next day. Four white settlers and twelve Indians died in the battle, 10 miles north of Lewisburg.

While all the men who slept upstairs in the attack were granted land as defenders of the country, Pointer continued to be enslaved for the next twenty-three years. In 1795 he petitioned for a pension. It was denied. When local citizens heard the news, they built Pointer a cabin. He was finally granted his freedom in 1801.

Pointer died in 1827 and was buried with full military honors in the African-American cemetery across the street from the white cemetery. Two plaques and a large monument topped with a stone cannonball mark Pointer's final resting place, and his musket is on permanent display a few hundred yards away at North House Museum. None of those other soldiers at Fort Donnally, even Pointer's former master, Colonel Andrew Donnally, is memorialized in this way.

BEST ATTRACTIONS IN THE NEW RIVER/GREENBRIER VALLEY REGION

The Greenbrier Resort
White Sulphur Springs
(304) 536–1110 or (800) 453–4858
www.greenbrier.com

**Tamarack: The Best of
West Virginia Crafts**
Interstate 77, exit 45, Beckley
(304) 256–6843
www.tamarack.com

**Outdoor Theatre West Virginia
at Grandview**
Beckley
(304) 256–6800 or (800) 666–9142

Pipestem Resort State Park
Pipestem
(304) 466–1800 or (800) or CALL–WVA

New River Gorge National River
Glen Jean
(304) 465–0508

Beckley Exhibition Coal Mine
Beckley
(304) 256–1747
www.beckleymine.com

**Canyon Rim Ranch ATV and
Horseback Riding**
Fayetteville
(304) 574–3021
www.canyonrimranch.com

Lost World is open daily, 10:00 A.M. to 4:00 P.M. from Thanksgiving until March 31, 9:00 A.M. to 5:00 P.M. in the spring and fall, and 9:00 A.M. to 7:00 P.M. May 15 through Labor Day. Rates are $10.00 for adults and $5.00 for kids under thirteen. To make wild caving reservations, call (304) 645–6677.

Five miles down U.S. Highway 219 from Lewisburg is the quiet town of Ronceverte (French for "Greenbrier") and its provocative *Organ Cave.* Pioneers discovered the cave in 1704 and used it for shelter. However, when Thomas Jefferson visited the site in 1791, members of his party found the remains of a large three-toed sloth.

During the Civil War, Organ Cave sheltered soldiers, and at one point it served as a chapel for a thousand of General Robert E. Lee's beleaguered Confederate troops. The cave provided them with much more than solace. Water collected inside the cave was laden with potassium nitrate, which, when evaporated, produced saltpeter, a main ingredient of gunpowder. The cave became a major Confederate saltpeter supply source, and today thirty-seven of the original fifty-two wooden saltpeter hoppers are preserved here.

Visitors to the cave, named for its "rock organ" formation resembling the pipes of a church organ, will discover there are more than 40 miles of mapped passageways. A one-hour guided tour will take you through cathedral-size rooms along a well-lighted path past calcite formations millions of years old.

Tours are available year-round. From November 15 through April 1, hours are 9:00 A.M. to 4:00 P.M.; the rest of the year, 9:00 A.M. to 7:00 P.M. Be sure to bring a jacket; underground temperatures remain a constant 55° F. Admission is $11.00 for adults and $5.00 for children six to twelve years old. For information on tours or on rodeos held on the property spring through fall, call (304) 645–7600 or (800) 258–CAVE.

Nearby is the southern terminus of the ***Greenbrier River Trail***, a 77-mile Rails-to-Trails project that presents excellent family outing options including hiking, biking, and horseback riding. For those who don't know, the Rails-to-Trails program converts abandoned rail lines into nonmotorized multiuse trails. This trail runs from Caldwell, in Greenbrier County, to Cass, in Pocahontas County, crossing thirty-five bridges along the way. The trail follows along the banks of the mild Greenbrier River, the longest free-flowing river in the eastern United States. A wide, level, gravel-covered trail makes for excellent family bicycling. Several area businesses offer bicycle rentals. The trail features a relaxed cycling atmosphere through some of the state's most beautiful scenery. The trail links two state forests, Greenbrier and Seneca. It also links two of the state's more popular state parks, Watoga and Cass. ***Free Spirit Adventures,*** in Caldwell, near Lewisburg, offers bike rentals, guided tours, shuttle services, and cycling instruction. For more information, call (800) 877–4749 or (304) 645–2093 or check the Web site at www.greenbrierrivertrail.com.

Unless you're an avid perennial gardener, you probably don't know a hellebore from a helicopter. But if you can appreciate the fact that deer eat almost anything green except hellebores, that most plants don't bloom in the winter, and that it takes a rugged flower to stay in blossom through three months of snow and rain, then you'll appreciate the hellebore for the truly exceptional flower it is.

Now you have to ask yourself if it is worth driving 10 miles over unpaved, mountain single-lane to see acres of hellebores blooming in the snow. Barry Glick, who owns the mountaintop ***Sunshine Farm and Gardens*** in northern Greenbrier

The Greenbrier River, which flows through Greenbrier County

OTHER ATTRACTIONS WORTH SEEING IN THE NEW RIVER/GREENBRIER VALLEY REGION

Bluestone Museum
Hinton

High Country Gallery
Lewisburg

Science Center of West Virginia
Bluefield

Greenbrier River Trail
Caldwell to Cass

Winterplace Ski Resort
Ghent

Organ Cave
Ronceverte

County, will assure you it is. But if you go, use caution on his driveway, a mile-long vertical shoot of mud and shale. A four-wheel-drive vehicle with high clearance is best.

Glick's 68,000 outdoor hellebores bloom maroon, black, white, yellow, and pink from February through June. On sunny days you'll see his crew dabbing paintbrushes into the flowers, doing the work of the hummingbirds and the bees and creating new varieties of the nodding, poppylike flower.

Besides the outdoor gardens, Glick nurtures four greenhouses of plants, almost 10,000 varieties of hellebores, cyclamen, primroses, anemones, and other species, some unknown to anyone else. Glick introduces them to the world through his wholesale business with nurseries around the globe. "You might say I have an obsessive love of plants," he says.

For information and directions to Sunshine Farms, call (304) 497–2208 or go to www.sunshinefarms.com.

Southeast West Virginia attracted visitors to its healing springs by droves some 150 years ago. White Sulphur Springs (now The Greenbrier) was one of the younger resorts. To see some of the older resorts, you can take a scenic drive south on State Route 311 down to *Sweet Springs,* swinging back and forth over the Virginia state line. This decaying 1790 resort looks like Versailles in West Virginia; the massive hotel, classical bath house, and several two-story guest houses still stand grand against their Peters Mountain backdrop. A new owner is attempting to revive the resort, and renovations are under way.

Pretty Sweet Springs Valley, however, has attracted several entrepreneurs and craftsmen. Beth and Dennis Potter make primitive early American furniture reproductions in the heart of the country where the original folk art was created 200 years ago. The Potters have researched milk paint recipes and developed twenty-five historic finishes for their furniture. You may recognize several of their pieces from back issues of *Country Living* magazine. They also sell authentic antiques collected in the Virginias, including a coffee bean counter, butter churns, and primitive boxes. Their ***Americana Homestead*** showrooms, featuring furniture, accessories, and folk murals in every room, are open from 10:00 A.M. to 5:00 P.M. Wednesday to Monday, May through August and weekends the rest of the year. Contact them at (304) 536–4320 or visit www.americana homestead.com. Their Mennonite neighbors on State Route 3 create oak chairs (Valley Springs Furniture), all manner of baked goods (Kitchen Creek Bakery), and cheeses, jellies, and jams (Cheese 'N More Store).

From near the bakery in Gap Mills, you can take the Mountain Shadow Trail scenic byway to County Road 15, up to Peters Mountain to a small parking lot on the right side of the road. From there, take the 1½-mile footpath to ***Hanging Rock Observatory.*** The little house braces on a rock outcropping atop 3,800-foot Peters Mountain, the perfect vantage point to watch the hawk migrations or the unfolding of the seasons. Visitors from twenty-three states and several countries have recorded their observations of eagles, hawks, and falcons at the observatory's Web site: www.hangingrocktower.org.

Returning to the valley, you can follow Route 3 to the little town of ***Union*** and its ***Union National Historic District.*** You'll pass the turnoff for ***Moncove Lake State Park,*** a secluded spot for fishing and camping. Just before you reach town, you'll see a sign for ***Rehoboth Church,*** a 1786 log structure reported to be the oldest Methodist church building west of the Alleghenies. In the dim interior, you can test the rough benches where parishioners listened to three-hour sermons. One of ten Methodist shrines, Rehoboth is open from 10:00 A.M. to 5:00 P.M. Tuesday through Saturday, Memorial Day through November 30.

Despite Union's name, a large limestone Confederate monument stands alone in a pasture just outside town. Apparently, town fathers expected more development when they erected the memorial in 1901. Or, some say, the town's Union sympathizers didn't want that symbol of the Confederacy to dominate downtown. This was divided territory during the Civil War, but both sides were relatively kind to Union. Twenty-nine antebellum structures sit within a 6-block area on Union's two main streets. And when your legs are tired, you can opt for a closer view of art and collectibles at ***Sydney's,*** on North Street just off Main Street. Sydney's carries antiques, candles, fragrances, and a display of the work of the Arts Alliance. Tea tastings are offered at the customer's request. Owner Susan Stidham makes candles in the back of the building, and her Guest Cottage of North Street (304–772–5900) is just down the street.

Sydney's is located within scent of ***Moxie Cafe***'s gourmet coffee, baked goods, and saucy entrees. Moxie (301 Main Street; 304–772–3068) is run by a former Greenbrier chef who took a liking to the laid-back ambience of Monroe County and began offering cooking classes in addition to lunches and dinners

Wednesday through Saturday. If you're feeling keyed up, be sure to request the herbal Moxie soda.

Heading south on US 219 for 3 miles, you glimpse the great stone lodge, bath house, spring house, and guest house of **Salt Sulphur Springs,** now a guest house open year-round. Owner Betty Farmer still bottles water for her family to treat various skin and stomach ailments. Call (304) 772–5891 for reservations.

From US 219, you can cut over to Greenville, home of **Creekside Resort** bed-and-breakfast and cottages (800–691–6420), then take State Route 12 and Route 3 to Pence Springs.

Only in West Virginia can you find a bed-and-breakfast that was once a women's penitentiary. Actually, that's not quite fair, because the historic **Pence Springs Hotel** was a thriving resort long before it was used as a prison. Located in the hamlet of Pence Springs, about 18 miles southwest of Ronceverte, the inn was first opened in 1897 by Andrew Pence, an entrepreneur who sought to capitalize on the idyllic location and famed springwaters of the region. (The village's water took the silver medal at the 1904 World's Fair.)

By 1926 the spacious sixty-room Georgian mansion was considered the grandest and most expensive hotel in the state, commanding an unheard-of daily rate of $6.00, which included all meals. During its heyday, fourteen trains stopped here daily, bringing in folks from as far away as Washington, D.C., Baltimore, and New York. The day after the stock market crashed in 1929, however, the inn closed its doors, only to be reopened briefly as a girl's school, a dude ranch, and then finally as a state-run women's prison from 1947 to 1977.

Renovated in the early 1980s by native son Ashby Berkley, the inn is once again bustling with activity and has earned a place on the National Register of Historic Places. Inside, a large sunroom and an elegant great room invite leisurely conversation with other travelers. Downstairs is the Cider Press Lounge, whose back bar was used as a set in the filming of *Matewan,* John Sayles's award-winning movie. The film chronicled one of southern West Virginia's bloodiest mining wars. Pence Springs's twenty-six guest rooms are simply furnished but comfortable. The portal windows on the bedroom doors are holdovers from prison days—guards once used these to look in on inmates; now they're reversed so guests can check the hall. Guests can also visit the solitary confinement cells on the third floor, where prison poetry scrawled on the dim walls can break your heart. Owner Berkley remembers pickup softball games with the inmates and can tell some stories.

Rooms for two with a full breakfast start at about $85. Breakfast, lunch, and dinner are served seven days a week. Dinner is available Tuesday through Saturday from 5:00 to 9:00 P.M. Berkley is a graduate of the prestigious Culinary

Institute of America, and the cuisine here (trout, salmon, rack of lamb, crab cakes with mustard sauce, to name just a few of the offerings) is outstanding. Between meals, guests play croquet, visit the old spring, or pick up some bargains at the Sunday Pence Springs Flea Market down the hill. Call (304) 466–2607 or (888) 675–1700 for reservations and more information.

There's an almost primeval quality to the smoky ravines and deep hollows of southern West Virginia. It's easy to sense that this was a land of courageous pioneers and rugged Native Americans, and nowhere is that feeling more acute than at nearby *Graham House.* It's an impressive log home dating from 1770, built for the express purpose of guarding Colonel James Graham's family from the Shawnee Indians, who quite understandably weren't too terribly keen on European encroachment into their region. In 1777 Colonel Graham's estate was raided, resulting in the death of his ten-year-old son and the capture of his young daughter. For eight years the determined colonel searched for the girl, finally rescuing her more than 100 miles away in what is now Maysville, Kentucky. Today the two-story house, considered extravagant for the times with its thick reinforced log walls and beams, is a National Historic Site. You'll see firsthand that living on the frontier of eighteenth-century West Virginia was an egalitarian experience. Not even the wealthy, such as Graham, were immune from the hardships of isolated life.

The house is located just south of Pence Springs along the river road. It's open Memorial Day through Labor Day from 11:00 A.M. to 5:00 P.M. Friday and Saturday and from 1:00 to 5:00 P.M. Sunday. For more information, call (304) 466–3321.

"Well, John Henry was a steel-drivin' maaaan, oh yeah." This famous line, popularized by Johnny Cash, is from the "The Ballad of John Henry," a song immortalizing West Virginia's and perhaps the nation's most famous railroad worker. In Talcott, a tiny village snuggled between the hills and the Greenbrier River south of Pence Springs, the legend of John Henry lives on at a small park commemorating the man and the myth.

According to both mountain storytellers and researchers, John Henry was an amiable, massively built man who could work a steel hammer like no one else. He was employed by the Chesapeake & Ohio Railroad, a company charged with clearing a tunnel through the concretelike red-clay shale of Big Bend Mountain. It was perilous work, to say the least. About 20 percent of the laborers lost their lives here, falling victim to all-too-frequent cave-ins or the more stealthy destroyer of lungs, silicosis from rock dust. One morning, one of the foremen bet John Henry $100, a huge sum of money in the early 1870s, that he couldn't beat a mechanized drill through one of the last stretches of the tunnel. Henry took the bet, grabbed his hammer, and won handily. As we all

John Henry statue at
John Henry Park

know, however, the extraordinary feat killed him soon after the race. (Most historians agree Henry's death was related to exhaustion, although some claim he died later in a cave-in.) In any event, Henry's hammer, bearing the initials J. H., was later found in the tunnel when a concrete floor was poured in 1932.

John Henry Park, containing the hammer and a statue of the famous railroad man, was built in 1973 and funded partly by a donation from Johnny Cash. The statue sits atop Big Bend Tunnel just off Route 3. The park is open year-round, dawn to dusk.

Peter Heus created *Enchanter's Garden* nursery in a hollow near Talcott after studying and growing native plants for more than twenty years. The beauty of the wild phlox, Dutchman's breeches, anemones, hepatica, trout lilies, lady slippers, and other wild plants romping over his grounds makes one rethink traditional landscaping. Heus's woodland and wetland flowerbeds attract hummingbirds, butterflies, frogs, and people, who are lured into Cale's Run Hollow to observe the seasonal transformations at the nursery. Heus has made his native plant nursery into a mail-order business selling trillium, Joe Pye weed, fringed gentian, blue flag, Virginia bluebells, and lesser-known flowers including wild quinine, cup plant, gaywings, and shale-barren pussytoes. While many of his specimens qualify as medicinals—ginseng, goldenseal, black cohosh, and wild yam—Heus advocates growing them for ecological reasons.

"The more you use natives in landscaping, the more you are reconnecting to the biological community of your area," he says. "Creating even a small natural area can entice fascinating creatures. You can provide stopover resting and feeding sites for neotropical songbirds and Monarch butterflies, maybe even provide safe haven for a beleaguered species."

But mostly, you notice that Enchanter's Garden is pretty, with its rock statues, random plantings, and pools. Although Heus discourages drop-in visitors ("We may not have time for you, and you won't want to meet us on our narrow driveway"), he does enjoy making appointments with visitors during the garden's productive period, April through October.

Homemade Instrument Capital of the World

Hinton, a quiet town of 2,700 surrounded by wild rivers, is emerging as the epicenter of a budding homemade musical instrument movement.

Recycled junk is how some might describe the materials used in instruments coming out of this New River burg. Hinton is home to the **National Cigar Box Guitar Museum,** an antique-guitar collection displayed at the Campbell-Flannagan-Murrell House Museum on Summers Street. The collection consists of everything from crude homemade guitars and fiddles from the early 1800s to more modern electric guitars made from cigar boxes for the likes of Lynyrd Skynyrd.

One guitar in the museum's collection uses golf tees for tuning pegs. A round candy tin has become a banjo. An old beer keg has been reincarnated as a bass. A hunting enthusiast whittled one cigar-box violin's scroll and bow to resemble antlered bucks, with silhouettes of deer forming the sound holes. Like most of the art in the collection, the piece is undated and unsigned by its creator.

The art of the homemade instrument was almost lost, says curator Ray Nutter. But a few people remember—including Nutter's friend Tom Hartwell of Hinton, who has made and sold at least 150 cigar-box guitars, including one played by Lynyrd Skynyrd guitarist Ed King. The cigar box gave "The Ballad of Curtis Loew" what King described as "a completely new sound" in a quote on Hartwell's Web site.

Carl Perkins, Roy Clark, and Jimi Hendrix are just a few of the musicians whose first guitar was a cigar box. Lyle Lovett is just now rediscovering the cigar-box guitar. His, in fact, is a bizarre instrument made from oak dowels and a wooden cigar box, with three guitar strings and a bass string, and played with a slide.

Nutter (aka "Rhythm Board" Ray) is himself a maker of musical washboards, one of only six such craftspeople in the nation. He and Hartwell, along with their blues band, Margo and the Bluegills, are key characters in a movement of musicians abandoning their "store-bought" instruments for the fun of building and using homemade instruments. At his riverside **Unkl Ray's Café,** Nutter has guest performers dropping their $2,000 instruments to pound out rhythms on pots and pans from the kitchen. He also encourages spectators to join in on the homemade instruments decorating his walls, things like PVC-pipe drums and, of course, cigar-box guitars.

"Hinton is now the self-proclaimed Homemade Instrument Capital of the World," says Nutter, a fifth-generation Summers County resident.

Hinton's free Festival of the Rivers, held each Labor Day weekend, features musicians from around the globe who play homemade instruments. The event always includes a workshop on how to build your own cigar-box guitar for $5.00. "We want Appalachian kids especially to know they don't even have to buy a guitar," Nutter says. "All you need is a box to resonate the sound out of."

Homemade instruments embody creativity, resourcefulness, and independence—the spirit of West Virginia, he says.

You can reach Heus by calling (304) 466–3154. To reach Enchanter's Garden, continue south on Routes 3 and 12 from Talcott and turn left on Route 12 after crossing Willowwood Bridge.

Deep in the heart of southern West Virginia's Summers County lies the little riverside community of **Hinton,** a picturesque railroad town that has escaped many of the urban trappings of the twenty-first century. The railroad arrived here in 1873, finding it the only practical route through the treacherous New River Gorge. The railroad brought prosperity and economic development. Today Hinton's beautifully restored courthouse, freight depot, 1890s passenger station, opera house, hotels, stores, warehouses, and gorgeous American Gothic, classical, and Greek-revival churches have been preserved. Even the original brick streets and gaslights have been saved from modernization.

The **Hinton Railroad Museum,** conveniently located in the same building as the Summers County Visitor Center (206 Temple Street), explains the railroad history of Hinton through vintage black-and-white photographs, recordings, documents, and train fixtures. Be sure to look for the old C&O Railroad baseball uniform worn by town resident Robert O. Murrell back in 1897. Murrell's team, perhaps the best company baseball club in the United States at the time, actually took on the Cincinnati Reds in an exhibition game and won. The museum's collection features tools that would have been used by John Henry, as well as the ninety-eight-piece John Henry woodcarving exhibit that took the carver Charles Pemelia three years and twenty types of wood to finish. It represents every 1870 railroad job that existed. The museum is open Monday through Saturday from 9:00 A.M. to 4:00 P.M. The museum is closed for repairs and upkeep during the months of January and February each year. Call (304) 466–5420 for more information.

Interestingly enough, the house Murrell lived in is now the town's oldest standing residential structure. You can visit the **Campbell-Flannagan-Murrell House Museum** at 422 Summers Street and get a feel for how a typical Hinton railroad family lived during the late 1800s. The wooden, three-story, Federal-style home was built in 1875; at the time, the basement level was used as a general store. Today it's used as a museum, with home furnishings dating from the golden years of the railroad. It's also the home of the nation's largest cigar-box guitar collection, as well as other homemade musical instruments. The house and shop are open Saturday from 10:00 A.M. to 5:00 P.M. and Sunday from 1:00 to 4:00 P.M. May through August only. Call (304) 466–1741 for more information.

The **Veterans Memorial Museum** in the old Carnegie library a few blocks away on Ballengee Street is another free attraction if you're visiting on a weekend afternoon in May through November. It is a treasury of artifacts of every conflict Summers County natives participated in—from the French and Indian War to the Gulf War. Special artifacts are General Douglas MacArthur's footlocker and a vintage 151A2 jeep.

Wild critters outnumber humans in Summers County, and to glimpse life from their perspective, take a side trip to *Three Rivers Avian Center* in nearby Brooks. This private, nonprofit organization provides rehabilitative care for West Virginia's wild birds. Staffers give tours of the facility on the first Saturday of the month May through October in an effort to educate the public about conservation. At any given time, you're likely to meet Robbie the barred owl, Horton hawk, or Apex the kestrel. For information on tours, call (304) 466–4683, or check the Web site at www.tracwv.org.

If you are ready for some outdoor adventuring, you've found the right spot. As you head south of Hinton along State Route 20, you'll pass over and through the beautiful *Pipestem Gorge.* Named for the native pipestem bush whose hollow, woody stems were used by Indian tribes to make pipes, the Pipestem is actually part of the much larger Bluestone River Gorge. The view of the 1,000-foot canyon from the main lodge of Pipestem State Park (also on Route 20, about fifteen minutes south of Hinton) is simply awesome. For a completely different perspective, head down to the base of the canyon and spend the evening at *Mountain Creek Lodge.* The remote but modern inn, also operated by the state park system, is accessible only by scenic aerial tramway. (The inaccessibility only adds to the charm.) The main lodge, with almost one hundred rooms, is accessible by road. Have the lodge set you up with a horseback riding trip through the gorge; or, if you'd rather wet a hook, the Bluestone is famous for its smallmouth bass fishing.

Communing with nature, however, isn't the only appeal. Lodge guests are but a short tram ride away from the resort's eighteen-hole championship golf course and adjoining nine-hole par-three links. Lighted tennis courts and a swimming pool also are located within the 4,000-acre preserve. Concerts and storytelling events draw folks into the amphitheater each summer Saturday and Thursday. Numerous interpretive programs covering subjects such as bats and snakes and including night hikes are held throughout the year. The park's visitor center regularly hosts arts-and-crafts sales and demonstrations by local artisans. When hunger pangs hit, the park has a nice, affordable restaurant. There's even a day care center on the property. Remote but hardly rustic describes the experience here.

Pipestem's rooms start at $69 for two and are open year-round. Mountain Creek Lodge takes guests from May 1 to October 31 only. The rest of the park is open year-round, 6:00 A.M. to 10:00 P.M. Call (304) 466–1800, or view the Web site at www.pipestemresort.com.

New River Gorge

Sometimes there's no overstating the obvious—this is a gorgeous place. The natural beauty coupled with the man-made attractions makes for a not-to-be-missed West Virginia experience.

The natural drama of Sandstone Falls seems an appropriate primer to this region, considered by many outdoor enthusiasts to be among the most scenic natural areas east of the Mississippi.

The **New River** is ancient—it's been flowing on its present course for as long as 225 million years, making it second only to the Nile as the oldest river in the world. Glaciers in the Ice Age buried it and diverted much of the water flow into two other rivers, the Ohio and the Kanawha. Another indication of its age: The New River flows across the Appalachian Plateau, not around it or from it as do most other rivers in the East. The New River existed before the Appalachians did, and these are the world's oldest mountains.

The river was virtually inaccessible along its entire length until 1873, when the railroad opened up the isolated region. The railroad followed the river and made possible the shipment of coal to the outside world. Today more than 50 miles of the New River (between Fayetteville to the north and Hinton to the south) and 40 miles of its tributaries are preserved and protected under the National Park Service as a wild and scenic watershed.

The best place to get acquainted with the gorge is at the **Canyon Rim Visitor Center** on U.S. Highway 19, about a mile north of Fayetteville. The center's

New River Gorge Bridge

overlook offers the most impressive views of the gorge and the awe-inspiring *New River Gorge Bridge,* which is actually part of US 19. This is the world's longest single steel-arch bridge, with a central span of 1,700 feet and a total length of 3,030 feet. It rises 876 feet above the riverbed. A number of television commercials and print advertisements have been shot here. In mid-October the locals celebrate *New River Bridge Day,* and it's worth attending if for no other reason than to watch the parachutists, who somehow muster the nerve to descend into the heart of the rocky abyss.

One of the area's best water attractions (at least in the warm-weather months) calls for a trip to the New River Gorge Bridge with *New River Jet- boats.* Travelers climb aboard the twelve-seat *Miss M. Rocks* at the *Hawk's Nest State Park* Marina. The trip is captained by a licensed river pilot, who'll

West Virginia Rafting Is Running Hot

Long before you see the first big rapids of West Virginia's lower New River, you hear their ominous song—a crashing like rocks barreling through a bowling alley. Your guide is grinning like a demon from the back of the raft, and you feel your heart beating in rhythm with the chopping of the waves. Your arm muscles tense as you gear up for what feels like the fight of your life. All you can think of as the raft bucks are the walls of mad white water closing in on you.

Some 250,000 people come to West Virginia every year to do this for fun. It's a contest between a boisterous river spirit and a bunch of neoprene-clad riders with something to prove.

The contest started back in 1965, when young West Virginia paddlers looking for thrills repeatedly sacrificed their canoes on the rocks of the New. Luckily, they discovered the Czechoslovakian slalom canoe and began emerging at Fayetteville Station intact.

The pioneers of the West Virginia white-water industry were made of the same stuff— college kids who really just wanted to have fun. Jon, Tom, and Chris Dragan began taking friends down the New in 1968 using army surplus rafts and asking everyone to chip in for food and shuttle gas. Rafting seemed like a pretty harebrained scheme to the bankers who turned down the Dragans' request for a $4,000 loan, so the young entrepreneurs borrowed money from their family for two used pickup trucks and two army rafts. The Dragans ran the river from the day they got out of school in June until classes started up again in September. Thus, Wildwater Unlimited was born.

These days, the New is so busy April through October that a state advisory board has been set up to regulate raft traffic on the nationally protected river. You can choose among more than twenty outfitters who operate state-of-the-art, self-bailing rafts, duckies, and kayaks in New River Gorge. Call (800) RAFT–WVA for a listing.

take you upstream on the New River through shoals and small rapids for an up-close view from beneath the massive bridge. The jet-boat trip affords an unforgettable vantage point. Don't forget your camera. New River Jetboats is open from 11:00 A.M. to 4:00 P.M. daily except Monday from Memorial Day through Labor Day, and on weekends in May and September from 11:00 A.M. to 6:00 P.M. For more information, call (304) 469–2525.

Outdoor recreation is plentiful here, to say the least. **White-water rafting** is among the popular sports on the river. The water churns and tosses as it begins its 750-foot descent along the 50 miles from Bluestone Dam to Gauley Bridge. (By way of comparison, the mighty Mississippi falls just over 1,400 feet on its 2,300-mile journey from northern Minnesota to the Gulf of Mexico.) The New boasts some of the best white-water conditions in the United States and is certainly among the top three rivers in the East for rafting. (The neighboring Gauley River and Tennessee's Ocoee River are in the same league.)

If you decide to take the plunge, more than twenty rafting companies, all certified and well trained, are eager for your business. Trips run the gamut from gentle, mostly flat-water affairs to gut-wrenching, heart-stopping rapids. Length and degree of difficulty are planned around participants' age and skill levels. Several outfitters also piggyback the water experience with a combination of hiking, camping, fishing, mountain biking, horseback riding, bird watching, rock climbing, llama trekking, river ecology, and even bed-and-breakfast trips.

One of the finest outfitters in this part of the country is **Class VI River Runners, Inc.,** offering beginner's floats on the Upper New, where you'll come across several Class I and II rapids (rapids are rated in order of difficulty from I to VI). More advanced floats can be had along the Lower New and Upper Gauley Rivers, with their world-famous (and not for the tame of heart) Class III to V+ waves. At the halfway point on most trips, rafters can expect fantastic riverside grub prepared by Class VI's own restaurants, Smokey's Charcoal Grill and Chetty's Depot. Fare includes barbecue chicken, ribs, smoked turkey, top sirloin, fresh seafood, vegetables, and salads. It's a welcome respite during a long day's journey.

Rafting prices vary widely—$60 and up—depending on the length and type of trip, the number of people in the group, and other factors. Trips are held from early spring through late fall. Class VI's base camp is located just north of the New River Gorge Bridge, off US 19 on Ames Heights Road. (You can't miss the signs.) Call (304) 574–0704 or (800) 252–7784. For more information on the other rafting companies in the region, call (800) CALL–WVA.

If your adrenaline is still running, why not try **climbing** the gorge walls? Some of the finest climbing rock in the East can be found here—solid, hard, mostly straight-up. The **New River Gorge Natural Recreation Area** claims

1,500 climbing routes up its rock cliffs within a 10-mile stretch. To set up your vertical adventure, contact the Southern West Virginia Visitor Center (800–847–4898) to get information on the half-dozen outfitters offering climbing expeditions.

Next to rafting, ***hiking*** is the second most popular activity in the gorge. Not only are there many trails for hiking, but there are several guided hikes offered by the National Park Service. Guided by park rangers, these hikes may have either a nature or history theme. Special hikes may be arranged with park service officials. For more information, call (304) 465–0508.

Several once-booming but now-abandoned mining communities await the inquisitive hiker all along the river. In the ghost town of ***Silo Rapids,*** you'll come across remains of silica sand storage vessels, while in ***Claremont*** vestiges remain of a giant coal preparation plant. In ***Beury,*** you can get a glimpse of a now-abandoned but once-spectacular twenty-three-room mansion owned by a local coal baron.

westvirginia southerners

Confederate flags wave from several roadside shops on eastern U.S. Highway 52. West Virginia became a Union state after it broke away from the rest of Virginia in 1861. But the story down here is different. When the Civil War first began, Mercer County sent ten full companies to the field under the Confederate flag—the highest proportional recruitment of any Virginia county.

There aren't many towns with populations of fewer than fifty people that have such colorful and sordid pasts as does ***Thurmond,*** which sits in about the geographic center of the gorge. The town grew up with the railroad and coal operators that opened the gorge in the early 1900s. In fact, the C&O Railroad was about the only way into town since Thurmond had no streets—the only such town in America with that distinction. Nevertheless, it became a commercial and social hub and a prosperous shipping center during its heyday. More freight tonnage was generated here than in Cincinnati and Richmond combined.

Thurmond also cultivated quite a reputation as a rough-and-tumble outlaw town. A common joke heard during the 1920s and 1930s was "the only difference between Thurmond and Hell is that a river runs through Thurmond." The town also had the distinction of hosting the longest-running poker game in history. The game began in the lively Dun Glen Hotel and ended fourteen years later, but only after the hotel burned down. Thurmond's demise came with the advent of the automobile, and its population dwindled to its present tiny state. It is now one of the smallest incorporated towns in West Virginia. As you hike through, notice the small wooden homes (some still occupied) that cling precariously to the hillside. Many of these were built by coal operators as company housing. Take a quick scan of this hardscrabble village, and it's easy to understand why director John Sayles chose Thurmond as the setting for his film *Matewan,* about the 1920s miners' uprising in southern West Virginia.

Thurmond is changing, though. A multimillion-dollar restoration, including a face-lift to the railroad depot, by the National Park Service is under way. A small museum greets tourists, many of whom will come in via the Amtrak *Cardinal.* Consequently, now might be the best time to visit the state's most off-the-beaten-path town—before the commercialization sets in. You can float into Thurmond by hooking up with a rafting company or drive down the county road leading into the gorge from the Glen Jean exit off US 19 north of Beckley, and follow the signs to Thurmond. If you elect to drive, park on the west side of the river and walk the bridge into Thurmond. Bring a camera, because you'll certainly want to document your trip to the "end of the earth."

Just west of Ansted on US 60 sits the antithesis of New River Gorge's natural beauty—**Mystery Hole.** Every road trip begs for at least one stop at a cheesy, hyped-up roadside attraction, and in West Virginia, the mysterious, gravity-defying Mystery Hole wins hands-down in the weird, offbeat attraction category. The enigmatic hole is hidden under a garishly painted Quonset hut with a VW bug smashed into its side. The tiny roadside gift shop is littered with signs urging you inside. After you pay your $4.00 admission ($3.00 if you're a child), you descend a staircase past eccentric art and fun-house mirrors to a tilted room where gravity has gone berserk. Some people say it made their vacation. Step right up. Come right in.

The Mystery Hole is open April through October on Thursday through Monday from 10:30 A.M. to 6:00 P.M. Call (304) 658–9101 for more information or to join their fan club.

Southern Coalfields

Seven rugged counties—Boone, Logan, McDowell, Mingo, Wyoming, Raleigh, and Mercer—represent a large share of West Virginia's coal industry. Although coal is found in other parts of the state, these counties cumulatively produce huge quantities of the stuff—as much as 60 percent of the state's total output in 1998.

In 1742 German immigrant John Peter Salley discovered coal along the Coal River in what became Boone County. The next century saw the introduction of railroads and coal mining to the area. By 1900 the combined coal output of Mingo, McDowell, and Mercer Counties alone was almost more than the entire state's production just a decade earlier. McDowell and Logan Counties were producing 5 million tons each by 1914, and to date over 4.1 billion tons have been produced in these historic coalfields.

The story of coal mining and the hard life of miners might not sound like the stuff of tourism, but West Virginia has done a good job promoting the cultural heritage of the region. And it's a heritage that's every bit as different and fascinating as the Cajuns of Louisiana and the watermen of the Chesapeake Bay.

The gateway to the coalfields is **Beckley,** located at the intersection of Interstates 77 and 64, about an hour south of Summersville. The city (population 18,000 and the region's largest) was founded and later named for General Alfred Beckley, the first Clerk of Congress during the administrations of Presidents Washington, Adams, and Jefferson. Beckley's home, **Wildwood,** a two-story log cabin on South Kanawha Street, is preserved as a museum and is open to visitors May through October on weekends. Call Wildwood House Museum at (304) 256–1747 for more information. Also of interest is the city's preserved uptown section, with its boutiques and restaurants situated around the town square.

The so-called city with a mine of its own is home to the **Beckley Exhibition Coal Mine,** located right off Harper Road (State Route 13) in what is now part of New River Park. More than 1,500 feet of underground passages have been restored in this once-working mine, originally operated by a family-owned coal company in the late 1800s. Ride aboard a clanking "man trip" car guided through the mine for a look at how low-seam coal mining developed from its earliest manual stages to modern mechanized operation. Former miners are your

One-ton car at the Beckley Exhibition Coal Mine

guides on the trips, and, as you can imagine, they provide colorful commentary. Be sure to bring a jacket—it's always 58° F down in the catacombs.

The mine is open from the first weekend in April through November 1. Tours run from 10:00 A.M. to 5:30 P.M. Rates are $12.00 for adults, $10.50 for seniors, and $8.50 for children. For more information, call (304) 256–1747.

After you've taken the tour, stop in at the park's mining museum, then head over to the museum's restored three-room house, which was once owned by the New River Coal Company and housed a miner and his family. The superintendent lived a little higher, you will see when you visit his house. You'll also view a coal-camp church and the Helen Coal Camp School. Also, don't miss the **Youth Museum** on the grounds, housed in four railroad cars and featuring, among other things, fascinating wood carvings depicting the legend of John Henry. An adjacent mountain homestead details the day-to-day lives of early mountaineers.

newriver/ greenbrier valleytrivia

Senator Robert C. Byrd, a native of Sophia, West Virginia, is widely renowned beyond political circles as one of the finest old-time mountain fiddlers in the United States.

Before you leave Beckley, you owe yourself a visit to **Tamarack.** This star-shaped building, just off exit 45 of I–77, is West Virginia's showplace for high-quality arts and crafts, food, and entertainment year-round. Not only can you observe West Virginia glassblowers and carvers in the studio, but you can hear mountain fiddle players or watch West Virginia's Swiss folk dancers in the auditorium. Local people line up early at Tamarack's cafeteria for economical meals prepared by Greenbrier chefs. Here you can sample ramps, the legendary mountain onion, with your salad or try a colonial bread pudding recipe. Tamarack's retail area stocks books, pottery, wearable arts, and more. For information on upcoming events, call 88–TAMARACK or (888–262–7225) or check www .tamarackwv.com.

Just fifteen minutes south of Beckley, you pass the exit for **Winterplace Ski Resort** (800–607–SNOW, www.winterplace.com) and **Glade Springs Resort** (800–634–5233, www.gladesprings.com), a 4,100-acre, all-season resort with two golf courses. Glade and Winterplace offer combined ski/lodging packages in winter. Winterplace, only open in winter, boasts the longest skiing day in southeast West Virginia and the largest tubing park. To warm up, guests can soak in Glade Springs' heated pool, even in January, or enjoy a session of hot rock therapy at the spa.

In summer Glade offers horseback riding, mountain biking, and all manner of off-resort expeditions, including a team-building rafting and climbing outing.

Taking to the Tubes

Snow tubing is a democratic sport. At Winterplace Ski Resort's tubing park, the young, the old, the unskilled, and the underimplemented are reclaiming the slopes.

I used to snow-tube back in 1960 in a snow-packed pasture, sharing the run with other kids on sleds, plastic trays, and even an old Pontiac hood. We didn't wear color-coordinated outfits or have much technique. But we loved speed and the jolt of hitting the knolls at screaming velocities.

Now folks are tubing in droves in West Virginia's tubing parks, where they pay a fee for canvas-covered tubes they ride up and down the slopes. Straddling the tube, they're pulled up the mountain on a tow lift, then released at the top to blast down an icy chute at speeds up to 30 miles per hour.

It's all perfectly safe, of course. But tubing can be an exercise in relinquishing control as your tube spins down the slope, backward, forward, all perspectives rushing together into a dizzying blur until force peters out at the end of the carefully banked lane.

At Winterplace, where skiers practice feline cool, negotiating clifflike precipices with nonchalance and maintaining silence through close calls, the tubing park is the emotional hot spot. Kids whoop; teens cheer; grandmoms yodel bloodcurdling screams the entire run.

Technique and skill aren't factors here. You can ride the tube butt-down in the doughnut or lie on your stomach; you start the tube down the incline with a shove, then jump on or get someone to push you off. The rest is up to gravity.

Tubing runs are open when the ski resorts are, usually early December through late March. Besides Winterplace, Canaan Valley Resort, Snowshoe Mountain Resort, Alpine Lake Resort, and Coolfont Resort have tubing parks.

And you don't have to work up an appetite to enjoy four-diamond clubhouse food prepared by Chef Louis Cressy, formerly executive chef of the Greenbrier.

An hour south of Beckley on the West Virginia Turnpike puts you in Princeton, a recovering coal-belt city with a huge new performance center near the center of town (Chuck Mathena Center for the Performing Arts; 304–425–5128). Go another mile on State Routes 20/104 (Mercer Street) and you'll come to *Sisters Coffee House*—at least that's its cover by day; on Friday and sometimes Saturday nights Sisters lets down its hair to become a blues cafe featuring some masters of the national circuit, such as Mem Shannon and Jimbo Mathus. Princeton's own legendary blues man, Nat Reese, is a monthly regular with the Sisters house band. By day, Sisters serves great coffee, mix-and-match sandwiches, and luscious desserts. Look over the murals and other art by local outsider artists.

Bluefield: Lemonade City

Bluefield is deceptive. A city of imposing commercial buildings and marble-facade storefronts, it seems very much at loose ends, serving a population of barely 12,000. Once a thriving city that boasted the nation's highest per capita ownership of automobiles, Bluefield now counts tire recapping and shoe repair prominent among its downtown businesses. But the edifices of the gilded era still dominate the skyline: the old Elks Lodge with its opera house; the Law and Commerce Building, which once housed a full bowling alley for lunching railroad men; and the Ramsey School, listed in *Ripley's Believe It or Not* for its seven entrances on seven levels. Old City Hall, now the Bluefield Arts and Science Center, boasts a virtual reality game of one-on-one hoops as well as an exhibit honoring John Forbes Nash Jr., the native son who won the Nobel Prize in economics in 1994 and was portrayed in the movie *A Beautiful Mind.*

Now the city's claim to fame is tied to its geography rather than its geology. At 2,612 feet, Bluefield is the highest city east of Denver. In 1939 the chamber of commerce voted to serve free lemonade on the day following any day when temperatures reached 90°F. Servers had to wait two years to offer their first glass and hit another dry spell between 1960 and 1982. In 1988, however, the Lemonade Lassies passed out free lemonade on seventeen days.

Call (304) 487–8701 or see www.sisterscoffeehouse.com for schedule and admission fees.

While in Princeton, you may notice a number of restaurants and sports bars with "club" entrances. This is code for "slot machines"—video games that children under 18 are not allowed to play. West Virginia differs from its neighboring states in that gambling is legal here.

In 2001, West Virginia lawmakers set out to control illegal gambling by creating a state-run industry that allows bars, restaurants, and clubs to operate video lottery machines. About 2,000 establishments statewide hold licenses to host such video games as slots, poker, blackjack, and keno. If you'd like to donate money to send West Virginia students to college, try your hand in these glittering arcades. You can find gaming machines in every West Virginia county but Webster—and the closer to the state border you are, the more slots you'll see.

Just south of Princetown is ***Bluefield,*** a little city that resonates with coal-mining history. Here you should make time to visit the ***Eastern Regional Coal Archives,*** housed in the Craft Memorial Library, 600 Commerce Street. Archivist Stuart McGehee has masterfully assembled a collection of coal-mining memorabilia, including company records, company store account books, correspondence, diaries, films, ledgers, maps, miners' tools, newspapers, and oral history

Disaster

In Maybeury, just over the McDowell County line, company houses radiate up the narrow hollows. This town was the site of the worst railway disaster in the history of the Pocahontas coalfields. On the evening of June 30, 1937, westbound Norfolk & Western freight No. 85 plunged off the east end of the Maybeury trestle, killing three crewmen and a pedestrian and creating an inferno that tied up rail and road traffic for weeks. Fifty-three boxcars spilled liquor, canned pineapple, and Vicks VapoRub over the site, and the explosions shattered windows a quarter mile away. Today the foundations of the old bridge are visible on the left side of the Maybeury curve.

Disaster seemed to lurk around these turns. A mile north on U.S. Highway 52 at Switchback, a deadly combination of coal dust and ignited methane at the Lick Branch Mine killed fifty miners on December 29, 1908. Less than two weeks later, sixty-seven miners died in another explosion, likely caused when an experienced miner overcharged his shot.

"I would hear the sirens going off and people screaming up and down the hollow when there was a mining accident," says Bramwell resident Jim Bishop, who grew up in a Mercer County mining town. "Everybody would run to the mine entrance and wait for them to carry out the casualties."

In 1907, 361 miners died in an explosion in Monongah. In 1914–1915, more than 400 miners died in separate incidents in Benwood, Leland, and Eccles. In fact, during World War I, West Virginia miners had a higher casualty rate than the American Expeditionary Force in Europe. While the dangers have subsided dramatically since the 1950s, risk still looms. In 1973, for example, a collapsed slag dam resulted in 175 deaths near Buffalo Creek.

tapes. Black-and-white photographs, some dating from 1919, capture the pain and pride of the miners.

The center is open on a variable schedule Monday through Friday. There is no admission charge. Call (304) 325–3943 for more information.

Bluefield itself makes for an interesting afternoon of touring. The city straddles the Virginia border and is incorporated in both states. It's known as "nature's air-conditioned city" on account of the unusually cool summers.

Like most towns in the coalfields, Bluefield blossomed with the arrival of the railroad. In the 1880s, when the Norfolk & Western Railroad began hauling coal out of the Pocahontas seam, Bluefield consisted of two large farms; six years later, the population topped 1,770, and it doubled every ten years thereafter for its first three decades. The Norfolk & Western hauled the world's finest coal out of this area for more than one hundred years, and the city has long been the industrial, financial, administrative, medical, and corporate center of the region. Its grand 1920s architecture is striking even today and is evident in a host of classical revival, neoclassical, and second-Renaissance revival buildings and homes. One of the most impressive is the elaborate West Virginia Hotel at Federal and Scott Streets. Twelve stories high, it's still the tallest building in southern West Virginia. The hotel once boasted a huge ballroom, dances, and a Paris-trained chef who was stolen away from the Greenbrier Resort. Today the building houses office space.

West Palm Beach, Newport, Beverly Hills, and Palm Springs: These cities are famous today for their affluence. About one hundred years ago, however, tiny **Bramwell,** West Virginia, was undeniably the richest town of its size in the United States. Located on a bend of the Bluestone River, about 7 miles northwest of Bluefield on U.S. Highway 52, Bramwell (current population 650) was home to most of the major coal barons of southern West Virginia. In the early part of the twentieth century, as many as fourteen millionaires lived within a 2-block radius. Their homes, needless to say, are spectacular. Perhaps the most opulent is the **Thomas House,** on Duhring Street. The revival Tudor-style home was built by coal operator W. H. Thomas between 1909 and 1912. Thomas actually had Italian masons brought over to do the stonework on the house and the retaining wall. It's estimated the house cost nearly $100,000 to build, an amazing sum of money at the time.

The nearby **Cooper House,** right on Main Street directly across from the downtown storefronts, is equally impressive. It was built in 1910 with orange bricks sent over from England. The compound contains an indoor swimming pool, among the first found in West Virginia.

To experience the life of an aristocratic coal family firsthand, you should try to spend at least one night at **Perry House,** now a bed-and-breakfast inn. It's located two houses up from Cooper House. The brick Victorian-style home was built in 1902 by the bank for the cashier of the Bank of Bramwell, an institution that had the highest per capita deposits in the United States at the time. (This powerful little bank helped finance the construction of the Washington, D.C., area's famous Burning Tree Country Club.)

Big comfortable rooms are de rigueur in the main house. They're decorated with southern West Virginia themes and elegant furnishings. Rates start at $75. Events in Bramwell include the home tours, a spring footrace, a wine-tasting festival, summer theater by equity actors, and an October fest. Call (304) 248–8145 or see www.perryhousebedandbreakfast.com for more information.

Bramwell's newly reconstructed train depot houses the **Southern Interpretive Center of the Coal Heritage Trail,** a national historic byway with exhibits depicting life during the coal boom. Sweet-talk Betty Goins, Bramwell tourism coordinator, and you may be able to get an inside tour of one of the mansions. Her number is (304) 248–8381. The little town of Bramwell has a full schedule of festivals and food events during May through October, so check the Web site at www.bramwellwv.com.

As you head out of Bramwell, look for the crumbling remains of a line of old beehive coke ovens. These coal-processing kilns are on the left as you climb the US 52 hill west toward Welch.

Continue west on US 52 to get deeper into Appalachian coal country. About five minutes out of Bramwell, you'll cross into McDowell County, or as some locals call it, the Free State of McDowell (in reference to its stormy political history and independent nature). Almost immediately you'll notice how the mountains begin to close in on one another; the valleys narrow to small canyons, and the sky disappears under heavily canopied forests. It's a claustrophobic feeling that's common to this part of the world. You start wondering how folks got into this remote country, let alone exploited it with coal operations.

Coal towns border US 52 through the coalfields—once 132 separate communities. The architecture varies with the distance from Bluefield; the older villages, built first in the railway's westward expansion, have a Victorian look. The wee town of Elkhorn is anchored by a gabled white clapboard home and matching schoolhouse, but Keystone and Kimball are composed of decidedly industrial redbrick row houses. The arched, brick **Elkhorn Inn** hugs a tight curve between US 52 and the Elkhorn Creek in Landgraff. The site began life as a wood-frame clubhouse for Empire Coal and Coke Company officials. When the original clubhouse burned, Empire erected a reinforced concrete and brick structure built to last till doomsday. And last it did—through years as a rooming house, two floods, and the widening of US 52 to its doorstep.

When Dan and Elisse Clark, former FEMA disaster recovery workers, found the place in 2002, it was a mud- and mold-filled mess. They purchased it and the little Shakespearean theater behind it and spent the next three years restoring them as a bed-and-breakfast and wedding venue. "We've laid out about ten times our purchase price on renovations," Dan says.

The inn may look familiar—its renovations have been featured on the House and Garden Television (HGTV) channel in 2004 and 2006. While adding air-conditioning and more bathrooms, the Clarks have left many of the 1922 architectural details, including the company pay-window, transom windows, and turn-of-the-century tile flooring. They've filled the inn's eight guest rooms with art deco furnishings, West Virginia quilts, and stunning paintings from Elisse's New York gallery. In addition to their gift shop/art gallery, the Clarks are setting up a small museum of coal-heritage artifacts found during renovations. The theater has become a venue for summer bluegrass concerts and other performances.

Coal Camps

Clusters of houses keep the U.S. Highway 52 coal camps of Simmons and Freeman alive in name, if not in activity. Englishmen John Freeman and Jenkin Jones opened Simmons Creek Mine with only one mule, one mine car, a few shovels, and their bare hands.

In 1889 the pair formed Caswell Creek Coal and Coke Company and made a huge fortune. Their story was not unusual in the southern West Virginia coalfields at the turn of the century, when mines could be opened with relatively little money.

All that was required were houses for miners, a store to supply them, and a tipple to dump coal into the railroad cars. Miners furnished their own tools—picks, shovels, breast augers, tamping bars, needles, and axes. Because of the low cost, many small companies were formed throughout the Pocahontas coalfield.

The inn is especially popular with rail fans, who sit on the balcony watching for some of the twenty or more trains passing the inn daily.

In the town of **Welch,** in the southern end of the Tug Fork Valley, US 52 will take you right by the stately **McDowell County Courthouse.** It was here in 1921, on the front steps of the building, that detectives hired by coal-company officials gunned down Matewan chief of police Sid Hatfield and union activist Ed Chambers in retaliation for the deaths of two of their colleagues during the Matewan Massacre a year earlier. The courthouse killings touched off a series of events that led to the Battle of Blair Mountain in neighboring Logan County, in which 10,000 miners took up arms against coal-company officials. It was the largest insurrection in the United States since the Civil War, and it was put down only after federal troops were called in and several lives were lost. Tours of the courthouse are available. For more information, call (304) 426–4239.

In an effort to honor the miners in their families and those of all West Virginia, Ivyrose and Elden Green have created the **History of Our Mountains Museum** in downtown Welch. Located in the pretty old Miners and Merchants Bank on 8 Wyoming Street, the museum contains memorabilia of the coalfields, from their earlier incarnation as a Native American hunting ground to the present. The Greens charge no admission to those who come in to look around or view the twenty-five-minute documentaries on coal mining and coal communities that alternate every month. Visitors may post a tribute to their own miner relatives or friends on the museum's mining wall. The museum complex contains a gift shop and the Almost Heaven Coffee Loft. All are open from 8:00 A.M. to 4:30 P.M., Monday through Friday. For information call (304) 436–3209.

Places to Stay in the New River/ Greenbrier Valley

ANSTED

Hawks Nest State Park Lodge
US Highway 60
(304) 658–5212
www.hawksnestsp.com
Inexpensive

BEAVER

Sleep Inn
1124 Airport Road
(304) 255–4222
(888) 259–8545
Inexpensive

BECKLEY

Comfort Inn
1909 Harper Road
(304) 255–2161
Inexpensive

DANIELS

Glade Springs Resort
200 Lake Drive
(304) 763–2000
(800) 634–5233
www.gladesprings.com
Moderate to expensive

FAYETTEVILLE

New River Hostel
State Route 16
(304) 574–1237
www.newriverhostel.com
Budget

White Horse Bed & Breakfast
120 Fayetteville Avenue
(304) 574–1400
www.historicwhitehorse.net
Expensive

HINTON

Coast to Coast Motel on the New River
junction State Routes 3 and 20
(304) 466–2040
www.coasttocoastwv.com
Budget to inexpensive

LEWISBURG

General Lewis Inn
301 East Washington Street
(304) 645–2600
(800) 628–4454
Moderate to expensive

Places to Eat in the New River/ Greenbrier Valley

DANIELS

Glade's Grill & Bar at Glade Springs Resort
200 Lake Drive
(304) 763–2000
(800) 634–5233
Very expensive

FAYETTEVILLE

The Cathedral Cafe
134 South Court Street
(304) 574–0202
Inexpensive

The Fat Tire Deli
103 Keller Avenue
(304) 574–0599
Inexpensive

HINTON

Unkl Ray's Cafe & Music Den
Hinton Bypass
(304) 466–3550
Moderate

LEWISBURG

The General Lewis Inn and Restaurant
301 East Washington Street
(304) 645–2600
(800) 628–4454
Moderate

Julian's Restaurant
1025 Lafayette Street
(304) 645–4145
Expensive

MULLENS

Twin Falls Resort State Park
State Route 16
(304) 294–4000
Moderate

PIPESTEM

Pipestem Resort State Park
State Route 20
(304) 466–1800
Moderate

PRINCETON

Sisters Coffee House
734 Mercer Street
(304) 487–8701
www.sisterscoffeehouse.com
Budget

WHITE SULPHUR SPRINGS

The Greenbrier Resort
State Route 92
(304) 536–1110
(800) 624–6070
Very expensive

FOR MORE INFORMATION

New River Convention and Visitors Bureau
(800) 927-0263
www.newrivercvb.com

Southern West Virginia Convention and Visitors Bureau
(304) 252-2244 or (800) VISIT-WV
www.visitwv.com

Summers County Convention and Visitors Bureau
(304) 466-5420
www.summerscvb.com

Mercer County Convention and Visitors Bureau
Bluefield/Princeton
(800) 221-3206
www.mccvb.com

Greenbrier County Convention and Visitors Bureau
(800) 833-2068
www.greenbrierwv.com

Metro Valley

Named for the population center stretching from the capital city of Charleston west to Huntington, the Metro Valley region is the most populated in the state. The area boasts an abundance of museums, restaurants, and theaters, but there are many places to get off the beaten path—especially along the byways of the southern counties.

Steeped in Appalachian history is the Mingo County town of **Matewan,** site of the Hatfield-McCoy feud (yes, it really happened) and the Matewan Massacre. Matewan is located on the Tug Fork River, a twisty hour-plus drive from the town of Welch along U.S. Highway 52 and County Road 9 (that is if there's not a coal truck in front of you).

Vestiges of the Hatfield-McCoy years surround you here. Snuggled into the hillside above Mate Street and the Norfolk & Southern Railroad is **Warm Hollow,** site of the Anderson Ferrell House, where Ellison Hatfield died in 1882 after an attack by three McCoy brothers. The retaliatory violence came on election day in August 1882 just across the river in Kentucky. After the young Hatfield died, "Devil" Anse Hatfield executed the McCoys in Kentucky. The killings went on for another eight years, but the sensationalism surrounding the feud continues today. Some accounts in major eastern newspapers of the time

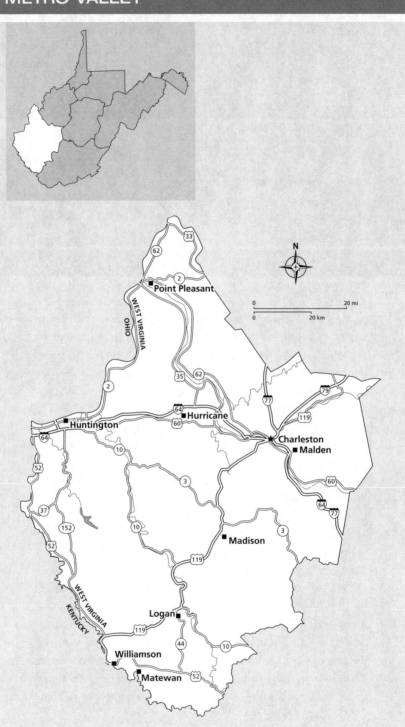

cited death tolls in excess of one hundred people. In reality, the ongoing feud resulted in twelve deaths. Today Hatfield and McCoy descendants meet peacefully on the banks of the Tug outside Matewan each June for a reunion.

A few years ago a fire swept through downtown Matewan and destroyed or damaged several historical buildings. A massive revitalization program is under way along the riverfront. New buildings are going up, older ones have received face-lifts, green spaces have been created, and an interpretive center is being constructed. The historical-minded restoration has had the result of giving Matewan the look it had in the 1920s.

The Matewan Development Center, a community economic development group that is spearheading much of the town's revitalization, has an interesting museum downtown in the 1920 Matewan depot. The stories of the region's bloody past, as well as its proud coal-mining traditions, unfold here through fascinating photographs and exhibits. The museum sits in the *Hatfield Building,* built in 1911 by Mingo County politician Greenway Hatfield. Ironically, right next door is the *McCoy Building,* built in 1925 by—you guessed it—a member of the famous Kentucky family. The exhibition area is open 10:00 A.M. to 5:00 P.M. Tuesday through Saturday. Call (304) 426–4239 for more information.

Over the past ten or twelve years, interest in Matewan and its past has undoubtedly been rekindled because of the award-winning 1987 film *Matewan,*

BEST ANNUAL EVENTS IN THE METRO VALLEY REGION

Annual WV Hunting and Fishing Show
Charleston; late January
(304) 768–9999

St. Patrick's Day Celebration
Huntington; mid-March
(304) 696–5954

Dogwood Arts and Crafts Festival
Huntington; late April
(304) 696–5990

Vandalia Gathering
Charleston; late May
(304) 558–0220

West Virginia Coal Festival
Madison; mid-June
(304) 369–9118

Sternwheel Regatta
Charleston; late August through early September
(304) 545–0244 or (800) 733–5469
www.sternwheelregatta.com

West Virginia Book Festival
Charleston; mid-October
(304) 343–4646
www.wvhumanities.org

Guyandotte Civil War Days
Huntington; early November
(304) 525–5720

a historical drama that featured James Earl Jones. The actual confrontation took place on May 19, 1920. At the time, the United Mine Workers of America (UMWA) was trying to organize the area's coal miners, but those who joined soon found themselves fired and evicted from their company-owned homes. When chief of police Hatfield encountered coal-company detectives hired to evict miners, shots were fired, resulting in the deaths of the town's mayor, seven detectives, and two miners. Hatfield emerged as a hero, both before and after the tragic events a year later in McDowell County.

As you walk through Matewan, head to the **Old Matewan National Bank Building** on the northeast corner of Mate Street and a small alley leading back to the railroad tracks. The massacre began in the alley here, and bullet holes from the confrontation are still visible on the side of the former bank building. The building located next door once housed Chambers Hardware, where the first shots of the massacre were fired. Down the street at the corner of Mate and Hatfield is the Buskirk Building, whose second-floor Urias Hotel served as headquarters for the coal-company detectives. The UMWA, interestingly, was headquartered almost directly across the street in the Nenni Building, adjacent to the Hatfield Building.

Using the Hatfield-McCoy names in an endeavor of unusual cooperation and community spirit, a group of southern West Virginia citizens, politicians, and corporations is building a multiuse trail system. The user-fee supported **Hatfield-McCoy Trails** has opened more than 500 miles of track in Logan, McDowell, Mingo, and Boone Counties, with plans for an eventual 1,800 more miles. Right now the system is open to motorcycles, ATVs, mountain bikes, and hikers. The unique part is that the trail system exists totally on private land, mostly resurfaced mining and logging roads.

metrovalley trivia

The Tug Fork River, which meanders along the Kentucky–West Virginia border, is the longest free-flowing river in Central Appalachia.

Developers hope the trails will provide both recreational and economic opportunities for the area; already several ATV and motorcycle repair shops have opened in Logan, Gilbert, and Delbarton near the trailheads. Annual activities on the trail include a summer hike, a dirt bike rally, a national ATV rally, and an October **Hatfield-McCoy Trail Fest.** Trail use fees are $25 annually for state residents and $37 a week or $19 a day for out-of-state visitors. For more information and detailed trail maps, call (800) 592–2217 or (304) 752–3255 or consult the Web site at www.TrailsHeaven.com.

Lodging is a rather scarce commodity in this corner of West Virginia, so you might want to start heading toward Charleston, the state capital and West Virginia's largest city, about two hours north. On your way up U.S. Highway 119, you'll pass through the town of Logan and by Chief Logan State Park. During the summer months the park stages productions of **The Aracoma Story,** an outdoor play depicting the struggle of the Shawnee Indians to survive in a changing land. It's based on both historical fact and local legend and tells the story of Chief Cornstalk's daughter Aracoma and her lover Boling Baker, a British soldier captured by her father. The Chief Logan Amphitheater also houses other dramatic productions, such as *Charlotte's Web;* the Aunt Jenny Wilson Folk Festival, a local event; and the annual Shawnee Living History Trail. A new museum at the park showcases the region's coal and railroad heritage along with a rotating art exhibit. For more information on the shows, call (304) 792–7125, or visit www.chiefloganstatepark.com.

The Capital Region

West Virginia is graced with one of the most beautiful state capitals in the United States. *Charleston* (population about 53,000) fans out along the banks of the Kanawha River, a major transport link to the Ohio Valley and the industrial Midwest. Charleston is actually a good five to six hours from the nearest major population centers of Pittsburgh and Cincinnati and as such has maintained a certain rugged "big small-town" charm. The relative remoteness of the capital city probably explains why so much of its beautiful architecture has been so well preserved.

There's lots to see and do in Charleston, starting with the *Capitol Complex,* located just off Washington Street 2 blocks up from the Kanawha River. The gold-domed Capitol Building and Governor's Mansion are both worth the hour you'll spend on the tour, not only for the beauty of the architecture, but for the inside stories you'll get. The first two capitol buildings in Charleston burned down, but this marble and limestone edifice was built to last in 1932. While the Capitol Building and Governor's Mansion are among the city's most on-the-beaten-path sites, few folks wander over to the impressive *West Virginia Cultural Center.* The contemporary building houses the 23,000-square-foot state museum, with displays tracing West Virginia's history from the great Native American migrations to the early-twentieth-century timber and coal boom. Some exhibits feature state artists and special Appalachian craft and folk collections. Don't miss the craft shop adjacent to the Great Hall, with its wide assortment of mountain arts, crafts, historical books, novels, and music.

If you love authentic old-time or bluegrass music, the cultural center is the place to be every Memorial Day weekend when the *Vandalia Gathering* comes to town. In addition to two full days of music featuring West Virginia

BEST ATTRACTIONS IN THE METRO VALLEY REGION

West Virginia Governor's Mansion
Charleston
(304) 558–4839

West Virginia State Capitol Complex
Charleston
(304) 558–4839

West Virginia State Museum and Cultural Center
Charleston
(304) 558–0220

Avampato Discovery Museum
Charleston
(304) 561–3575
www.avampatodiscoverymuseum.org

Heritage Farm Museum
Huntington
(304) 552–1244
www.heritagefarmmuseum.com

Camden Amusement Park
Huntington
(304) 429–4321 or (866) 8CAMDEN
www.camdenpark.com

musicians—many of whom are world renowned—Vandalia is spiced with plenty of food and folklife demonstrations. You'll also hear some feats of imaginational gymnastics at West Virginia's biggest-liar contest. If you missed the show, head back into the cultural center shop and get a copy of *The Music Never Dies: A Vandalia Sampler,* a tape of some of the festival's finest musical performances over the years.

Also found in the cultural center is a concert theater that offers a variety of performances, including **Mountain Stage,** the eclectic music program produced by West Virginia Public Radio. The live, two-hour show is taped almost every Sunday from 6:00 to 8:00 P.M. The show regularly hosts nationally and internationally recognized musicians and features some of the best jazz, folk, blues, and new music in America. Past shows have included the likes of R.E.M., Buckwheat Zydeco, Los Lobos, Mary Chapin Carpenter, Warren Zevon, and the Cowboy Junkies, to name a few.

Tickets are available through TicketMaster at (304) 342–5757 or (800) 594–8499 for $10 to $20 or at the door for $12 to $30. The cultural center, meanwhile, is open weekdays from 9:00 A.M. to 8:00 P.M. and weekends 1:00 to 5:00 P.M. For more information on the center's services and programs, call (304) 558–0220 or check www.mountainstage.org.

From the Capitol Complex, hop a trolley that'll take you through Charleston's *East End Historic District.* Here you'll find more than twenty historic buildings and mansions, most dating from the 1890s, Charleston's gilded age. The grand homes give way to downtown, with modern hotels, fine restaurants, a large civic center, and interesting shops.

Charleston has been called one of the most northern of the southern cities and the most southern of the northern cities. Its past is just as full of contradictions and contrasts, but now that just means many things are possible. You can cruise the Kanawha on a sternwheeler or play the slot machines in nearby Cross

World Music from West Virginia

West Virginia's live public radio show may be called *Mountain Stage,* but the music doesn't always come from the hills of West Virginia. You could hear a bluegrass musician from Japan or a Hungarian ensemble teamed up with Jerry Jeff Walker and a traditional Irish band.

"We play world music here," says host Larry Groce. "We have a show that is radically eclectic."

Mountain Stage gives airtime to folks who don't necessarily fit neatly into today's radio formats, particularly in the singer/songwriter and Americana genres. Groce, who is best known for his 1976 pop hit "Junk Food Junkie," is the mix master who has blended the music of the known and not so well known for more than two decades. "We've been able to feature people who aren't famous yet, but who become famous later," he says. Some of those who have taken the stage of the West Virginia Cultural Center before they were stars were Mary Chapin Carpenter, Phish, and Sheryl Crow.

Each week more than a quarter of a million people worldwide listen to the show on 110 radio stations in the United States, in Ireland, and on the Voice of America. It's public radio's longest-running live musical variety show, and the three men who launched it still take the stage every Sunday evening. Groce teamed with producer Andy Ridenour and sound engineer Francis Fisher to kick off the first live show in Charleston in December 1983.

On Sunday at 6:00 P.M., Ridenour ambles onstage of the intimate theater in his faded blue jeans and baseball cap to introduce the show. It takes a minute for the band to saunter in—Ron Sowell, Bob Thompson, Michael Lipton, John Kessler, and Ammed Solomon—all 40-ish and 50-ish guys who started playing together in the days of tape decks.

"If you only listened to *Mountain Stage* on radio and had illusions about us, this could be sad," Groce says to the live audience. Then the Mountain Stage Band kicks off and nobody cares about anything but music.

"We're relaxed because we're like family," Groce explains, "and because it's the West Virginia way. We're an international show, but the pressure is off because we're in West Virginia. Artists like that. They relax. You hear music here you won't hear on their recordings. There's just something magical about live music."

OTHER ATTRACTIONS WORTH SEEING IN THE METRO VALLEY REGION

Wine Cellar Park Dunbar	**Chief Logan State Park** Logan
Huntington Museum of Art Huntington	**Beech Fork State Park** Barboursville
Blenko Glass Company Milton	**Mountain State Mystery Train** Huntington

Lanes. You may spend an evening with the city's Light Opera Guild or participate in the state turkey-calling contest at the WV Hunting and Fishing Show. You might go virtual caving at Avampato Discovery Museum's IMAX theater or learn the fine points of appliqué at Cabin Creek Quilts.

Charleston may be a small capital, but it's the hub of business, industry, and government for a surrounding metropolitan area that consists of more than 6,000 businesses and 250,000 people. However, taking care of business is not the only priority of this sweet city. Embracing a sense of community, Charleston has maintained one of the lowest crime rates in the nation.

The downtown *Clay Center for the Arts & Sciences* (399 Leon Sullivan Way) combines a first-class performing arts center and concert hall with the high-tech *Avampato Discovery Museum,* complete with planetarium and hands-on educational programs for children of all ages.

metrovalley trivia

Contemporary country music star Kathy Mattea is a native of Cross Lanes.

Whether it's exploring earth science through a series of water troughs, learning about health by stretching a giant intestine, or making music with a spider, kids have fun learning. The art gallery showcases West Virginia and international artists and has cultivated a permanent collection of nearly 800 works. The Avampato is open Tuesday through Sunday, noon to 5:00 P.M. For more information call (304) 561–3573.

A night at the *Charleston Ballet, Chamber Music Society,* or *Symphony Orchestra* is the perfect complement to delectable fare at one of Charleston's fine restaurants. You can enjoy a spectacular view of the river and city while sampling dishes at the *Chesapeake Crab House* atop the Charleston House Holiday Inn. For a truly gourmet experience, visit *Wellington's of Scarlet Oaks Country Club* (304–755–8219), which specializes in Continental French cuisine. A stop at the **Sitar of India, Joey's Downtown,** or **Mykonos Café** will satisfy cravings for something more exotic. Top off the evening with some original live music at the **Empty Glass,** where Mountain Stage performers sometimes let their hair down after the radio show.

Casual dining is the rule at **Blossom Deli and Soda Fountain,** located at 904 Quarrier Street. The smoked salmon sandwich and lean quiche are popular for lunch, with a butterscotch milkshake from the deli for dessert. For dinner, folks often choose tuna carpaccio or walnut-crusted salmon, or they create their own pasta dish from among a potpourri of toppings—pine nuts, gorgonzola cheese, roast sausage, Thai barbecue, and scallops, to name a few. Hours are 8:00 A.M. to 9:00 P.M. Tuesday through Thursday, 10:00 A.M. to 10:00 P.M. Friday and Saturday, and 8:00 A.M. to 3:00 P.M. Monday. For a look at their current menu, see www.blossomdeli.com.

metrovalley trivia

Charleston's Craik-Patton House, a 166-year-old Greek-revival home, was once owned by Colonel George S. Patton, grandfather of General Patton of World War II fame.

Southern Kitchen, located at the corner of MacCorkle Avenue and Fifty-third Street, has been offering country cooking since it first opened in 1947. House specialties include chicken and dumplings, baked steak, and fried chicken. The restaurant is open twenty-four hours a day and closes only for Christmas. Call (304) 925–3154 for more information.

Other downtown attractions include the Charleston Civic Center and one of the largest downtown malls in the East, and **Taylor Bookstore** (226 Capitol Street; 304–342–1461), which manages to blend an art gallery, book readings, sculpture studio, live music, and a cafe all in one store. Taylor is the place to find work by your favorite West Virginia artist, whether it's Mountain Stage violinist Julie Adams or West Virginia–born author Mary Lee Settle. Across the street is **Ellen's Homemade Ice Cream,** a favorite for its cappuccinos, light lunches, and super-premium ice cream in flavors both beloved and as offbeat as pawpaw and pumpkin.

Ten minutes east of downtown on U.S. Highway 60 is the boyhood home of African-American educator Booker T. Washington. The riverside village of **Malden** seems dedicated to his history, from the life-size replica of **Booker T. Washington's cabin** to the **Women's Park** dedicated to his sister.

"Kick a rock in Malden, and you wonder if Booker T. kicked that same rock," says West Virginia state senator Larry Rowe, whose office stands near Washington's homesite. "I tell kids they could be the next world leader to come out of Malden."

In 1865 nine-year-old Washington walked 225 miles with his family from the Virginia farm where he had been enslaved to his freedom home in Malden. Here he labored in the saltworks with his stepfather, eventually becoming a garden helper for the wealthy Ruffner family, who encouraged his education. By the time of his death in 1915, he was called "the most important leader of any race to come out of the South after the Civil War" by his arch-critic, W. E. B. Du Bois.

A replica of Washington's small cabin has been built behind the church where he learned to read. *African Zion Baptist Church* was organized in the 1850s as the first black Baptist church in western Virginia. After his graduation from Hampton Institute, Washington taught Sunday school here and also got married here.

At *Cabin Creek Quilts Cooperative,* two doors down, you'll find folks practicing a craft that was old during Washington's time. Inside the pink brick Hale House, you can learn anything you want to know about quilts, ramps, or life in the mountains. Since the cooperative was formed in 1970 by VISTA volunteers, these women have stitched quilts for three U.S. presidents, Jackie Onassis, Barbra Streisand, and scores of other celebrities. Here you can buy a staggering variety of quilted objects—from hand-pieced quilts to vests to cell-phone jackets to credit card holders. Cabin Creek Quilts is staffed by quilters Monday through Saturday from 10:00 A.M. to 4:00 P.M. Call (304) 925–9499 for specific information.

metrovalley trivia

African-American educational pioneer Booker T. Washington is one of three West Virginians elected to the Hall of Fame for Great Americans.

Directly across the street from Cabin Creek is a park dedicated to the women of Malden, built on the site where the home of Washington's half-sister, Amanda, once stood.

A block to the west is an antiques shop/museum on George's Creek, where Kelly Bratton displays his antique gas station. The sign says GREYHOUND MUSEUM, but Bratton repairs anything with wheels. His collection includes a 1954 Nash, a 1908 five-ton electric truck with all the batteries, an 1897 horse-drawn hearse, and a 1913 Ford Model T.

If you ever thought of going to the dog track, you probably had South Florida and swaying palm trees in mind. The Sunshine State comes to the Mountain State via the *Tri-State Greyhound Track and Gaming Center* in Cross Lanes, about 13 miles west of Charleston off Interstate 64. In fact, Tri-State is owned by the same people who own the Hollywood Greyhound Track in Florida, and you can expect to watch some of the best dog racing in the United States right here in West Virginia. Casual seating is available in the 3,000-

seat grandstand; more formal viewing is offered in the clubhouse area, which seats 1,200 and includes the rather nice French Quarter Restaurant. Clubhouse patrons can also watch and bet on simulcast horse racing from around the country. For dinner reservations, call (304) 776–1000 or (800) 224–9683. The center also features 1,000 slot machines in its 33,000-square-foot casino. It all makes for a fun afternoon or evening.

The park is open from 11:00 A.M. to 3:00 A.M., with matinee races beginning at 1:30 P.M. and evening races beginning at 7:30 P.M. Live races run from the second week of April through mid-October. No races are held on Tuesday. Another facet of the center is *Friends of Greyhounds Adoption Services* (800–SAVE-A-PET), which finds homes for retiring dogs.

The Tri-State Area

The Tri-State Area begins just west of Charleston and extends westward about 60 miles to Huntington and the confluence of the Big Sandy and Ohio Rivers, the point where the states of Ohio, Kentucky, and West Virginia meet. It contains portions of Putnam, Cabell, and Wayne Counties, and it's among the most densely populated and industrialized parts of the state. Of course, comparatively speaking, what's considered densely populated in West Virginia would be thought of as largely rural in most other states.

The Tri-State is marked by low rolling hills that don't seem all that intimidating until you try driving the back roads over and around them. Most of the secondary roads here aren't going to take you anywhere particularly fast. But because they're so close to the population corridors of Charleston and Huntington, you can ramble off the beaten path without ever worrying about getting totally lost—a claim that could never be made in the more mountainous and isolated parts of the state.

Head west on I–64 from Charleston and you'll venture into the heart of West Virginia's *glass country.* The area, along with the Mid-Ohio Valley, was once pocketed with dozens of companies that specialize in the difficult and beautiful art of glassmaking. West Virginia's prized sandstones and sands have been used over the years in a variety of ways, from extracting silica and minerals to oil and natural gas production to the making of some of the world's finest glassware.

The small community of *Hurricane* was named by George Washington when, as a young surveyor, he came across a spot near the Kanawha River where all the trees were bent in the same direction. Legend had it that a hurricane, or at least a strong windstorm, must have come through just prior to

"Mad Anne" Bailey Was Here

The exploits of "Mad Anne" Trotter Bailey are legendary in the Kanawha Valley. Not only did the frontierswoman evade the Indians as a colonial spy on the old war trail between Fort Union and Point Pleasant, West Virginia, but her tales have added to the intrigue of these historical spots. You can visit her grave at Point Pleasant Battle Monument State Park (also known as Tu-Endie-Wei State Park), where the museum contains her hair and other memorabilia.

Anne didn't start out mad. Anne Hennis came from Liverpool, England, and married fellow indentured servant Richard Trotter when their servitude expired. They settled in the mountains near Covington, Virginia, and were raising a family when Richard enlisted with Colonel Andrew Lewis's forces to fight the Shawnees in 1774. He was killed fighting against Chief Cornstalk's Indians at the Battle of Point Pleasant.

When Anne heard of her husband's death, she became obsessed with revenge. She immediately put on leggings, armed herself with a tomahawk and rifle, and left her son in the care of others as she rode about attending every muster of soldiers she could find.

In a few years she married an army ranger named John Bailey and went off to serve with him at Fort Lee in Clendennin's Settlement, where Charleston now stands. When the officers saw her skill with the rifle, they offered Anne a career as a spy and messenger.

Soon after the murder of Cornstalk at Point Pleasant, Indians surrounded Fort Lee. The colonials were almost out of gunpowder, and not a man would risk his life to ride to a distant warehouse. Anne mounted her steed, Liverpool, and took off alone. She rode day and night for 100 miles, often pursued by Indians, until she arrived at Fort Savannah (Lewisburg). Anne loaded up two horses with ammunition and stole back to Charleston, saving the fort.

Anne never did put up her long rifle or her buckskins. She was called "Mad Anne" for her eccentricities, but she was loved and welcomed for her bravery in the homes of settlers wherever she traveled.

Washington's arrival. The town existed as a stagecoach stop and livestock center for another century before the railroad arrived in 1873 and the community began to thrive in earnest.

Although strip malls do lure travelers from I–64 in other towns, downtown Hurricane has managed a comeback by attracting small specialty shops. Across from the Victorian bandstand on Main Street, you'll see a costume shop, an antiques store, a coffee shop, and two gift shops—one run by the Humane Society and staffed by a calico cat. The ***Root Cellar*** with its ***Ferguson Tea Room*** offers everything from balm of Gilead to high tea. It's open Tuesday to

Saturday 11:00 A.M. to 3:00 P.M. Next door at the ***Glass Amulet,*** Lesia Null sculpts her own glass beads, buttons, pendants, and perfume vessels. Her technique, called lampwork, involves shaping glass rods with a glassblower's torch. Her studio is just off the shop, so customers are welcome to observe studio work, even try it themselves at Null's bead-making classes and bead parties. Hours for the studio and Null's adjacent coffee shop are 11:00 A.M. to 6:00 P.M., Tuesday through Saturday. To schedule an individual class or studio time, call (304) 562–2774.

West Virginia may be landlocked, but you can still catch a wave in Hurricane. If you're traveling with young children, start your day here at ***Waves of Fun,*** located off I–64 on State Route 34. This county-operated water park is complete with a gigantic wave pool, an aqua tube slide, and a giant slide. If the natural white water of West Virginia's raging rivers seems too intimidating, try the park's equally fun—and markedly safer—white-water tube run. This is a great place to cool off and wind down in the summer months, when the lower elevations of the Ohio River Valley can turn a bit sultry, to say the least. The park is open Monday through Saturday, Memorial Day through Labor Day, from 11:00 A.M. to 7:00 P.M. and Sunday from noon to 7:00 P.M. The park closes at 6:00 P.M. during August and September. General admission is $8.00 for adults, and children ages five to eleven get in for $7.00, or half price if you arrive after 4:00 P.M. Call (304) 562–0518 for more information.

Next door to Waves of Fun stands the new ***Museum in the Community,*** which considers itself a three-dimensional teaching tool as well as a cultural center. Everything about the single-story, Japanese folk-art building is conscious—from the exposed green water pipes to the wiring visible behind transparent covers to the meters showing energy consumption in the building. Signs identify elements of the exposed roof structure, so that you'll never again be in the dark about soffits, fascia, or rooflines. The museum's exhibit areas have held art shows as well as quirky collections of snow-globe paperweights, Pez dispensers, and automobiles. The museum is open from 10:00 A.M. to 5:00 P.M. Tuesday through Friday, as well as Thursday evenings and Saturday afternoons. For more information, call (304) 562–0484, or check the Web site www.museuminthecommunity.org.

After a lunch or early dinner, head over to downtown Hurricane for shopping and sights. In a minipark beside the fire department on Main Street, you can commune with the ***Maiden of the Rock.*** The 7-foot petroglyph was found on the roof of a natural stone shelter in Putnam County, and although it looks a lot like other petroglyphs found in the Mountain State, controversy has flared over whether the Maiden is authentic or the work of local teenagers in the 1920s. You be the judge.

There are also several interesting off-the-beaten-path shops in Hurricane, some of which are standouts. ***Reflections of Judy,*** named for its owner, who has more than twenty years' experience in floral design, offers custom floral designs, collectibles, and a wide assortment of Victorian and country accessories. Here you'll find the largest lace doily collection in the state. Judy's is open from 9:00 A.M. to 6:00 P.M. during the week but closes at 4:00 P.M. on Saturday. It's closed Sunday. Call (304) 562–1027. It's located on Morris Court between Main Street and Route 34.

On Putnam Avenue is ***Plantation Corner,*** located in the oldest house in Hurricane. Especially enticing are the regional antiques, reproductions, gifts, and home accessories. Proprietor Renee Wiles-Johnson offers an interior design service, with clients who own some of the finest homes in this Victorian-tinged village. Plantation Corner is open from 11:00 A.M. to 6:00 P.M. Thursday and Friday and from 10:00 A.M. to 2:00 P.M. Saturday. Call (304) 562–1001 for information.

The ***Whispering Wisteria House*** features American primitive dolls, doll cabins, full-size primitive furniture, and gift items. If you could be shrunk and go back in time, you should choose to hang out in this dream of a place: pioneer life made beautiful. It's located on Morning Road and is open from 10:00 A.M. to 5:00 P.M. Tuesday through Saturday. Call (304) 562–6941 for details.

Back on I–64 and heading west from Hurricane, detour into another delightful little town, ***Milton.*** Downtown, take a left on US 60 and head to the city's most impressive attraction, the ***Blenko Glass Factory,*** founded in 1922 by William Blenko, a British glassmaker. Today it's recognized worldwide for its exquisite handblown stained glass, some of which is found in the great museums and art galleries of the world.

The factory is run by the fourth generation of Blenkos, who beam with pride over their most notable creations, including the colorful windows found in the chapel at the United States Air Force Academy, in St. Patrick's Cathedral in New York City, in Washington Cathedral in the nation's capital, and at Riyadh Airport in Saudi Arabia. These folks are also responsible for making the beautiful, clear, rocket-shaped trophies of the Country Music Awards and were the original manufacturers of Williamsburg reproduction glassware. The lighting globes in the U.S. Capitol were created here.

The factory offers a free tour, which includes a stop at an observation deck for a how-do-they-do-that, up-close view of the craftspeople. There's also a funky and eclectic visitor center next door, with a factory outlet on the lower level and a glass museum, military exhibit, and stained-glass showcase upstairs. The fascinating complex can consume the better part of a day. And beware, you could fall in love with the sparkling glass and be compelled to return for the early February clearance sales.

Tours are available from 8:00 A.M. to noon and from 12:30 to 3:15 P.M. Monday through Friday, except for a week or so around July 1 and the week between Christmas and New Year's Day. The visitor center is open from 8:00 A.M. to 4:00 P.M. Monday through Saturday and noon to 4:00 P.M. on Sunday. Both the plant and the visitor center close for holidays. For more information, call (304) 743–9081.

Handblown glass pieces at the Blenko Glass Factory

Still haven't had enough? There's another glass factory in town, **Gibson Glass,** located just past Blenko in a residential area. Gibson is known for its gorgeous flower paperweights, marbles, angels, and figurines. Most of the glassmaking is supervised by Charles Gibson, who is one of the few remaining old-time masters of the craft. His Vaseline glass and cracklework is widely collected. In the observation area take a peek at the glassmakers, then stroll over to the gift shop where they sell seconds and other items. Gibson's is open Monday through Friday from 8:30 A.M. to 2:00 P.M. The gift shop is open until 4:00 P.M. Monday through Saturday. Call (304) 743–5232 for directions or information.

If you're ready for some fresh air and a picnic lunch, head over to Camp Arrowhead, just off US 60, and take a hike on the beautiful, serene **Kanawha Trace.** The 32-mile trail (you don't have to walk the entire trail—a short stroll provides plenty of beautiful scenery) runs from Barboursville, where the Mud and Guyandotte Rivers come together, to Fraziers Bottom on the Kanawha River. The trail was created by the Boy Scouts for hiking and is open year-round. Call (304) 523–3408 for more information or see http://members.tripod.com/~Trace42/.

If you're spending the weekend in Milton, don't miss a visit to the **Mountaineer Opry House,** a nationally known venue for country and bluegrass music stars. Performers Ricky Skaggs, Doyle Lawson, Rhonda Vincent, and others come here to play on weekend nights year-round. The cinder-block theater, just off I–64, is nothing fancy to look at, but you're not here for the visuals. This is all about old-time and country music with a West Virginia twang. Grab a goody at the concession stand (no alcohol allowed) and let the good times roll. Shows begin at 7:00 P.M. Admission is $12.00 for adults, $10.00 for senior citizens, and $4.00 for children. Call (304) 743–5749 or 8428 for more information.

Back on I–64 and heading west toward Kentucky, plan to spend a few hours—or better yet, a few days—in the charming but often overlooked town of *Huntington,* West Virginia's second-largest city. Nestled right up against the Kentucky and Ohio borders, this historic riverside community offers a number of interesting diversions. Here you'll find *Marshall University,* whose football team, the Thunderin' Herd, is a perennial NCAA powerhouse. Marshall also hosts regular concerts in its new jazz center with its digital recording studio. Huntington is also home to the *Huntington Cubs,* a minor league baseball team; the Huntington Railroad museum; and a beautiful downtown.

metrovalley trivia

Huntington, one of the largest cities in West Virginia, is also the westernmost city in the state.

A good place to start is at the *Huntington Museum of Art,* located on a wooded hilltop near downtown. The museum was started by the benevolent Herbert L. Fitzpatrick, who donated the land on which it sits as well as his own art collection. Several other wealthy local art patrons have since given generously to the museum, including Henry and Grace Rardin Doherty, who helped fund the 300-seat *Doherty Auditorium,* home of the Huntington Chamber Orchestra. Additions and studios were designed by Walter Gropius, founder of the Bauhaus school of architecture. Clerestory windows flood the rooms with natural light.

Here, at the largest museum in the state, you'll discover room after room of eighteenth-century European and American paintings, Ohio River historical glass, contemporary art glass, Georgian silver, Oriental prayer rugs, American furniture, Appalachian folk art, and contemporary furniture. The *Herman Dean Firearms Collection* includes eighteenth-century powder horns inscribed with maps, breech-loading rifles, and a Kentucky flintlock. Don't miss the hands-on *Young People's Gallery* if you're traveling with young children.

Admission is free to everyone. Hours are 10:00 A.M. to 5:00 P.M. Wednesday through Saturday, 10:00 A.M. to 9:00 P.M. Tuesday, and noon to 5:00 P.M. Sunday. Closed Monday and most major holidays. Call (304) 529–2701.

Huntington is also home to another museum, the *Museum of Radio and Technology,* the largest of its kind in the eastern United States. It seems rather appropriate to honor such technology here, since radio has long helped open up remote areas of the state with national and global information and entertainment.

Exhibits here will fascinate today's electronically sophisticated kids and teenagers. On display are hundreds of old radios from the 1920s to the 1950s, telegraph items, and early televisions and computers. A favorite stop is a re-creation of a radio station studio from the 1950s. Listen closely and you'll hear the sounds of the King himself, Elvis Presley. An adjoining gift shop features recordings of old radio programs, posters, and other early radio memorabilia reproductions. Music lovers will want to browse the large collection of 78 rpm, 45 rpm, and LP records. The museum is open from 10:00 A.M. to 4:00 P.M. Saturday, and Sunday from 1:00 to 4:00 P.M. Admission is free, but donations are encouraged. The museum, in a former elementary school at 1640 Florence Avenue, is located very near the city's antiques district, just off I–64. For more information call (304) 525–8890.

While in Huntington, don't miss **Heritage Village,** an award-winning shopping and entertainment complex housed in the downtown former B&O Railway Station. There's much activity here, along with the Heritage Station Restaurant and a renovated Pullman car. Also take note of one of the quieter attractions—the statue of city founder Collis B. Huntington, sculpted by Gutzon Borglum, the same man who created Mount Rushmore.

The nearby **Heritage Farm Museum,** which opened in spring 2002, is a place where you can get lost in another era. Stop by an old log church, visit the village smithy in his blacksmith shop, tour a broom-making workshop, drop by a one-room schoolhouse, and shop a general store, then head over to the kitchen-through-the-ages exhibit to revel in how lucky we are that washing and food preparation don't monopolize our time. Children will especially love the petting zoo and find vicarious terror in the nineteenth-century dentist's office. The new Transportation Building includes a 1908 electric truck. The village's fifteen authentically outfitted buildings will be an educational experience to visitors of any age. The Heritage Farm Museum is open March through November, Monday through Saturday 10:00 A.M. to 3:00 P.M. Admission is $8.00 per adult and $6.00 per child. The four, two- to three-bedroom log homes rent for $150 to $200 a night. For more information visit www.heritagefarmmuseum.com or call (304) 522–1244.

If you love green landscapes, river vistas, and city views, there are at least three in Huntington that you shouldn't miss. At Tenth Street and Veterans Memorial Boulevard (directly across from Heritage Village) is the **David Harris Riverfront Park,** deemed one of the nation's most beautiful urban green spaces. It sits on a wide expanse of the Ohio River and is the base for several sightseeing cruise boats and a popular riverfront amphitheater (complete with a floating stage). Call (304) 696–5954 for a park schedule.

Across Heritage Village and away from the river is **Ritter Park,** a seventy-acre park where it's almost mandatory to stop and smell the roses. Ritter's nationally acclaimed rose garden contains more than 1,500 bushes. The park's second must-see stop, especially if you're toting children, is the playground—and not just any playground. This one was voted one of the ten best children's playgrounds in America by *Child* magazine. The fairy-tale-like play area is cut into a hillside and features bigger-than-life stone columns, arches, and triangles to climb on and hide in. Ritter Park is also home to the outdoor *Huntington Railroad Museum,* open Sunday afternoon from Memorial Day to September 30. The park includes an H-6 steam locomotive, a caboose, several velocipedes, and a steam tank engine. Admission is free.

The Mountain State's only remaining amusement park, the *Camden,* just west of Huntington, claims not one, but two vintage wooden roller coasters and authentic old bumper cars, as well as the state's third-largest Indian burial mound. The 20-foot conical mound is right beside the Big Dipper roller coaster and was once used as a bandstand. The Little Dipper has the distinction of being the only wooden kiddy coaster still operating in the United States, while the Big Dipper has been voted into the American Coaster Enthusiasts' Hall of Fame. Camden's carousel has been spinning each summer since the park opened in 1903.

Camden has also earned a reputation for its superlative corn dogs. The twenty-six-acre park has twenty-five rides, as well as games, a cafeteria, rest-room facilities, and a new interactive and delightfully educational bat house tour. It's open weekends only in May, September, and October and from 11:00 A.M. to 10:00 P.M. daily, except Monday, in June, July, and August. For more information call (304) 429–4321 or (866) 8CAMDEN. Admission is $19 for adults, $12 for children under 4 feet tall, and $12 for senior citizens.

Don't leave Huntington without taking a look at the *East End Bridge,* a mile-long steel spiderweb of a bridge connecting Huntington's Thirty-first Street to Ohio's Route 7 in Proctorville. It's the second concrete cable-stayed bridge built in the United States and the first to use triple-strength concrete. It cost $38 million and took twenty years to plan, ten years to build. It was completed in 1985.

A forty-five-minute drive north of Huntington, along the lazy Ohio, puts you in *Point Pleasant,* which is also the terminus of the Kanawha River. The town's *Tu-Endie-Wei State Park* (Point Pleasant Battle Monument State Park) memori-alizes a battle fought here on October 10, 1774. The name was officially changed in early 2000 from Battle Monument to Tu-Endie-Wei, a Native Ameri-can term meaning "the mingling of the waters." More than a thousand Virginia militiamen fought against as many Shawnee Indians, keeping them from form-ing an alliance with the British. The fighting allowed white settlers to push far-ther west into the frontier of Ohio and beyond. The two-acre park has several monuments to the brave that fell here, along with the *Mansion House,* the first hewn-log house in the county. It was so large for its day, with two stories and real glass windows, that the settlers felt justified in giving it such a grandiose name. First used as a tavern, it now houses battle artifacts. The park is open year-round, and donations are appreciated in lieu of an admission fee. Mansion House is open May through October, 10:00 A.M. to 4:30 P.M. Monday through Saturday and 1:00 to 4:00 P.M. Sunday. Call (304) 675–0869 for more information.

Krodel Park, on the southern edge of Point Pleasant, offers fishing, camping, miniature golf, and camping along its twenty-two-acre fishing lake. A walking path leads to *Fort Randolph,* a replica of the 1774 fort built here against Indian attack. The structure includes two blockhouses and a log blacksmith shop. Demonstrations and reenactments are held here most summer weekends. Colonial crafts portrayed include carpentry, broom making, candle dipping, basket weaving, soap making, spinning yarn, flintlock riflery, flint napping, and blacksmithing. For more information call (304) 675–2366 or (304) 675–3844.

For more recent history, head downtown and look for an antebellum mercantile station within splashing distance of the Ohio River. The *Point Pleasant River Museum* uses displays and demonstrations to highlight topics such as major floods in history, boat construction, local river industries, and the collapse of the Silver Bridge. The museum is open Tuesday to Saturday 10:30 A.M. to 3:00 P.M. and from 1:00 to 5:00 P.M. on Sunday. Admission is $4.00 for adults and $1.00 for children. For information, call (304) 674–0144 or visit www.pp rivermuseum.com.

At your next stop you'll learn a lot about what farm life in West Virginia was like in the 1800s. Just 4 miles north of Point Pleasant is the *West Virginia State Farm Museum,* with more than fifty acres of grounds and thirty-one period buildings demonstrating the hardy lifestyle of West Virginia farmers past and present. This is a working museum where crops are grown, harvested, and processed using nineteenth-century equipment and methods. On your tour take particular note of *General,* a Belgian gelding (now stuffed) on record as the third-largest horse ever to have lived. The museum is open April through November, from 9:00 A.M. to 5:00 P.M. Tuesday through Saturday and from 1:00 to 5:00 P.M. Sunday. Admission is free. Call (304) 675–5737 for information.

Places to Stay in the Metro Valley Region

CHARLESTON

Charleston Marriott Town Center
200 Lee Street East
(304) 345–6500
(800) 228–9290
Expensive

Red Roof Inn
Interstate 64 at MacCorkle Avenue
(304) 925–6953
(800) THE–ROOF
Budget

Sleep Inn
Interstate 79, exit 1
(800) 216–0661
Moderate

CROSS LANES

Comfort Inn
102 Racer Drive
(304) 776–8070
(800) 798–7886
Inexpensive

HUNTINGTON

Radisson Hotel
1001 Third Avenue
(304) 525–1001
Moderate to expensive

MATEWAN

Historic Matewan House
Mate Street
(304) 426–5607
(866) 878–8178
www.historicmatewanhouse
.com
Inexpensive

Places to Eat in the Metro Valley Region

CHARLESTON

Charleston Marriott
Town Center
200 Lee Street East
(304) 345–6500
Moderate

Chesapeake Crab House
Holiday Inn
600 Kanawha Boulevard
(304) 344–4092
Moderate to expensive

Harding's Family
Restaurant
Interstate 79, exit 1
(304) 344–5044
Inexpensive

Sahara Restaurant
189 Summers Street
(304) 346–9800
Inexpensive

HUNTINGTON

Coach Pruett's Steak-
house at the Radisson
1001 Third Avenue
(304) 525–1001
Moderate

FOR MORE INFORMATION

Cabell-Huntington Convention
and Visitors Bureau
(800) 635–6329
www.wvvvisit.org

Mason County Convention
and Visitors Bureau
(304) 675–6788

Charleston Convention
and Visitors Bureau
(800) 733–5469 or (304) 344–5075
www.charlestonwv.com

City of Hurricane Convention
and Visitors Bureau
(304) 562–5896
www.hurricanewv.com

South Charleston Convention
and Visitors Bureau
(800) 238–9488
www.southcharlestonwv.org

Putman County Convention
and Visitors Bureau
(304) 562–0518
www.putnamcounty.org/tourism

Mid-Ohio Valley

The Ohio River Valley sits at the western edge of the Mountain State, extending northward along the namesake river from Huntington to the Northern Panhandle.

The valley was the site of some of the first western expansion movements in the United States as settlers came down from Pennsylvania on the Ohio River, and as such it was open to attack from Native Americans, backed by the British, who still held frontier outposts. Today this area of sloping hills, small riverside towns, and prominent glass factories is gaining ground as a tourist mecca, with many visitors coming from Ohio and Kentucky to shop, fish, hunt, and spend weekends in out-of-the-way bed-and-breakfasts.

Of course, the mighty Ohio River is the defining feature here, and there is plenty to do on or near the water. But there are also numerous treasures to be found away from the riverbank, in the rich green folds and ravines of the Appalachian foothills.

Sharing qualities of both the Midwest and the upper South, the valley is a warm, friendly place where no one is about to get in a hurry or demand that you do, either.

The slow-paced, easygoing Mid-Ohio Valley includes the large swath of country extending north along the Ohio from the Jackson County line, below Ravenswood, up to the Pleas-

MID-OHIO VALLEY

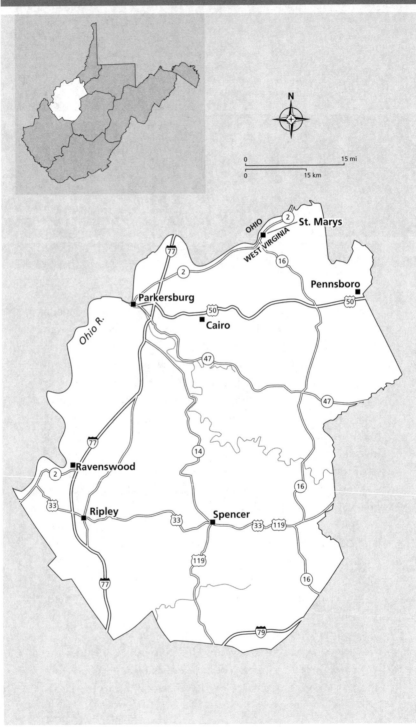

ants County line, north of St. Marys. It's a patchwork of forests, farmland, and serene river roads. It's also among the state's least traveled tourist destinations; hence, virtually everything here is off the beaten path.

Heading east from Point Pleasant on State Route 2 will take travelers "round the bend" of the Ohio River—that is, to the small community of **Ravenswood.** The village bears the distinction of hosting West Virginia's only naval battle. On July 19, 1863, U.S. Navy armored steamers fought Confederates in the Battle of Buffington Island. Earlier, the site of the future town received accolades from none other than George Washington when he made his living as a land surveyor. He surveyed much of the Ohio Valley and wrote about the area in his journal. That bit of history is preserved, along with many other artifacts, at **Washington's Lands Museum,** found in the upper two floors of a converted river-lock building and a restored log cabin. Land-grant documents signed by Patrick Henry, a log house furnished in 1840s style, and the trappings of an old country store are the highlights here. Take the Ravenswood exit to Route 2, then follow the signs to the Ritchie Bridge over the Ohio south of town. The museum is riverside. Hours are 1:00 to 5:00 P.M. Sunday, Memorial Day through October (longer if weather permits); otherwise by appointment. Call (304) 372–5343.

If you're in an artsy frame of mind, head south on Interstate 77 to the **Cedar Lakes Craft Center** in Ripley. The center stages the annual **Mountain State Arts and Crafts Fair,** a prestigious showcase for more than 250 of West Virginia's best artisans and mountain musicians held every Independence Day weekend. At the festival you're likely to find woodcarvers making ladderback

BEST ANNUAL EVENTS IN THE MID-OHIO VALLEY

Mid-Ohio Multi-Cultural Festival
Parkersburg; mid-June
(304) 424–3457

Mountain State Arts and Crafts Fair
Ripley; early July
(304) 372–7860

Rail Trail Festival
North Bend State Park
Cairo; early June
(304) 628–3777
www.northbendsp.com

West Virginia Honey Festival
Parkersburg; late August
(304) 485–6437 or (800) 752–4982

West Virginia Black Walnut Festival
Spencer; mid-October
(304) 927–5616
www.wvblackwalnutfestival.org

chairs or mountain dulcimers (many of which are played on the spot) and specialty craftspeople churning out intricate quilts, dried-flower wreaths, sweaters, and jewelry. A big hit at one of the most recent festivals was a line of ladies' accessories woven out of pine straw.

If you're passing through at another time of year, there's still plenty to see and do at Cedar Lakes. From March through mid-November, some of the country's best artisans teach others new ideas, designs, and techniques for handcrafted art. People come from all over the United States to spend a week at the center (you can stay in a dormitory, in the campus hotel, in cottages, or off campus), learning pottery making, woodworking, bookbinding, rag-rug weaving, quilting, watercolor painting, basket weaving, chair making, and more. The center also participates in the Elderhostel program, an international network of colleges and other institutions that offers special classes for senior citizens. More than 300 seniors participated at Cedar Lakes in 2003. For information about the center, call (304) 372–7860, or check the Web site at www.cedarlakes.com.

The Western Frontier

The northern Ohio Valley counties of Wood, Pleasants, Ritchie, and Wirt were once considered outposts of the western frontier, a wild and woolly region of hardscrabble farms and low, forested hills. Though the pioneers continued on much farther west, the region still retains a certain rustic charm. **Parkersburg** is the only town in the region with a population over 30,000. Nevertheless, this somewhat lonely stretch of the Mid-Ohio Valley also might be the most scenic and fascinating.

Plan to spend at least two days in Parkersburg, for this friendly community on the banks of the Ohio has much to offer. The best place to start, naturally, is the **Visitors and Convention Bureau,** downtown at 350 Seventh Street. Here you can pick up loads of information on local points of interest. The bureau is open Monday through Friday from 8:00 A.M. to 4:30 P.M. One interesting site is just down the street. **Point Park** is where local residents built a flood wall after a series of devastating floods. Marks on the wall show where the river crested each of the last three times; the most recent, in 1913, was 38 feet above normal.

mid-ohio valleytrivia

The Ohio Valley was the site of West Virginia's first oil boom; the region still contains some active wells.

While you're down by the flood wall, don't miss the **Little Kanawha Craft House,** a large shop that displays high-quality handmade crafts of almost

BEST ATTRACTIONS IN THE MID-OHIO VALLEY

Blennerhassett Island
Historical State Park
Parkersburg
(304) 420–4800
www.blennerhassettislandstatepark.com

Trans Allegheny Bookstore
Parkersburg
(304) 422–4499
www.abebooks.com/home/TABOOKS/

Fenton Art Glass Company
Williamstown
(304) 375–6122
www.fentonartglass.com

West Virginia Motor Speedway
Mineral Wells
(304) 758–0558 or (304) 758–2934
www.wvspeedway.com

Cedar Lakes Crafts Center
Ripley
(304) 372–7860
www.cedarlakes.com

North Bend State Park
Cairo
(304) 643–2931 or (800) CALL–WVA
www.northbendsp.com

600 area artisans. The selection of baskets, ceramics, quilts, furniture, and other items is amazing. Prices range from $1.00 to several hundred. From May to October hours are 10:00 A.M. to 6:00 P.M. Monday through Saturday, and noon to 6:00 P.M. Sunday. From October through April hours are 9:00 A.M. to 5:00 P.M. Monday through Saturday. Call (304) 485–3149 for more information.

Point Park is also where visitors board the stern-wheeler that takes them to **Blennerhassett Island.** The Blennerhassett story is a unique and tragic one. Wealthy Irish immigrants Harman and Margaret Blennerhassett bought an island in the Ohio River, built "the most beautiful private residence in the Ohio Valley," and lived in unsurpassed splendor for several years.

Their downfall came when a prominent figure in American history, **Aaron Burr,** arrived in their lives. Burr, already notorious for killing Alexander Hamilton in a duel, had just lost the presidency to Thomas Jefferson and was very bitter. He hatched a scheme to set up his own country by seizing Spanish territory in the Southwest. He enlisted Harman Blennerhassett's help, but local officials discovered the plot and arrested the pair for treason. Though both were eventually acquitted, the Blennerhassetts were ruined financially and politically after the ordeal (the mansion had already burned to the ground in an accident). They tried briefly to resurrect their lifestyle in Mississippi by running a cotton plantation, but it failed and they moved to England. Harman died there, and Margaret returned to the United States seeking financial aid from her sons. One son disappeared; she and the other son died in poverty.

Despite the tragic tale, there's much to see on Blennerhassett Island, now on the National Register of Historic Places. The state reconstructed the Italian Palladian–style mansion on the original site using research and information from archaeological excavations. Resembling George Washington's Mount Vernon, the mansion has more than 7,000 square feet of space and is resplendent with oil paintings, Oriental rugs, opulent antiques, Italian sculptures, and other treasures. Wagon rides and craft demonstrations are featured from June through August. Margaret Blennerhassett herself returns to socialize and entertain visitors over brunch on the third Thursday in June, July, and August. Call (304) 420–4800 for reservations.

Ruble's Sternwheelers (740–423–7268) leaves the mainland from Point Park for the island every half hour between 10:00 A.M. and 4:30 P.M., May through October (weekends only in September and October; closed on Monday). The trip on a steam-driven paddle-wheeler boat, once a common site on the Ohio River, and tours of the mansion and museum cost $12.00 for adults, $9.00 for children ages three to twelve.

savingsbond capital

Parkersburg is the savings bond capital of the nation. Since 1957, every U.S. bond bought or redeemed has passed through the U.S. Treasury's Bureau of Public Debt in Parkersburg. If you want to know the amount of the debt or who owns it, you can write to the Bureau of the Public Debt, P.O. Box 2188, Parkersburg, WV 26106-2188 or visit their Web site at www.publicdebt.treas.gov.

The boat launch is near the *Blennerhassett Museum,* Second and Julianna Streets, where you can begin with a twelve-minute video about the Blennerhassetts. The island itself is believed to have been inhabited as early as 11,000 years ago. So before boarding check out the glass-encased displays of ancient relics found there (don't miss the mastodon bones) as well as other exhibits unrelated to the Blennerhassetts. The museum is open 10:00 A.M. to 5:00 P.M. Wednesday through Saturday and Sunday afternoons, March through October, and on weekends November through March. Call (800) CALL–WVA for information.

After you return from the island (or before you go), there's still lots to see and do. If you remain in a Blennerhassett frame of mind, head over to the hotel bearing the same name. The redbrick turrets and Palladian windows of the *Blennerhassett Hotel* (now on the National Register of Historic Places), Fourth and Market Streets, take visitors back to another time, when horses galloped by and gunshots sometimes rang in the rowdy Parkersburg streets. It remains the showcase today that it was when it was built in 1889 by banker Colonel William Chancellor. It was also one of the first hotels in the country to boast a bank branch in its lobby. Its elegance and sophistication made it the

Victoriana

Probably the residents of Parkersburg's Julia-Ann Square Historical District know they're living in the twenty-first century—they have a Web site, www.juliannsq.org, after all.

But those who live in the 125 homes of this elegant historic district seem to have immersed themselves in the ambience and trappings of the Victorian era when these homes were built. It's not enough that residents spend their time researching nineteenth-century gas streetlights, Irwin and Russell hardware, brass newel posts, and pocket doors. Now the avid homeowners association organizes an event almost every month in which they can indulge their zeal for all things Victorian.

The whimsy of the Easter Parade is fun for residents and tourists alike. As they did at the turn of the twentieth century, the wealthy turn out in their newest hats and dress to parade down the avenue for the admiration of all. The hat contest is the biggest draw.

The year continues with Victorian garden tours, teas, historic street fairs, craft demonstrations, yard sales of the rich and not-so-famous, and a Christmas home tour. But any time of year, a walking tour of the mansions yields a visual feast of Second Empire, Gothic revival, Italianate, Queen Anne, and Federal styles, occasionally all in one home.

The district's elegant bed-and-breakfast, the **Harnett House,** for instance, combines Gothic revival, Italianate, and French Second Empire features in one gorgeous, thirty-two-room house—oops, thirty-four rooms: two are accessed by hidden passageways. In a house with standard 15-foot ceilings, it's not too hard to misplace a chamber or two.

For more information about the district and Harnett House, call (304) 483–1029 or (304) 295–0127.

Harnett House

OTHER ATTRACTIONS WORTH SEEING IN THE MID-OHIO VALLEY

Holl's Chocolates
Vienna

Julia-Ann Square Historic District
Parkersburg

Davis Handmade Marbles
Pennsboro

R.C. Marshall Hardware Company
Cairo

Thistle Dew (Honeybee) Farm
Proctor

Blennerhassett Museum
Parkersburg

Smoot Vaudeville Theatre
Parkersburg

grandest hotel in the state, and those qualities are still evident, thanks to a renovation in the 1980s. The elegantly refurbished guest rooms are decorated with Chippendale reproductions and offer high-speed wireless Internet service, bedtime chocolates, and plush bathrobes. Its restaurant, *Spat's,* has a reputation for fine Continental cuisine. For reservations or information, call (304) 422–3131 or (800) 262–2536.

While you're still downtown, check out Parkersburg's *Oil and Gas Museum.* Not interested? Don't be so hasty. This exhibit offers a fascinating look at what could be a dry subject, no pun intended. Housed in a turn-of-the-twentieth-century hardware store is an impressive collection of engines, pumps, tools, models, documents, maps, photos, and more. Visitors can trace the development of West Virginia's oil and gas industry, from the Indians (yes, the first Americans used oil, which was so abundant that it rose to the surface and oozed into the river) to the 1870s when Standard Oil arrived to the present day. In fact, Parkersburg is still known as "the town that oil built." Outside note the enormous pieces of drilling equipment adjacent to the building. Be sure to catch the video story of the birth of West Virginia's oil and gas industry. It examines the links between the accumulation of wealth in this section of the state and West Virginia's separation from Virginia. The museum is open seven days a week, noon to 5:00 P.M., April through November. Admission is $2.00 for adults, $1.00 for children. Call (304) 485–5446 or (304) 428–8015 for information.

Remember Ruble's Sternwheelers, the folks who took you over to the Blennerhassetts' place? Well, they've got even more to offer than the island tour. Their boats will take you on a dinner-dance cruise or, in the fall, a beautiful foliage excursion, during which you can admire the leaves as they reflect off the water. One of their best cruises, especially for young children and nature enthusiasts, is the *Critter Cruise,* which has those on board scanning the river for wildlife. *Valley Gem Sternwheelers* (740–373–7862) also offers daily history cruises and dinner excursions in the summer and on weekends in May and September.

Now on to the more fanciful. Parkersburg's *Smoot Theatre,* 5 blocks from the flood wall, is a restored movie house and the city's most popular venue for performing arts. The original, glitzy theater was built in 1926 at the height of vaudeville, and for a while it was home to some of the most colorful acts of the era. That changed when vaudeville died. It then served as a movie house for half a century—promising nurses and smelling salts for *Frankenstein* showings during the Depression—but eventually lost out to new competition. Today, after a renovation largely completed by local contributions and elbow grease, the theater stages jazz, ragtime, opera, bluegrass, and rock performances. Call the visitor bureau at (800) 752–4982 or the theater at (304) 422–7529. Prices per person range from $3.00 to $20.00.

Try to arrange to spend a few extra minutes at your next stop, *Trans-Allegheny Books* on Eighth and Green Streets. This is no ordinary used/rare/new bookstore. It's on the National Register of Historic Places, thanks to millionaire philanthropist Andrew Carnegie, and its home is the former *Parkersburg Carnegie Public Library,* built in 1906. The building itself is a gem: a brick, neoclassical structure with glass insets in the floor, a three-story spiral iron staircase, and behind it, a stained-glass window bearing the Carnegie coat of arms. Four floors house 700,000 volumes, as well as magazines, newspapers, postcards, sheet music, old photos, prints, hymnals, and more. West Virginia's largest used-book store also specializes in book searches—finding out-of-print books for patrons. The library is open Monday through Saturday from 10:00 A.M. to 6:00 P.M. Call (304) 422–4499 or look at www.transalleghenybooks.com for more information.

African Americans hold a proud heritage in the Mid-Ohio region. It was here in Parkersburg that a small group of black citizens founded the first free public school for African-American children south of the Mason-Dixon Line. When the Sumner School was established in January 1862, West Virginia was not yet formally a state of the Union, though it had severed its ties to Confederate Virginia. The Sumner School continued on into the twentieth century to become the first West Virginia high school to racially integrate. Although the original building has been razed, its 1926 gymnasium remains, now reincarnated as the *Sumnerite Museum.* Here you can browse through photographs and documents of the school's early years, as well as community artifacts that include a "beaten biscuit machine" used by an early caterer. The museum is open by appointment. For information call (304) 422–0985 or (304) 485–1152.

Parkersburg's shopping possibilities are enticing, but none more than **Holl's Chocolates.** The chocolatier beckons from nearby Vienna, where you can sometimes watch Dominique Holl making truffles in the demonstration area. His father, Fritz, learned the fine art of candy making in his native Switzerland as an apprentice to the masters in Zurich and passed the techniques and recipes down to his son. Although Fritz supervised a research kitchen for many years in the United States, the elder Holl kept on making chocolates, selling them through a local wine shop. In retirement, this activity blossomed into a full-time job, and Dominique came into the business, using his college education to blend old recipes with new automation. Holl's continues to use the traditional recipes, as well as fine Caillier chocolate from Switzerland and real cream, in their handcrafted, always fresh chocolates. Recently, they added a line of sugar-free chocolates, just as tasty but without the guilt.

The shop on 2001 Grand Central Avenue in Vienna is the main outlet, but Holl's chocolates can be ordered through their Web site, www.holls.com.

Parkersburg can also boast a woodworker's mecca, the **Woodcraft** shop, with its specialized tools, demonstrations, and classes. In any given season, woodcrafters can choose among such offerings as Federal-period inlay techniques, basic hand planing, carving a walking stick, building Windsor chairs, and box making for women. If you know what to do but don't have the equipment, you may rent workshop time for an hour or several days. The store is located at 4420 Emerson Avenue and is open 9:00 A.M. to 6:00 P.M. seven days a week. Call (304) 485–4050 or (800) 225–1153 for information.

Just north of Parkersburg on Route 14 is **Boaz,** where gun enthusiasts will find a treat. **Mountain State Muzzle Loading** at the **Early Americana Museum** has all the parts and equipment needed for building and collecting these types of weapons. The large log building also houses a collection of historic American firearms, Native American artifacts, and farm implements and tools. Call (304) 375–7842 for more information.

A bit farther north on I–77 is **Williamstown,** within waving distance of the Ohio border. It was named for Pennsylvania backwoodsman Isaac Williams, who helped to settle the area. A few miles south of town is the lovely **Henderson Hall.** Talk about curb appeal! This redbrick, Italian villa–style manor house is jaw-dropping, so imposing as it sits on a hilltop amid gentle rolling hills looking down on the Ohio River. The three-story house has been called the most significant historic site in the Mid-Ohio Valley, and it is awesome. Today the estate, built beginning in 1836, sits on sixty-five acres, though the Henderson estate once held more than 2,000 acres. It is the oldest standing residential home in the area, and it is still owned by Henderson descendants.

Stepping across its threshold into the giant great hall is like a step back in time. Both the structure and its contents are intact and preserved in pristine condition. All the original furnishings, right down to the parlor wallpaper, are still there. The Hendersons, aside from being very wealthy, also apparently never threw anything away—even a letter from an escaped slaved asking to return. (He escaped again, this time with nine other slaves from the plantation.) All the Hendersons' personal papers, from daily shopping lists to the original grant to the land signed by Virginia governor Patrick Henry, are still in the house—two centuries of memorabilia. Family portraits and photos add to the feeling that the original occupants aren't deceased, just merely away.

The home is open Sunday, June to September, from 1:00 to 4:00 P.M. Admission is $4.00 for adults, $2.00 for children. Call (304) 375–2129 for more information.

In Williamstown make time for another old classic, ***Fenton Art Glass Factory and Museum.*** This more-than-ninety-year-old business, run by the third generation of Fentons, uses old-time, hand glassmaking techniques and modern technology to make carnival, hobnail, milk, cranberry, and Burmese glass.

Glass Dancing at Fenton

Cajoling screaming-hot, molten glass into art is an intense dance. This is not something you realize right away when you first step onto the factory floor with a tour group at Fenton Art Glass. The terse moves of the glass crafters are so carefully orchestrated, the duties so precisely configured and intuitive for these relaxed masters in tennis shoes that you don't realize a second's delay will turn the glass unworkably sluggish; a second more heat will melt it into amorphousness. Too much pressure cracks the molding glass; too little produces weak stems.

"Heat is life for glass. You do your work when the glass is about 1,800° F. When you lose its heat, you lose its life—the glass goes brittle," says Fenton's associate historian James Measell.

So these master craftspeople step lively as they work—from the gatherer, winding a gob of fiery taffy on the end of his punty rod; to the gaffer, who straightens stemware with a wooden paddle; or the swinger, twirling glowing glass to give it shape.

Water breaks are important here where temperatures routinely hit 100° F. Sunglasses and even shorts are de rigueur for folks who face red-hot furnaces all day. Once "snowbird" glassworkers picked up work in the warm factories during the winter but set out hunting or fishing with the first warm breezes of spring. Now workers toil year-round, serving an apprenticeship of two to twelve years to become a skilled member of the glassworkers' union.

A tour starts with a twenty-four-minute movie in the upstairs museum about the Fenton glassmaking process, then heads downstairs for a forty-five-minute tour of the factory floor. Here you'll watch up close as craftspeople stir together sand, soda ash, and lime, plus special ingredients, depending on the color of the glass. This "batch" is put into a 2,500-degree oven until a "gatherer" collects some of the molten liquid and drops it into a mold or gives it to another craftsperson to be blown into shape. Other procedures, such as hand decoration, also are exhibited.

After the tour, head to the gift shop and factory outlet where seconds are discounted. Tours begin every forty-five minutes from 8:15 A.M. to 3:15 P.M. Monday through Friday. Children under two are not allowed on the factory floor, but they can visit the museum, movie, and gift shop. Admission is free. The factory closes on weekends, national holidays, and two weeks in July. For more information call (304) 375–7772 or (800) 319–7793.

Don't leave Williamstown without a visit to the **Williamstown Antique Mall** on Highland Avenue, where several dealers display beautiful collections in a two-story mall. Lustrous glassware and tableware, stoneware, flow blue china, dolls, clocks, quilts, furniture, and more are a delight to both the educated and the novice collector. Hours are 10:00 A.M. to 6:00 P.M. Monday through Saturday and noon to 6:00 P.M. Sunday. The antiques mall can be reached at (304) 375–6315.

If you're craving a little outdoor activity, head north on Route 2 to **St. Marys,** where the natives claim "the livin' is easy and the fishing is great." They're probably right on both counts. Here the deceptively named Middle Island Creek, wide and rolling, joins the Ohio River, creating one of the state's best spots for sportfishing. Trophy muskie are common in these waters, and the

A Vision of St. Marys

Legend has it that the town of St. Marys got its start from a vision of the Virgin by an eastern Virginia businessman. It seems Alexander Creel was traveling by steamer to Wheeling one night around 1834 when he was awakened by a vision of the Virgin Mary, who told him to look upon the Virginia (now West Virginia) side of the river.

"There," she said, "you will behold the site of what someday will be a happy and prosperous city." Creel looked out the door of his stateroom and saw the lower end of Middle Island illuminated in the moonlight. Beyond it was a large cove surrounded by wooded hills. Creel returned to buy the land and eventually devoted his energies to fulfilling his dream. In 1849 the town was named in honor of the mother of Jesus.

bass fishing is so good that the town holds a Bassmasters tournament each June. A few miles south the waters are still ripe. ***Willow Island Locks and Dam*** on West Virginia Route 2 boasts largemouth bass, striped bass, white bass, northern pike, channel catfish, and a few more species that regularly bite hooks.

Running just above St. Marys down to Parkersburg is the ***Ohio River Islands National Wildlife Refuge,*** a haven for fishermen and bird-watchers created in 1992. The area's 3,300 acres are spread across eighteen islands on the Ohio.

mid-ohio valleytrivia

Throughout the late eighteenth and early nineteenth centuries, the mighty Ohio River was the single busiest waterway in North America.

The Last West Virginia Ferry

For almost 200 years, a ferry has operated on the banks of the broad Ohio River between historic Sistersville, West Virginia, and Fly, Ohio. The *City of Sistersville* ferryboat is still the fastest way for residents on the Ohio side to reach a hospital, so the town police chief occasionally gets calls from expectant parents who need transport across the Ohio after the ferry's 6:00 P.M. closing.

Until 1889 the boat was powered by paddles driven by a horse on a treadmill. A steamboat took its place for the next four decades. Now, pilot Joe Frye takes about eight minutes to make the crossing on a calm day. In its busiest times, the diesel craft transports one hundred vehicles in a twelve-hour day. It's a break-even venture for the town during the ferry's operating season April through mid-October, but no one wants to put an end to the last West Virginia ferry operating on the Ohio.

Sistersville Ferry

The pristine setting is home to more than 130 species of birds, including all kinds of waterfowl, wading birds, peregrine falcons, and bald eagles. Rare plants and freshwater mussels (more than thirty species) are resplendent here. There are no bridges connecting the islands to the mainland; at the present time they are accessible only by private boats.

mid-ohio valleytrivia

The North Bend Rail Trail, which begins just east of Parkersburg and runs nearly 72 miles east to Clarksburg, was considered an engineering marvel when it was completed as the Baltimore & Ohio railroad line in 1857. Today it guides cyclists through thirteen tunnels and over thirty-six bridges.

After a busy afternoon of exploring, you'll need a place to rest up and call it a night. You have your choice. You can head north on Route 2 about 30 miles to **Sistersville,** a collection of Italianate villas and other Victorian period mansions on the Ohio. The restored **Wells Inn** (304–652–1312) serves guests comfortably in three stories with an indoor pool, dining room, and tavern. The surrounding National Historic Register district pays tribute to a city once at the heart of America's first oil boom. At one point during the 1890s, at least twenty millionaires lived here, more than any city its size in the United States. Visitors will enjoy antiquing, golf, touring the historic district, or taking West Virginia's last surviving ferry over to Ohio for dinner. The **Sistersville Ferry** has been in continuous operation for almost 200 years and still operates between April and October when the river is not flooding.

If you want modern accommodations, drive to nearby **North Bend State Park,** near Cairo. This family-oriented, 1,405-acre park stretches along the banks of the Hughes River and has a beautiful twenty-nine-room lodge, with restaurant, as well as eight deluxe cottages. The park offers the usual array of outdoor amenities, with one special surprise: a playground designed for visually impaired and physically challenged children.

Another option is the **Rose Hill Inn Bed and Breakfast** in Pennsboro. The 1860s-era home boasts five guest rooms, a large continental breakfast, and a great view overlooking the **North Bend Rail Trail,** which runs along the old B&O Railroad line between Parkersburg and Wolf Summit near Clarksburg. It's part of the larger American Discovery Trail, which runs clear across the nation. This gravel section of the path passes through wooded park, farmland, and thirteen tunnels. If you're staying at Rose Hill, you'll be happy to know that they operate a small bike repair shop and shuttle business. B&B rates are $70 to $75 for a room with a private bath. Call (304) 659–3488 for reservations and information.

The Longest-Running Picture House in America: The Robey

You won't get Surround Sound or a selection of movies, but the old Robey Theatre in downtown Spencer has the charm of soda fountain drinks, a wide screen, and a history you won't find at other movie houses. The theater, which opened in June 1907, lays claim to being the oldest continuously running movie theater in the nation.

When Hamond Robey opened the theater during Spencer's oil and gas boom days, people had read about moving pictures, but most had never seen one. They turned out two or three times a week to see the same movie (for 10 cents), and it wasn't uncommon for the theater to run a show four or five times a day to accommodate the crowds.

Compared to other movie theaters, the Robey is still a few dollars cheaper, and its candy costs only $1.50. To stay afloat in this small town, owner Mike Burch rents videos from the backstage area by day.

The theater went through five name changes—Dreamland, Wonderland, Lyric, Auditorium, and the Robey—and traded locations on Main Street three times. It was one of the first theaters in the state to install sound equipment for the "talkies."

During its 1926 renovations, the Robey temporarily set up as a "Tentatorium," showing movies in a tent on the high school athletic field for a few months. During that time, actor Hoo Ray of *Our Gang* fame dropped by to do a live dance performance.

Although innovations have transformed some parts of the Robey's operations, the artifacts remain. The projection room still has the fireproof doors from the days when film was made with flammable nitrate, and a toilet still sits in the corner from the days before projectionists had automatic film systems.

Although the Robey's 400 seats are seldom filled in this small town, owner Burch hopes he can keep the Robey going at least until 2007, when the theater turns one hundred. General admission tickets are now $5.00; children get in for $3.00.

For current movies, call (304) 927–1390.

Or, if you still have plenty of daylight ahead of you, head south from Harrisville on State Route 16, then turn on State Route 53 and then State Route 5 to **Burning Springs.** This circuitous route through the rolling countryside takes you to the banks of the Little Kanawha River and the site where Confederate soldiers burned what was in 1863 one of the three major oil fields in the world. Nestled in the green hollows of Wirt County, this spot, because of its value to Federal troops (it provided oil for machinery and illumination), was burned on the direction of General Robert E. Lee. It burned with such ferocity that the river became, as locals described, "a sheet of fire." More than 300,000 barrels of oil were destroyed, as well as every sawmill, business, and private dwelling in Burning Springs, a city with 10,000 residents at the time.

Bluegrass Heartland

The moniker here applies to both the predominant music and the landscape of bucolic Calhoun and Roane Counties—agricultural areas rich in timber, pastureland, and old-time musicians.

The routes given here take a bit of pioneer spirit if you are to discover the treasures of life hidden off the interstates. So grab a cup of coffee and a road map and give yourself some time, for there's much to see in this quiet and pretty corner of West Virginia.

After you leave Burning Springs on Route 5, jump over onto State Route 14 and head into Roane County to *Spencer,* where, in the middle of October, the locals are celebrating their black walnut harvest in grand style. They host a four-day festival complete with singing, dancing, fiddling, turkey calling, flea markets, black walnut bake-offs, and the nuttiest parade you've ever seen. If you need a break, check what's playing at the old *Robey Theatre,* one of the nation's most economical spots for movies and movie food. The Robey opened in 1907 as a vaudeville house, making it one of the oldest continuously operating theaters in the nation. Nearby *Arnoldsburg,* in Calhoun County, is also busy in late September celebrating the *West Virginia Molasses Festival,* an event dripping with homegrown mountain music and delicious food.

In this part of the state, there are many wonderful places to shop, but don't look for any malls. Stores are tucked away—small gems just waiting for the adventurous shopper. One of them is found just south of Arnoldsburg on Route 16 in the town of *Chloe.* Here you'll uncover some of the country's finest basket weaving, resulting in baskets that sell for anywhere from $20 to $3,500. Local artisans Tom and Connie McColley, for instance, have a studio where Tom also specializes in turned wooden bowls. The *McColley Studio and Basketry School* is open by appointment only. If you're lucky, the McColleys might entertain you with a demonstration of their meticulous craftsmanship in West Virginia white oak. Call ahead for tours and times at (304) 655–7429. Sales of the studio's work are handled by the Poplar Forest Co-op in Flatwoods.

Places to Stay in the Mid-Ohio Valley

CAIRO

Log House Homestead B&B
Homestead Cove Lane
(304) 628–3249
www.loghousehomestead
.com
Moderate to expensive

North Bend State Park
Exit 176 off
U.S. Highway 50
(304) 643–2931
www.northbendsp.com
Inexpensive

PARKERSBURG

Blennerhassett Hotel
Fourth and Market Streets
(304) 422–3131
(800) 262–2536
Moderate

Comfort Suites
Interstate 77 and State
Route 14 South, exit 170
(304) 489–9600
Moderate

Historic Harnett House
1024 Juliana Street
(304) 483–1029
www.harnetthouse.com
Moderate

Manor Retreat & Conference Center
1016 Market Street
(304) 422–4277
www.themanorretreatand
conference.org
Moderate

Old Carriage House B&B
118 Twelfth Street
(304) 428–9588
www.oldcarriagehouse.com
Moderate

Places to Eat in the Mid-Ohio Valley

PARKERSBURG

Spat's at the Blennerhassett
Fourth and Market Streets
(304) 422–3131
Moderate

Third Street Deli
403 Third Street
(304) 422–0003
Moderate

PENNSBORO

P&H Family Restaurant
206 Kimball Avenue
(304) 659–3241
Budget

WILLIAMSTOWN

Da Vinci's Restaurant
215 Highland Avenue
(304) 375–3633
www.villadavinci.com
Inexpensive

FOR MORE INFORMATION

Parkersburg/Wood County Visitors and Convention Bureau
(304) 428–1130 or (800) 752–4982

Ritchie County Tourism
(888) 379–7873
www.visitritchiecounty.com

Northern Panhandle

Like neighboring Pennsylvania, the Northern Panhandle of West Virginia is a region of intensive mining, industry, and agriculture. It's an oddly shaped region whose northernmost point is actually closer to Canada than it is to the southern border of West Virginia. The four "Yankee" counties of West Virginia—Marshall, Ohio, Brooke, and Hancock—and the two counties of Tyler and Wetzel collectively make up the Northern Panhandle region. All of the Northern Panhandle proper lies north of the Mason-Dixon Line (Tyler and Wetzel counties are south of the line), and the residents here tend to have strong affiliations with such nearby northeastern industrial cities as Pittsburgh and Cleveland. Although industrial, the Northern Panhandle is also surprisingly green, with heavy forests, gentle hills, and fertile pastureland found along the Ohio River. The city of Wheeling is the industrial hub of the region.

Prehistoric man left his imprint on West Virginia in a grand fashion at *Grave Creek Mound,* a massive burial site located in the village of Moundsville. The Adena people, a native Indian tribe, were common to this part of West Virginia and what is now Indiana, Kentucky, Ohio, and Pennsylvania during the Woodland Period, an era lasting from about 1000 B.C. to A.D. 700. The Adena, a hunter-gatherer society, were referred to as

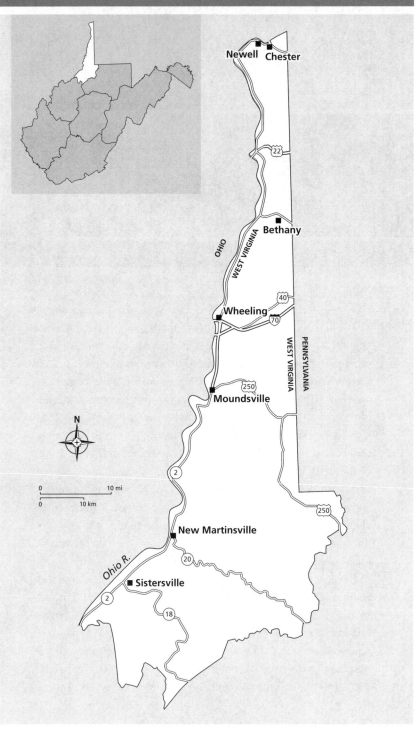

the "mound builders" on account of their passion for constructing earthen burial mounds and other earthworks. Grave Creek Mound, now part of the West Virginia State Parks system, is the largest and certainly the most impressive of the Adena mounds and is probably the largest conical type of mound ever built. The mound measures 69 feet high; the diameter at the base is 295 feet. The mound was also once encircled by a 40-foot-wide, 5-foot-deep moat. In all, about 60,000 tons of earth were moved in the building of the burial place.

Grave Creek Mound, which dates from 250 B.C., took more than 100 years to build, as evidenced by the multiple burial levels found here. Most of those buried here were probably cremated at death, placed in small log tombs, and covered with earth. Important members of society were often buried in the flesh and laid to rest with valuable personal belongings such as flints, beads, mica, copper ornaments, and pipes.

The story of the Adena and the mounds is told at the adjoining *Delf Norona Museum,* which has an exhaustive collection of Adena and Hopewell culture artifacts, including an inscribed sandstone tablet (whose meaning has been guessed at by a number of amateurs and professionals) found in the mound during the first excavation in 1838. A gift shop is located in the museum complex. The museum and park are open year-round, except for major holidays, from 10:00 A.M. to 4:00 P.M. Monday through Saturday and 1:00 to 5:00 P.M. Sunday. There is a $3.00 admission charge. Call (304) 843–4128 for more information.

Just across the street from Delf Norona is one of the 500 best places to visit in the United States, according to *U.S. News & World Report.* The **West Virginia State Penitentiary** is a defunct maximum-security prison, closed in 1995 after

BEST ANNUAL EVENTS IN THE NORTHERN PANHANDLE REGION

Celtic Festival
Wheeling; early March
(304) 233–7709 or (800) 828–3097

Jamboree in the Hills
Wheeling; mid-July
(304) 234–0050 or (800) 624–5456
www.jamboreeinthehills.com

Oil and Gas Festival
Sistersville; mid-September
(304) 652–1312 or 2939

Marble Festival
Sistersville; late September
(304) 652–4030

Oglebayfest
Wheeling; early October
(304) 243–4010 or (800) 624–6988
www.oglebay-resort.com

Winter Festival of Lights
Wheeling
November 1 through January 2
(304) 243–4000

A Penitentiary Experience

In West Virginia you can have the experience of going to prison without ever breaking the law. No, state troopers aren't unduly severe with speeders—the old West Virginia State Penitentiary in Moundsville is now a tourist attraction. Its doors were shut to felons in 1995 after the West Virginia Supreme Court ruled its standard 5-foot-by-7-foot cells were cruel and unusual punishment. (In the 1950s, inmates had been triple-bunked in these tiny cells.)

Nowadays, the 1866 Gothic fieldstone prison makes for an eerie tour, with its execution area and Old Sparky, the electric chair constructed by an inmate. Those who visit the facility (Tuesday through Sunday between April 1 and November 15) will see the guns used by guards, the isolation cells on North Hall where the worst inmates were confined, and the area where sixteen correctional officers were taken hostage during a 1986 riot.

Depending upon your tour guide, often a former guard, you'll learn about the personalities of individual prisoners, famous escapes, the workings of the prison coal mine, and other stories.

the inmates sued the state over deplorable living conditions. You understand their perspective within minutes after passing through the high-walled Gothic prison. The Pen still casts a sinister presence over Moundsville and has been called one of the most haunted places in America. All of the cells have original graffiti, and you get the chance to be locked behind bars briefly, if that's what you like. The tour's highlight is Old Sparky, the state's original electric chair. Sparky was responsible for nine executions before West Virginia outlawed capital punishment.

In addition to the regular tours, adventuresome visitors can now participate in monthly overnight "ghost hunts" with flashlight tours, spooky movies, and pizza. To register visit www.pentours.com or call (304) 845–6200. Regular tours are conducted Tuesday through Sunday April 1 through November 15 at 10:00 A.M., noon, and 2:00 P.M. and cost $8.00 for adults and $5.00 for children under eleven. Groups can schedule midnight tours that last until dawn. The annual Elizabethtown Festival is held within the gates in mid-May.

After this experience you may need to see a bit of the lighter side of life to balance your psyche. You can find that at the *Marx Toy Museum,* a few blocks away at 915 Second Street. This place is rigged out like a child's dream Christmas in the 1940s or '50s. You'll encounter legions of action figures, play sets, and other toys, all from the former Marx factory. The museum is open April through December on Thursday through Sunday afternoon. Admission is $6.50 for adults and $4.25 for children. Call (304) 845–6022 for more information.

Another good stop in Moundsville is the ***Fostoria Glass Museum*** on Sixth Street, where you can see 37,000 pieces of crystal from the famed company's one-hundred-year existence. Some of these one-of-a-kind pieces were made by employees experimenting during their lunch break. The factory, abandoned in 1986, stands several blocks away. At one time Fostoria was the largest producer of handmade glass in the nation, employing more than 1,000 people. Its American pattern, introduced in 1915, is still being made by Lancaster Colony. The museum is open Thursday through Saturday from 1:00 to 4:00 P.M., and admission is $4.00. Call (304) 845–9188 for other information about Fostoria.

If you like the glitter of Fostoria crystal, just wait until you see the next stop on the tour, the ***Palace of Gold*** in New Vrindaban, a 10-mile trip northeast of Moundsville, in the steep green hills of Marshall County.

Baby Boomer Dream Museum

If the baby boomer going into his senior years with the most toys wins, then Francis Turner is the state champion, hands-down. By his count, Turner owns at least 300 Marx play sets and hundreds of other vintage Marx tin and plastic toys, including Ben Hur, Robin Hood, and the Giant Blue and Gray, in his Moundsville Marx Toy Museum.

Ironically, Turner never owned one of the West Virginia–produced toys until he was well into middle age.

"In those days it was hard to justify buying a new play set for $12.95 when the family car cost only $10," Turner said. Turner never laid a hand on a Marx toy in rural West Virginia. None of his friends could afford them either.

Turner didn't have the Marx experience until 1982, when he impulsively bid $500 for three rooms of unseen items at a Marx factory going-out-of-business auction. He planned to resell the tools, workbenches, and other industrial items. The boxes of mint-condition toys were incidental.

"I gave away the toys to kids or sold them at flea markets. I didn't know what I had," Turner said.

Turner was hitting himself in the head later when he found out the value of his toys. By the 1990s, he was an ardent collector of Marx toys and multiple-figure play sets. Turner owns play sets for the Revolutionary and Civil Wars, as well as the Untouchables and other valuable collections. He has service stations, construction sites, western towns, firehouses, and dollhouses complete with all the accessories.

Turner's museum, on Second Street in Moundsville, includes not only legions of Marx action figures and other toys, but footage from the once nearby factory showing how Marx toys are made. The museum, he says, honors not so much the toys, but the creators—Louis Marx and his employees—whose labors touched many of the children of the baby boomer generation.

Palace of Gold

During the late 1960s, when religious and alternative lifestyle communes were cropping up throughout isolated and "live and let live" Appalachia, the Hare Krishnas came to this rural stretch of the Northern Panhandle and forever changed the complexion of the place. Between 1973 and 1979, Krishna devotees built this extraordinary palace as a memorial to Srila Prabhupada, founder of the religious movement. Today some one hundred residents maintain the sprawling palace—nicknamed America's Taj Mahal—and the surrounding 5,000-acre estate. A tour of the 3,000-square-foot palace includes stops in the west gallery, a room bedecked with marble flooring, giant stained-glass windows, and chandeliers, as well as a peek into the temple room with its awesome mural containing 4,000 crystals depicting Lord Krishna's life, radiating from the 25-foot-high dome ceiling.

The whole project, from architecture through inlay, was a challenge for unskilled devotees armed with how-to books and courage. The palace is a stunning tribute to the power of devotion. Ritual swan boats rock in a domed boat house, and peacocks strut along the shore. The sign by the lodge spells out the desired ambience here: YOU ARE ENTERING A SACRED PLACE. NO SMOKING OR INTOXICANTS. NO NON-VEGETARIAN FOODS. PLEASE KEEP THE GROUNDS CLEAN. Vast gardens and smaller temples are spread over the compound, which visitors are allowed to roam at will. If you have images of Krishnas hounding guests, don't fret; this is a laid-back experience where visitors can tour without intrusions. You may be invited to a midday meditation and curry meal, but efforts to proselytize are restrained. It's a bit surreal, maybe even excessive, but there's certainly nothing else like the Palace of Gold in West Virginia or, for that matter, the nation.

The palace and grounds are located off U.S. Highway 250 in a gorgeous setting of lush hills and pastures. Tours are available daily from April through

August, 10:00 A.M. to 8:00 P.M., and from September through March, 10:00 A.M. to 5:00 P.M. The snack bar is open May through October, noon to 4:30 P.M. during weekdays and noon to 8:00 P.M. on weekends. Adult admission to the palace is $6.00; ages six to eighteen, $3.00; young children are admitted free. Overnight accommodations are available in cottages or lodges for $30 per room or $150 to $200 per cottage. Meals are provided on a donation basis. For more information call (304) 843–1812 or (304) 845–5905.

There's a tendency among folks who've never been to West Virginia to dismiss **Wheeling** as an industrial has-been, a Rust Belt relic with little or no tourism appeal. Nothing could be further from the truth. Not only is Wheeling loaded with interesting historical and cultural diversions, but it's also a beautiful city with one of the highest concentrations of Victorian homes in the country, lovely parks (including 1,500-acre Oglebay Park, one of the largest and more heavily used municipal parks in the country), a scenic riverfront, and graceful tree-lined neighborhoods.

This northern city is the birthplace of West Virginia statehood, and you can retrace those tense pre–Civil War times at **Independence Hall**, Sixteenth and Market Streets downtown. This stately 1859 Italian Renaissance building was easily the most state-of-the-art structure in Wheeling at the time of the secession debates, claiming both flush toilets and an air-circulating system, a predecessor to modern air-conditioning. The cooling effect was needed for the heated debates that sprung up here in 1861, when it was decided that the western region

BEST ATTRACTIONS IN THE NORTHERN PANHANDLE REGION

Jamboree U.S.A., Capitol Music Hall
Wheeling
(304) 232–1170
(800) 624–5456
www.jamboreeusa.com

Independence Hall
Wheeling
(304) 238–1300
www.wvculture.org

Wheeling Artisan Center
Wheeling
(304) 233–4555

Oglebay's Stifel Fine Arts Center
Wheeling
(304) 242–7700
(888) 696–4283
www.oionline.com

West Virginia State Penitentiary
Moundsville
(304) 845–6200
www.wvpentours.com

of Virginia would break free from the rest of the Old Dominion and form its own Union-aligned state, the Reformed State of Virginia. From 1861 to 1863 the Customs House (as it was called then) served as the state capitol. In 1863 President Lincoln declared West Virginia the thirty-fifth state in the Union. Following official statehood the capital moved to Charleston, and the three-story building fell into a number of other uses, including a post office and federal court.

In 1912 Independence Hall was restored, and today it houses exhibits relating to the state's history along with period rooms, an interpretive film, and, from time to time, special historical reenactments. Admission price is $3.00 for adults, $2.00 for students, and free for children under six. Group tours with Miss Busbey, an 1860s-attired docent, are $3.00 a person but require a minimum of seven people. Smaller groups may purchase the guided tour for a flat fee of $20. The newest exhibit, on the first floor, is *West Virginia: Born of the Civil War.* Independence Hall is open daily year-round from 10:00 A.M. to 4:00 P.M. except for Sunday. Call (304) 238–1300.

The Mountain State has always been a hotbed for country music, producing both large audiences and more than its share of performers who've moved on to Nashville. Wheeling is the state's undisputed music capital, thanks to the ongoing success of **Jamboree U.S.A.,** the second-oldest live-radio show in the nation. Every Saturday night since 1933, the country music show has been broadcast over radio station WWVA to fans along the eastern seaboard and six Canadian provinces. The first show was broadcast on April 1 at midnight at Wheeling's Capitol Theatre; the cost of attending was a whopping 25 cents.

In 1969 the wildly popular show, featuring the rising and established stars of Nashville, moved to its present location at the luxurious **Capitol Music Hall,** 1015 Main Street. Lodged in the middle of downtown, the 2,500-seat theater is heralded for its acoustics and intimate seating. Performers who've graced the stage over the past few years include the likes of Willie Nelson, Styx, Trace Adkins, the Oak Ridge Boys, Frankie Avalon, Sammy Kershaw, John Michael Montgomery, Tanya Tucker, Ricky Van Shelton, and the Charlie Daniels Band. *Jamboree U.S.A.'s* own 11–70 band deserves a hearty round of applause for the way it serves up country, rockabilly, and bluegrass. Tickets to the shows, almost as coveted as those for West Virginia University football games, are available by calling (800) 624–5456 or dropping by the box office on Main Street. Tickets typically start at about $10 and work their way up, depending on the performer.

After the show, you can head over a few blocks to **Ernie's Cork & Bottle,** 39 Twelfth Street, for a fabulous Greek kabob or steak and probably the best salad bar in the Northern Panhandle. The bar, resembling something out of New Orleans' French Quarter, stays open until 4:00 A.M. Sunday through Friday nights and until 3:00 A.M. on Saturday nights, with live jazz or acoustic rock for those who can't get enough music. You can also grab a burger or a Cajun-influenced chicken sandwich and wash it down with one of the many wines on hand, including some native West Virginia vintages. The restaurant is open daily from 11:00 A.M. to midnight and on weekends until 2:00 A.M. Reservations are accepted and encouraged on weekends. Call (304) 232–4400.

Within a few blocks of the Capitol Music Hall, you can stroll the magnificent Victorian homes district. If your idea of nirvana is literally shopping till you drop, then head over to the ***Eckhart House Tours and Gift Shoppe,*** 810 Main, where you can browse through an assortment of exquisite handmade arts, crafts, and furniture; stroll through the interior design studio; and then tour some of the area's Victorian homes. Home tours, high teas, and dinners may be arranged through the Eckhart House. Tours leave at 1:00 P.M. Wednesday through Saturday, May through December. Call in advance for tour or dinner arrangements at (304) 232–5439 or (888) 700-0118.

You really mustn't leave the Wheeling area without a stop at the ***Wheeling Island Racetrack and Gaming Center,*** if only to listen to the music of the gaming machines and sample the seventy-item Islander Buffet. This will give you a chance to drive over the ***Wheeling Suspension Bridge,*** the first bridge over the Ohio River and, at the time of its construction (1849), the longest single-span suspension bridge in the world. With its striking arched stone entrances, the bridge is considered the nation's most important pre–Civil War engineering structure.

The Northern Panhandle's other toy museum, ***Kruger Street Toy and Train Museum,*** engenders a special fondness from train lovers. If the lemon-yellow 1926 Baltimore & Ohio caboose C-2019 in the yard doesn't signal the founders' passion for trains, the O-gauge train layout filling an entire room should. In the middle 1970s Allan Robert Miller and his son, Allan Raymond, began actively collecting Lionel toy trains. By the early 1980s, the collection had expanded to include Louis Marx trains, then all toys by Marx and others—classic 1950s play sets, dolls, dollhouses, and other items. They virtually grew out of the house. A museum seemed the natural mode of displaying the extensive collection, and the Victorian schoolhouse at 144 Kruger Street in the Elm Grove section of Wheeling was the perfect fit. The museum has hosted the Marx Toy and Train Collectors National Convention and visiting collections of Mego and NASCAR toys. Toys, trains, and other mementos are on sale in the gift shop. The museum is open from 10:00 A.M. to 5:00 P.M. daily June through December and 9:00 A.M. to 5:00 P.M. Friday, Saturday, and Sunday the rest of the year. Admission is $8.00 for adults, $7.00 for seniors, and $5.00 for students. Children under ten are free. For specific information call (340) 242–8133 or (877) 242–8133.

Pickin' and Fiddlin'

Nashville may claim the title of Music City, USA, but the seeds of American country music were planted in the fertile mountain hollows of southern Appalachia, far from the neon glow of Music Row. Music scholars will give credit to such places as Galax, Virginia; Bristol, Tennessee; and Monticello, Kentucky, as well as the coal camps and logging towns of central and southern West Virginia.

The roots of country music date from seventeenth-century Ireland and came to the Appalachians with the Scots-Irish settlers a century later. Those Irish ballads, jigs, and reels were transformed into distinctly American mountain music, which evolved into old-time string music and bluegrass, country, and honky-tonk sounds. Although today's prevailing Nashville sound has strayed far from its roots, you can still hear real mountain music throughout the southern Appalachians, especially at the festivals, music parks, and picking parlors of the Mountain State.

For examples of this, check out the Allegheny Echoes workshops in Pocahontas County (304–799–7121), the Appalachian String Band Festival at Clifftop (304–558–0220), and the Augusta Heritage Center in Elkins (800–624–3157). You may also want to take in Charleston's Vandalia Festival, the Sunday jams at Kanawha County Library in Charleston, the Mountain State Arts and Crafts Fair in Ripley, Spencer's Black Walnut Festival, and the Wednesday-night jams at Davis and Elkins College's Hermanson Center.

More informal gatherings are tucked away in country stores, campgrounds, and coffeehouses. They're not hard to find. Just inquire at any local music store, or, if the area is very rural, any store. You're bound to find a pickin' parlor or a front porch fiddlin' within a short drive.

Toys still captivate the adult heart, all right, but some grown-up boys (and girls) prefer the bigger, louder toys at *Cabela's* massive outdoor store. The 175,000-square-foot mecca for outdoor enthusiasts features giant aquariums of freshwater fish that you seem to walk through, as well as an indoor mountain, an archery range, and herds of wildlife specimens in a naturalistic setting. Oh yeah, and there's stuff for sale, too. The retail departments include camping, hunting, fishing, marine equipment, all-terrain vehicles, boots, clothing, a bargain cave, a general store, and a 180-seat restaurant. Cabela's sits on a 110-acre site near the Dallas Pike exit of Interstate 70.

Wheeling's most popular destination, *Oglebay Resort,* can keep a family busy for days. In a setting of 1,650 pastoral acres, Oglebay offers a zoo, two museums, three restaurants, 212 lodge rooms, 49 deluxe cottages, trails, gardens, seven specialty shops, an art gallery, a laser show, stables, tennis, fishing, and seventy-two holes of golf. It's also a municipal park—one of the largest in the nation. Oglebay is known for its stunning Winter Festival of Lights, Easter egg hunt, flower show, and golf tournaments on its Arnold Palmer course. Oglebay is located on State Route 88 North. For more information call (800) 624–6988 or (304) 243–4000 or go to www.oglebay-resort.com.

Continue north on Route 88 through the peaceful countryside and you'll come to West Liberty, where you will usually find the ***Women's History Museum*** at 108 Walnut Street. Usually, but not always. Because this museum is on wheels, interpreter Jeanne Schramm occasionally drives it off to schools or festivals. In fact, Schramm can be very much a part of the show; she does costumed portrayals of feminist Susan B. Anthony, union activist Mother Jones, author Julia Ward Howe, and other famous women. But even without Schramm's spirited interpretation, the exhibit stands powerfully on its own through signed documents, letters, portraits, and even hair from twenty women who made a difference in U.S. history. Among the offerings are a Planned Parenthood pamphlet signed by Margaret Sanger, a handwritten poem by Harriet Beecher Stowe, a Christmas card signed by Helen Keller, and recordings of the voices of Sanger, Keller, Florence Nightingale, Jane Addams, Eleanor Roosevelt, and Carrie Chapman Catt. The museum is usually open from 10:00 A.M. to 2:00 P.M. on Saturday, but it is wise to check by calling (304) 336–7159. Admission is $1.00 per adult and 50 cents for children twelve and younger.

The urban facade of Wheeling gives way to peaceful countryside as you wend your way up Route 88 to the historic village of Bethany. Here you'll find

northern panhandle trivia

The Ohio River, which first flows into the Mountain State near the town of Chester, actually begins in Pittsburgh, Pennsylvania, at the confluence of the Allegheny and Monongahela Rivers.

OTHER ATTRACTIONS WORTH SEEING IN THE NORTHERN PANHANDLE REGION

Oglebay Resort and Museum
Wheeling

Homer Laughlin China Company
Newell

Wheeling Downs
Wheeling

Fostoria Glass Museum
Moundsville

the redbrick, Gothic-influenced **Bethany College,** a prestigious liberal arts institution that conjures up images of the film *Dead Poets Society*. Dominating the ivy-covered and tree-lined campus, the oldest in West Virginia, is "Old Main," a National Historic Landmark with a 122-foot tower and central building of brick and stone stretching more than 400 feet and punctuated by five arched entrances. It was styled after a similar structure at the University of Glasgow in Scotland.

Also on the college grounds is the **Alexander Campbell Mansion,** the home of Bethany College's founder and a leading figure in the nineteenth-century religious movement that spawned the Disciples of Christ, Churches of Christ, and Christian Church. The impressive, twenty-five-room home was built in four periods, beginning in 1793, and entertained such important figures of the day as Henry Clay, Daniel Webster, Jefferson Davis, and James Garfield. The mansion is open Tuesday through Saturday, typically from 10:00 A.M. to noon and 1:00 to 4:00 P.M., and Sunday from 2:00 to 4:00 P.M., April through October. The rest of the year, tours can be arranged by calling (304) 829–4258.

While on campus you may also want to see the nineteenth-century **Pendleton Heights,** the college president's house, as well as the **Old Bethany Meeting House** and the **Delta Tau Delta Founders' House.**

About a thirty-minute drive north of Bethany puts you in the Chester/ Newell area, the top of the Mountain State. This part of the Northern Panhandle is barely 5 miles wide. Although famous for its Mountaineer Race Track and Gaming Resort and its house-size teapot, this region has also garnered a respectful reputation for its **Homer Laughlin Fiestaware.** The world's largest manufacturer of dinnerware—from china for White House banquet tables to the art deco Fiestaware prized by collectors and recently reissued in new colors, the Newell-based Homer Laughlin plant has produced quality china for 134 years. You can watch this bold china coming off the assembly line during plant tours Monday through Thursday at 10:30 A.M. and 12:30 P.M. and buy economically priced dinnerware at the outlet store, open 9:30 A.M. to 5:00 P.M. Monday through Saturday and Sunday from noon to 5:00 P.M. For more information call (800) HL–CHINA.

There's a range of accommodations up here in the northern tip of West Virginia—from camping in nature at Tomlinson Run State Park to deluxe rooms at Mountaineer Race Track and Gaming Resort, where the lights never go off.

Not everyone who likes an occasional night in the woods invests in a tent, cookstove, and all the other necessary paraphernalia. Realizing this, **Tomlinson Run State Park** recently constructed four weather-tight canvas yurts to accommodate carefree campers. Each little round hut is equipped with one or two bunk beds, a lantern, propane stove, cookware, cooler, and picnic table, all for under $55 a night. A convenience store and bathhouse with hot showers are a short stroll away. During the day, you can fish, play miniature golf, hike, or swim. The campground is open April 1 to October 31 and features melodious wake-up calls by songbirds. For reservations, call (800) CALL–WVA.

At the other extreme stands *Grande Hotel at Mountaineer Race Track and Gaming Resort* in Chester. The resort features 3,220 slot machines, a year-round thoroughbred racetrack, golf course, theater, spa, fitness center, indoor pool, and four restaurants. Each of the expansive guest rooms is equipped with fluffy bathrobes, oatmeal soap, and all the amenities. If you don't feel like sleeping, you can usually party till dawn at the Roaring Twenties theme casino. For hotel prices and reservations, call (800) 489–8192.

Anyone for a Large Spot of Tea?

In the middle of the intersection of West Virginia Routes 2 and 30 north of Chester sits the world's largest teapot, its claim to fame emblazoned on its sides. This chunk of kitsch lured bargain hunters into Devon's pottery outlet during the golden years of highway travel before interstates.

The 14-foot teapot was erected in 1938 by William "Babe" Devon in front of his Chester shop on Route 2. Rumor has it that the teapot is actually a hogshead barrel used in a Hires Root Beer publicity campaign, with a spout and a tin covering added. Nevertheless, for almost fifty years, the teapot coaxed tourists to shop for Fiestaware and other locally produced china. The teapot served as a natural symbol for the region's leading industry, and the home of the world's largest pottery plant and manufacturer of dinnerware, Homer Laughlin. The mile-long plant is located just a few miles down the road.

In 1987 the deteriorating teapot was in danger of demolition. After a grassroots Save the Teapot campaign, the teapot was donated to the city of Chester, and renovation began. In 1990 the world's largest teapot was moved to its present location beside the ramp to Jennings Randolph Bridge.

Places to Stay in the Northern Panhandle

CHESTER

Grande Hotel at Mountaineer Race Track and Gaming Resort
(304) 387–8300
www.mtrgaming.com
Moderate to expensive

GLEN DALE

Bonnie Dwaine Bed & Breakfast
505 Wheeling Avenue
(304) 845–7250
Moderate

WHEELING

Best Western Wheeling
949 Main Street
(304) 233–8500
(800) 528–1234
Inexpensive

Oglebay Resort
State Route 88 North
(800) 624–6988
(304) 243–4000
Moderate

Ramada Plaza City Center
1200 Market Street
(800) 862–5873
Moderate

Places to Eat in the Northern Panhandle

WHEELING

Abbey's Wheeling Island
145 Zane Street
(304) 233–0729
Moderate

Bella Via
1 Burkham Court
(304) 242–8181
Moderate

Coleman's Fish Market
Twenty-second and Market Streets
(304) 232–8510
Budget

Oglebay Resort, Ihlenfeld Dining Room
State Route 88 North
(304) 243–4000
Moderate

River City Ale Works
(Artisan Center at Heritage Square)
1400 Main Street
(304) 233–4555
Inexpensive

FOR MORE INFORMATION

Wheeling Convention and Visitors Bureau
(304) 233–7709 or (800) 828–3097
www.wheelingcvb.com

Hancock County Convention and Visitors Bureau
(304) 564–4800

Mountaineer Country

Mountaineer Country, probably because of its industrial and coal-mining heritage, is also the most ethnically diverse part of the state, with particularly large Italian and Polish populations. Of course, ethnic festivals and eateries are popular here, and the astute traveler won't ever leave hungry.

Traveling north on Interstate 79 into Harrison County, have a look at what early American farm life was like. Between Lost Creek and West Milford lies **Watters Smith Memorial State Park,** a 523-acre farm established in 1796 on land originally patented by Patrick Henry and owned by four generations of the Watters Smith family, pioneers in this region. It still contains a hand-hewn eighteenth-century livestock barn, carpenter and blacksmith shops, a modest 130-year-old home built by a Smith family descendant, and a small museum with frontier farm equipment. Start at the visitor center, then take the self-guided tour. After you've learned a bit of history, cool off in the swimming pool located in the park's recreation area. Then maybe go horseback riding or at least visit the "adoptable" steeds. Docent tours are conducted from 11:00 A.M. to 7:00 P.M. every day of the week from Memorial Day through Labor Day. Tours at other times of the year are available by reservation only. Small

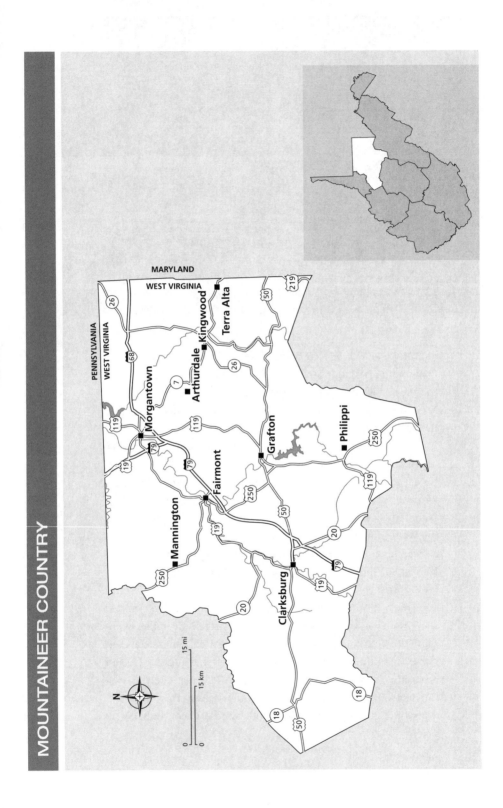

MOUNTAINEER COUNTRY

donations are accepted. Call (304) 745–3081 or see www.watterssmithstate park.com.

From here, you're only about 10 miles south of Clarksburg, one of the prettiest and most historic cities in the state. Just off the interstate, it's at the intersection of U.S. Highways 19 and 50. Clarksburg was established in 1785 and is, among other things, the birthplace of native son Stonewall Jackson. One of the best places to get started on your tour of the city is downtown at *Waldomore,* an 1839 Greek-revival mansion that houses exhibits and information on West Virginia history and culture. It's chock-full of museum-quality pieces from the mid-1800s and holds works by local authors and historical documents from the life and times of Stonewall Jackson.

Also of note at Waldomore is the *Gray Barker UFO Collection,* one of the nation's largest undentified flying object exhibits, featuring documents from investigations and sightings as well as a slew of provocative photographs, official records, and correspondence among various international UFO societies. As you might imagine, West Virginia's rural nature—and amazingly dark nighttime skies—make it a rich trove for all things UFO. Buckhannon native Gray Barker amassed this large personal collection, and after his death Waldomore assembled it into a museum-quality collection, one that attracts folks from around the world. Waldomore and the Gray Barker UFO Collection are open Tuesday, Wednesday, and Friday 9:00 A.M. to 5:00 P.M.; Thursday 1:00 to 8:00 P.M.; and Saturday 9:00 A.M. to noon. David Houchin maintains the collection. Call ahead to be sure he is there; the hours fluctuate with his schedule. Telephone at (304) 627–2236 or e-mail houchin@hp9k.clark.lib.wv.us.

BEST ANNUAL EVENTS IN MOUNTAINEER COUNTRY

Arthurdale New Deal Festival
Arthurdale; second week in July
(304) 864–3959
www.arthurdaleheritage.org

Arts on the River Festival
Morgantown; mid-June
(800) 458–7373 or (304) 292–0168

West Virginia Italian Heritage Festival
Clarksburg; weekend before Labor Day
(304) 622–7314
www.wvihf.com

West Virginia University Mountaineer Football
Morgantown; September through December
(800) WVA–GAME

Buckwheat Festival
Kingwood; late September
(304) 329–0021
www.buckwheatfest.com

Mountaineer Balloon Festival
Morgantown; mid-October
(304) 296–8356

Also in the 16-block downtown historic district is the 1807 ***Stealey-Goff-Vance House,*** 123 West Main Street (304–842–3037; open May through September) with its large collection of Indian artifacts. On Main Street on the courthouse grounds is an impressive bronze sculpture, *The Immigrants,* a tribute to the Belgian, Czech, Greek, Hungarian, Irish, Italian, Romanian, and Spanish immigrants who came to the Clarksburg area during the 1880s to work in the glass factories and coalfields. The monument conveys the spirit in which these diverse immigrants pulled together to form a harmonious community that still exists today.

Just north of Clarksburg on US 19 is the historic town of ***Shinnston,*** settled in 1778 when Levi Shinn built a home in the area. Today the town has a population of about 2,500. It supports several pizza places, as well as the ***Chapel of Perpetual Adoration,*** where people of all faiths can go for prayer any hour of any day. Shinnston is located at the southern terminus of the ***West Fork River Trail,*** a 16-mile-long path running north to Fairmont. On the north

Don't Worry; You're in West Virginia

When I considered walking the West Fork River Trail's 16 miles between Fairmont and Shinnston, I wasn't as concerned about my physical ability as my safety. Fairmont State College cyclists patrol the rail trail on bicycles daily, I knew; but would a solitary hiker be safe from human harm in the long stretches of lonely forest?

"Oh, honey, you're in West Virginia," said Kathleen Panek, owner of Gillum House B&B in Shinnston. "If you see a man on the trail, he's just going to ask if you're doing all right and if you need anything."

OK, I said, if you say so. But I pocketed my mace as I headed out of town along banks quivering with white trilliums. I saw kingfishers and a green heron trolling the West Fork River. (West Fork of what? It should be the Monongahela, but nobody says so.) I spied wild turkeys and a nesting goose, but no humans until I approached Monongah.

There, beside an abandoned coal yard, a young man with big tattoos on his arms was approaching me at a fast clip. Nobody else was in sight.

I clutched my mace in my pocket. He smiled. "How are you, ma'am? Been hiking long?"

"An hour or so."

"Bet you're thirsty. My house is right next to the trail behind the fire station. Nobody's home. Just go in the front door—it's unlocked—and get you a drink out of the fridge."

I thanked him and unclenched. Honey, you're in West Virginia.

BEST ATTRACTIONS IN MOUNTAINEER COUNTRY

Prickett's Fort State Park
Fairmont
(304) 363–3030

West Virginia Public Theatre
Morgantown
(304) 598–0144 or (877) 999–9878

Cheat River White-water Rafting
throughout the region
(800) CALL–WVA

Monongalia Arts Center
Morgantown
(304) 292–3325

side of Fairmont, you can connect with the McTrail to Prickett's Fort State Park, and from there to the Mon River Trail through Morgantown to the Pennsylvania border. Someday soon you'll be able to pedal a network of trails all the way to Pittsburgh, Pennsylvania, or Washington, D.C., should you choose such an aerobic holiday. But for many the West Fork River Trail is plenty, thank you, as it wends along its flat course past wildflowers and waterfalls through the company towns of Worthington, Enterprise, and Monongah.

With the active traveler in mind, *Gillum House Bed & Breakfast* can set up bicycle rentals, horse boarding, and shuttle services for those who want to do the scenic trail one-way. Horses get to enjoy the horse B&B (Wade Maley Stables) right on the rail trail, just minutes from the Gillum House, and owners get to meet Punjab the camel, who lives at the stables. Hosts Kathleen and John Panek also offer motorcycling inn-to-inn packages and will give you an itinerary of covered bridges, craft shops, glass outlets, and other interesting places to visit. They love the challenge of making breakfasts for special diets, so throw your requirements at them, whether they're sugarless, low-carb, low-fat, or gluten-free. Call (304) 592–0177 or (888) 592–0177.

West of Clarksburg on State Route 50 is the town of *Salem,* settled in 1792. This is a little city with an unusual history. It was settled by Seventh-Day Baptist families from New Jersey after a two-and-a-half-year journey westward in search of religious freedom.

Just east of Clarksburg on Route 50 is the little town of *Bridgeport.* Founded as a trading post in 1764, it still serves as a good spot to stop for a rest and a bite to eat. There are a number of national chain hotels/motels and restaurants along the highway, but for a real taste of local flavor, go shopping! Sample the local retail scene by stopping at *Shabady's,* a three-story antiques store filled to the rafters with quality glassware, art, housewares, and collectibles. Shahady's is open Tuesday through Saturday from 10:00 A.M. to 5:00 P.M. It's downtown, where there is quite a jumble of intriguing shops, including **Provence Market, A La Carte Chocolates,** and **Mustard Seed Primitives.** Call (304) 842–6691. You'll want to save a few coins to give to the folks at **West Virginia Mountain Products,** at I–79, Stonewood exit. Housed

The Mummies of Philippi

They spent much of their short lives hidden away in a mental hospital, but after death these women traveled widely. The mummies of Philippi, two women embalmed shortly after their deaths by a rural storekeeper and inventor, toured with P. T. Barnum's circus and got as far as Paris, France, in the late nineteenth century.

Now they are the most popular attraction at the Barbour County Historical Society Museum in Philippi. For a paltry $1.00, visitors can enter the former railroad station restroom to peep at the small, leathery women lying adorned with artificial flowers in their caskets.

They are preserved with Graham Hamrick's Mummifying Fluid; that's also stored in the museum, although a description of his patented formula is not. He claimed his formula was based on the recipe used in the embalming of Jacob in the Bible and that the ingredients were available in any country store.

The label on his embalming fluid reads: "Best in the World, Absolutely Prevents Decomposition, No Such Bleacher is Known, The Fluid that is Always Dependable. Antiseptic, Deodorizer, Disinfectant, Germicide." Hamrick said on his patent application that he wanted to offer a simpler, less expensive method of embalming. Descriptions of his process compare it to smoking meat.

Hamrick experimented with embalming vegetables and small animals for years before he drove his wagon to the West Virginia Hospital for the Insane in Weston and emerged with the cadavers of two unknown women. Mortuary officials examined the bodies two months later, noting they were perfectly preserved.

Old records suggest that Hamrick also preserved a baby's body, but that disintegrated in the flood of 1985. The mummified women were also damaged, and some say they were laid out on the post office lawn to dry. The mummies belonged to several private citizens before they were reclaimed by Philippi town officials for the museum. Exhibitions of the mummies have been used locally to raise money for scholarships and for the library.

The Barbour County Historical Society Museum is located in an old railroad station beside the Philippi covered bridge. Hours are 11:00 A.M. until 4:00 P.M. Monday through Saturday and 1:00 to 4:00 P.M. on Sunday, mid-May through mid-October. Arrangements for visiting the mummies at other times may be made by calling (304) 457–4846 or (304) 457–3349.

OTHER ATTRACTIONS WORTH SEEING IN MOUNTAINEER COUNTRY

Valley Falls State Park Fairmont	**Mon River Trail** Morgantown
Coopers Rock State Forest Bruceton Mills	**Anna Jarvis House** Grafton
Clarksburg Downtown **Historical District** Clarksburg	**Adaland Mansion** Philippi

in the old Quiet Dell School, this is the state's largest artisans' cooperative, rich with handmade quilts, stained glass, baskets, pottery, and dolls made by local artists. If your interests go beyond just admiring and purchasing the handiworks, you might want to watch one of the craft demonstrations held here throughout the year. Courses include basket weaving, ceramics, and stained-glass making. Hours are 10:00 A.M. to 5:00 P.M. Monday through Saturday and 1:00 to 5:00 P.M. Sunday. Call (800) 524–4043 or (304) 622–3304 for information.

Now put away those shopping bags and head south on State Route 76 into beautiful Barbour County. There's lots of water here, notably from the lower half of gigantic Tygart Lake. *Audra State Park,* south of the lake off U.S. Highway 119, contains the beautiful Middle Fork River, with its huge rocks for sunbathing and its clear, cool water for diving or kayaking. Meandering back to the north on U.S. Highway 250 places you in *Philippi,* the Barbour County seat. This is where you'll find a treasure of another kind—*Philippi Bridge,* one of the prettiest covered bridges in the country and certainly the most scenic south of New England. In fact, almost half of West Virginia's remaining covered bridges are in the Mountaineer Country region. The Philippi Bridge is located just west of town on US 119/250 and spans the width of the Tygart River. It's the only wooden covered bridge that is still a part of a federal highway, and it is also the state's oldest covered bridge, built in 1852. North and South fought the first land battle of the Civil War in Philippi on June 3, 1861, over this bridge. The battle, known in these parts as the Philippi Races because the Confederates retreated so fast, is now commemorated annually with a festival, reenactment, and footrace. The conflict was an easy victory for Union forces, who used the covered bridge as a barracks. Confederate soldier J. E. Hanger was the first man to lose a leg in the Civil War, but he gained a profession. Hanger was hit by a cannonball, had his leg amputated by a Union doctor, and later invented an artificial leg. He was asked to create wooden legs for other Confederate soldiers and eventually started a company that became one of the largest manufacturers of wooden legs in the world. A plaque in Philippi commemorates the fateful cannon blast. For more information about reenactments of the Battle of Philippi, call (304) 457–1225.

The **Barbour County Historical Society Museum,** home of the Philippi mummies, sits on the bank of the Tygart beside the bridge. Located in a renovated railroad station, the museum contains Civil War memorabilia, antiques, books, and the mummified remains of two women who lived in a Weston mental hospital. It's open Monday through Saturday 11:00 A.M. to 4:00 P.M. and Sunday 1:00 to 4:00 P.M., May 15 to October 15, and by appointment the rest of the year (304–457–4846).

For another glimpse of West Virginia history, go 4 miles north of Philippi to the **Adaland Mansion,** where you can tour a stately 1870 home and learn about crafts as they were practiced in the nineteenth century. Call (304) 457–1587 for more information. Adaland is open May 1 to December 31, Wednesday, Thursday, Saturday, and Sunday afternoons.

The Northern Heartland

Rich soil and scenery define this quiet corner of Mountaineer Country, which covers all of Preston, Taylor, and Marion Counties. From the south, the gateway to the region is **Grafton,** a tranquil, tree-lined community perched on the upper shores of Tygart Lake. Like most of the towns in the area, Grafton emerged along a wilderness road that opened this part of the Mountain State to civilization in the East. What is now US 50—the brainchild of French engineering genius Claude Crozet—runs through the middle of town. Crozet surveyed and blazed much of the wilderness road (which now extends from Maryland to California) and is credited with being one of the founders of Grafton.

Perhaps the most interesting sidelight here is a shrine that will go straight to the heart of any good mother and child. It's the **International Mother's Day Shrine,** located at Andrews Methodist Church on Main Street, about a mile south of the US 50/119 intersection. Grafton native Anna Jarvis is credited with organizing the first celebration of Mother's Day at the pretty redbrick church in 1908. Miss Jarvis, who was living in Philadelphia at the time, thought it would be a nice gesture to have the church where her mother taught Sunday school for more than twenty years recognize the first Mother's Day on the third anniversary of her mom's death.

The International Mother Day's Shrine, depicting a mother, infant, and small child, was erected adjacent to the 130-year-old church in 1962. A special

Mother's Day service is held at the church on that day each year at 2:30 P.M. Guided tours of the historic church and grounds are available year-round by special appointment. The church is also open to the public from April 15 through October 15 every Monday through Friday, 9:30 A.M. to 3:30 P.M. Call (304) 265–1589.

The restored farmhouse where Anna Jarvis was born is now a museum containing 5,000 period artifacts, ranging from Anna Jarvis's clothes to Civil War relics. To visit the **Anna Jarvis Birthplace Museum,** go 4 miles south of Grafton on US 119/250. It is open for tours March through December, Tuesday through Sunday, 10:00 A.M. to 6:00 P.M. Admission is $4.00 for adults and $2.00 for students. Call (304) 265–5549 for more details.

There's another important shrine in Grafton, albeit of a different sort. The **Grafton National Cemetery** is the final resting place for 1,251 Union and Confederate soldiers who fell victim to the violent clashes that broke out near Grafton, which was a strategic railroad center connecting the interior of West Virginia with Union supply and industrial plants in Parkersburg and Wheeling. The beautiful, maple-draped cemetery, dedicated in 1867, is open to the public year-round from dawn to dusk.

mountaineer countrytrivia

Mountaineer Country is the most ethnically diverse area of the state, with significant populations of residents of Italian, Polish, German, Czech, and Hungarian descent.

If you can grab some fishing line, a bobber, and some fresh night crawlers, head over to the trout pond at Fellowsville's **Cool Springs Park,** also located on US 50, just at the base of rugged Laurel Mountain. At the park you'll find a display of antique farm implements, including fascinating old tractors and threshing machines, reminders of the county's agricultural roots. The park's restaurant serves up a tasty hamburger, and after your meal you can browse through the adjoining gift shop, which is full of local arts and crafts. For information call (304) 454–9511.

From the park, continue east on US 50 for about another 20 miles to majestic **Cathedral State Park,** certainly one of West Virginia's most unusual natural attractions. Before the timber barons of the early twentieth century began exploiting the state's vast forests of pine and hardwoods, much of the West Virginia wilderness once looked like Cathedral State Park, a dense canopy of giant, towering trees. This 132-acre reserve, open for day-use only, contains virgin hemlocks and hardwoods, some measuring several feet in diameter and more than 100 feet tall. It's West Virginia's finest primeval forest, and because of its location right off US 50, it's also one of the nation's most accessible old-growth forests.

West Virginia: Birthplace of Mother's Day, Father's Day, and Grandparent's Day

Call them sentimental if you want, but give West Virginians credit for starting all three family holidays: Mother's Day, Father's Day, and Grandparent's Day. Whether it's the importance of family, the precariousness of life in mining towns, or the urge to memorialize loved ones, West Virginians were the first to make a day for it.

It all started with Mother's Day. Although Anna Marie Reeves Jarvis was memorialized by her daughter in the first known Mother's Day service in 1905, the elder Jarvis herself formed Mother's Day Friendship Clubs in Taylor County in the mid-1800s. She taught sanitation methods to rural women, and by instructing mothers in the importance of preventing food spoilage, sterilizing bottles, and disinfecting wounds, she is credited with saving countless lives.

When the Civil War broke out, Jarvis and her clubs refused to take sides, nursing North and South alike. Jarvis let Union general George McClellan use her home in Webster, West Virginia, as he planned the war's first land battle. But she had one stipulation—her house was open to any wounded soldiers, blue or gray.

After the war Jarvis organized a family picnic honoring mothers, called Mother's Friendship Day, to reunite warring sides of the community. While the band played "Auld Lang Syne," teary-eyed neighbors shook hands and hugged.

After Jarvis's death in 1905, her daughter Anna Jarvis organized a memorial service for her on the third anniversary of her death, and, the next year, a memorial service for all mothers. Services for the first Mother's Day were held at Andrews Methodist Episcopal Church in Grafton, now the Mother's Day Shrine. In her mother's former church, 407 people celebrated the first official Mother's Day on May 10, 1908.

But the younger Jarvis's work didn't end there. She persuaded West Virginia governor William Glasscock to proclaim a statewide Mother's Day in 1910 and then started working on U.S. president Woodrow Wilson. He ordered the second Sunday of May be recognized nationally as Mother's Day, and the holiday is now celebrated in at least fifty countries.

The historical Mother's Day church, built in downtown Grafton in1873, is open for tours weekdays. An annual Mother's Day service still recognizes all mothers. The Anna Jarvis Birthplace Museum in Webster hosts a two-day festival on Mother's Day weekend.

The trees, incidentally, were spared during the timber boom because they were on private property, a mountain resort. Later the land was donated to the state. Among the park's many ancient trees is a 500-year-old hemlock with a circumference of 21 feet that was 121 feet tall until lightning lopped off a segment of the tree's top a few years ago. Among the park's maze of well-

The Birth of Father's Day

Just two months after the first official Mother's Day was celebrated, on July 5, 1908, the first Father's Day observance was held 20 miles away at Williams Memorial Methodist Episcopal Church in Fairmont.

The preceding December a mine explosion in nearby Monongah had killed 362 men, leaving 250 widows and more than 1,000 children grieving. Grace Fletcher Clayton, a minister's daughter still missing her own father, persuaded her pastor to perform a special Mass to honor and remember fathers. Although it didn't become an annual event until 1972, the hundreds who attended long remembered the service.

Clayton didn't follow through to get West Virginia to proclaim an annual Father's Day, so credit for the national observance goes to a Washington woman who petitioned her state for the holiday in 1910. But the fact remains that Rev. Robert Webb's service in 1908 was the first Father's Day, and signs at Fairmont's entrances proclaim this.

Although the original Father's Day church building was torn down to make way for a new church in 1922, the congregation, now called Central United Methodist, still celebrates Father's Day with special services on the third Sunday each June. The site on Third Street and Fairmont Avenue is marked with a West Virginia historical marker.

Grandparent's Day Started by Mother of Fifteen Children

A younger holiday, Grandparent's Day, came about through the efforts of Marian McQuade, but you'll find no shrine in her hometown of Oak Hill, only a sign on US 19 commemorating her efforts. This mother of fifteen lobbied for five years until West Virginia governor Arch Moore proclaimed May 27, 1973, as the first official Grandparent's Day.

McQuade, who had started the "Past 80 Party" in Richwood for all West Virginia octogenarians, was saddened by the chronic loneliness of many nursing home residents. She hoped a national holiday would bring attention to their plight. "They load these people up with gifts at Christmas," she said, "but leave them alone the other 364 days. I want there to be another day to visit."

West Virginia's Grandparent's Day was only the beginning. Buoyed by her success, McQuade worked through U.S. Senators Robert Byrd and Jennings Randolph to create a national observance. The date was changed to September to signify "the autumn years." In 1978, President Jimmy Carter designated the first Sunday after Labor Day as National Grandparent's Day when the proposal received unanimous approval in Congress. The first observance occurred in 1979.

manicured trails, you'll come across imposing stands of yellow birch, red oak, black cherry, maple, chestnut, and beech. As you might imagine, the scene here during the mid-October foliage season is unforgettable.

Cathedral State Park is about a mile east of the town of Aurora. It's open year-round from 6:00 A.M. to 10:00 P.M. Guided park-ranger tours are available by appointment, from spring through fall. Call ahead for hours and special programs (304–735–3771).

After a hike through Cathedral, you might come away feeling a bit spiritual. Hold on to that sensation, because just down the road in Horse Shoe Run is *Our Lady of the Pines,* supposedly the smallest church in the forty-eight states and one of the smallest Roman Catholic churches in the world. The 16-foot-by-11-foot stone structure, with six West Virginia–made stained-glass windows, a tiny altar, and six pews, can seat at best a dozen worshippers. It was built in 1957 by a local family and today is visited by thousands each year who come to pray, walk the beautiful grounds, and send postcards from the adjacent post office, also one of the smallest anywhere.

Our Lady of the Pines is open daily during daylight hours from spring through fall. The church is tucked away on a small knoll off U.S. Highway 219 near Thomas. There is no admission charge—though donations are welcome—and there is no phone.

Every great river starts with a trickle from a spring. The Potomac River is no exception. About 6 miles south of Horse Shoe Run is the source spring of the mighty Potomac, a river that serves as a border between West Virginia and Maryland for more than 100 miles. Marking the spot of the spring is *Fairfax Stone,* a boundary point established by the wealthy British colonist Thomas Lord Fairfax. The spring marked the northwestern border of Fairfax's land holdings, a vast real estate empire that included what is now almost half of Virginia and most of the West Virginia Eastern Panhandle. You can visit this spot and pay homage to Fairfax and the river that went on to define so much of the history of these states. It's located 6 miles south of Silver Lake off a gravel road off US 219 (look for the sign on 219) in a remote stretch of country that must have looked much the same as when Fairfax himself was surveying the area. The Fairfax Stone State Monument is open year-round dawn to dusk. However, do not try to negotiate this road in heavy snowfall. The marker is actually a couple of miles down the gravel road, and if you get stuck there's not a whole lot of traffic coming in or out of this way-off-the-beaten-path site.

More outdoor adventures await north at Terra Alta. The serpentine drive on County Road 53 qualifies as an escapade on its own. At Terra Alta, you can pause at *Alpine Lake Resort,* a former hunting preserve now operating as a 2,300-acre community with its own lake, beaches, indoor swimming pool, tubing run, eighteen-hole golf course, and Nordic ski trails. For reservations at the thirty-five-room motel or restaurant, call (800) 752–7179.

The town's *Americana Museum* is one of the few places you can examine a sleigh taxi, which shares space with twenty horse-drawn vehicles, a Diamond T pickup, and an antique fire engine. Visitors may also wander through an old country store, a nineteenth-century post office, a weaver's cabin, a blacksmith shop, and a nineteenth-century doctor's office outfitted with both bloodletting implements and early X-ray equipment. Costumed interpreters demonstrate the trades and answer questions. The museum is open Sunday afternoon from the last Sunday in June through the second Sunday in October. Call (304) 789–2361 for an appointment. Admission is $2.00 for adults and $1.00 for children under sixteen.

About 10 miles north in **Cranesville Swamp,** you enter a "frost pocket," set aside by The Nature Conservancy as a living artifact from earlier, colder times. Described as Canada in the South, this high, bowl-shaped preserve is the southernmost tamarack (a deciduous pine) forest, a spot where you also see red spruce, insectivorous sundew plants, and cranberries. Birders tramp these boardwalk paths to sight golden-crowned kinglets, saw-whet owls, alder flycatchers, and other rare birds. The swamp has been designated a National Natural Landmark, and its trails are open year-round at no charge.

Isolation and poverty have long been associated with the largely impenetrable hills and hollows of West Virginia. As such, the state has seen its share of social engineering experiments, including the nation's first federal New Deal homestead, **Arthurdale.** This western Preston County community on State Route 92 about 25 miles southwest of Cranesville was the pet project of then first lady Eleanor Roosevelt. The federal homesteading plan she helped craft served two purposes: to provide affordable, quality housing and to help boost the Depression-era economy of America's rural areas. Arthurdale became the prototype community, with more than 165 houses built here during 1933.

All but one of the original homes are intact in this tidy community of wide green lots and little white houses. A number of the original homesteading families, many from impoverished mining camps, remain at Arthurdale and help to organize reunions, dinners, and old-time dances. The original Great Hall and some of the stone shops where cooperative craft and manufacturing ventures were housed can be visited. Although the first lady would bring in her wealthy friends to buy quilts and furniture, Arthurdale was not a business success. But many children had healthier, more enriched lives in the experimental agricultural settlement. While the Arthurdale Cemetery is the only cooperative still functioning, Arthurdale Heritage is very much alive in its programs, tours, and July New Deal Festival. Now a National Historic District, Arthurdale's homes, Esso station, New Deal Homestead Museum, and craft shop make an interesting tour. On summer weekends interpreters introduce visitors to the farm animals and life in the settlement houses. Arthurdale Heritage is open weekdays year-round from 10:00 A.M. to 2:00 P.M. and from May through October on Saturday from noon to 5:00 P.M. and Sunday from 2:00 P.M. to 5:00 P.M. Admission is $5.00 for adults, $4.00 for senior citizens, and $3.00 for children under twelve. You can visit their Web site at www.arthurdaleheritage.org or contact them at (304) 864–3959.

Virtually splitting Preston County into two equal halves is the **Cheat River,** which comes out of the mountains of the Potomac Highlands and flows north through the state before emptying into Cheat Lake and ultimately the Monongahela River north of Morgantown.

The Cheat, with its boulder-strewn shoreline and glaciated gorges, is easily the premier white-water river in northern West Virginia and perhaps third in the state, behind only the Gauley and New Rivers. Consequently the area has attracted several professional river outfitters. For rafting trips on the Cheat, as well as the Potomac, Shenandoah, and other fabled rivers of this region, hook up with either **Appalachian Wildwaters** (304–454–2475 or 800–624–8060; www.awrafts.com) in nearby Rowlesburg or **Cheat River Outfitters** (304–329–2024 or 888–99–RIVER) in Albright. Both outfitters offer a range of trips, including overnight, weekend, and extended camping trips. Late-spring trips tend to be the most exciting (because of the high water levels) and are often the most crowded.

When the hunger pangs hit, head west to Fairmont, the seat of Marion County, and get ready for an epicurean masterpiece. **Muriale's,** 1742 Fairmont Avenue, on the south side of town, is probably the best Italian restaurant in the state. The local landmark is famous for its huge portions of wonderful lasagna, ravioli, rigatoni, spaghetti, and cavatelli. Included in the *Who's Who in America's Restaurants,* Muriale's is testament to northern West Virginia's rich Italian heritage. With six separate dining rooms, it's a family-friendly kind of place that attracts regular diners from as far away as Pennsylvania and Maryland. Although the star attraction is the pasta, made fresh on the premises, Muriale's also serves hearty steaks, hoagies, pizza, and a wide variety of seafood. It's open daily year-round (except Christmas) from 11:00 A.M. to 9:00 P.M. Call (304) 363–3190.

One of northern West Virginia's unique treats is the pepperoni roll, invented by Giuseppe Agiro in 1927 as a one-hand lunch for coal miners. His **Country Club Bakery** on Country Club Road in Fairmont still makes those 6-inch buns baked around two sticks of pepperoni. It's best hot out of the oven. The Country Club is open daily, except Wednesday and Sunday. Of course, you can now find pepperoni rolls at Morgantown, Clarksburg, Weston, and out-of-the-way delis in between.

If you've already paid homage to mothers by visiting the International Mother's Day Shrine in Grafton, now you've got your chance to salute fathers. Following Grafton's lead, Fairmont's Central United Methodist Church, 301 Fairmont Avenue, was the site of the first observance of Father's Day on July

5, 1908. You can even have your Father's Day cards imprinted here with a special stamp. The so-called **Father's Day Church** is available for tours by calling (304) 366–3351.

While you're in Fairmont, drop over to the **Marion County Museum** on Adams Street beside the courthouse. The former sheriff's home contains three stories of rooms, each room furnished with the artifacts representing a different era in U.S. history. History seen through West Virginia eyes, that is. The emphasis here is on West Virginia's history and its contribution to our nation. The young at heart will love the collection of antique toys and kiddie-scale furniture in the Children's Room. It's open Monday through Saturday, 10:00 A.M. to 2:00 P.M. in the summer and weekdays only (the same hours) September through May. For special arrangements call (304) 367–5398.

Just north of Fairmont, a rustic log fort perches on a slope above the confluence of Prickett's Creek and the Monongahela River. A re-creation of the original 1774 Prickett's Fort, this building serves up living history of the late eighteenth century in **Prickett's Fort State Park.** Costumed interpreters demonstrate colonial crafts such as spinning, blacksmithing, weaving, and gunsmithing. The fort sheltered colonists in sixteen tiny cabins within its stockade walls. When Indian attack threatened, up to eighty families would rush into the fort and stay for days or weeks. During its summer season the park also offers concerts, Elderhostel classes, and a three-day camp, which allows older children to learn spinning, dyeing, blacksmithing, and natural history. The park is open mid-April through the end of October, Monday through Saturday 10:00 A.M. to 5:00 P.M. and Sunday from noon to 5:00 P.M. Admission is charged for the historical attractions, but the trails and picnic area are free. Call (800) CALL–WVA or (304) 363–3030 for more information.

Immediately west of Fairmont is the small community of Monongah, a coal-mining town that was the scene of a devastating mine explosion that killed 362 men in 1907. Congress reacted by toughening mining laws, but in 1968 another explosion less than a mile from Monongah killed 78 men. The victims of these tragedies—and others like them that too often plagued the Mountain State—are remembered at the **West Virginia Miner's Memorial,** a moving, bronze sculpture located in Mary Lou Retton Park, named in honor of the famous Olympic gold medal winner and Marion County native. The park, just off US 19, is open daily from dawn to dusk. A stone monument also stands in the town of Monongah.

The gently rolling countryside around Fairmont is dotted with beautiful dairy farms and pastureland. Agriculture is still an important part of the economy, and here you can trace its colorful roots by visiting the **West Augusta Historical Society Round Barn** in Mannington, 10 miles west of Fairmont on

US 250. The striking round, wooden barn, commonly known as the Mannington Round Barn, was built as a dairy barn in 1912 by Amos Hamilton. Its unusual architecture was commonplace on dairy farms in Pennsylvania, West Virginia, and Virginia during the late 1800s and early 1900s. This particular barn is the only such restored structure in the state and one of the few remaining south of the Mason-Dixon Line.

Most round barns, including this one, were built into the side of a small hill, enabling the farmer to drive a hay wagon directly into the loft from the rear. Farmer Hamilton's round barn not only sheltered cows and feed, but also was the main residence for the family. Your tour will undoubtedly start in the kitchen and wend around the three stories of living space, which is now full of family heirlooms and farm artifacts—milk coolers, lard presses, butter churns, a children's sleigh, a carriage, and a horse-drawn potato picker. There are even some early West Virginia coal-mining tools on display.

The round barn is open on Sunday, May through September, 1:30 to 4:00 P.M. Special tours also can be arranged any time of the year for small groups. In addition, the barn hosts a quilting exhibition every Thursday from 9:00 A.M. to 1:00 P.M., and visitors are encouraged to join the circle. A small admission price of $2.00 per person is charged. Nearby, the ***West Augusta Historical Society Museum*** contains three floors of Civil War–era Americana, from brass ox-horn covers to music boxes. For more information contact the historical society at (304) 986–2636 or (304) 986–1089.

West Augusta Historical Society Round Barn

Morgantown

From Mannington, head east back into Fairmont and pick up US 19 north to Morgantown. One of the most interesting communities in the Mountain State, Morgantown is a harmonic blend of blue bloods, blue collars, bohemians, and college students. It stands as its own subregion in this book because it's really unlike any other community in West Virginia. It is to the Mountain State what Austin is to Texas, Boulder is to Colorado, Madison is to Wisconsin. It's an industrial town with long ties to the nearby northern coalfields and famed glass factories, but it's also a high-tech town anchored by research laboratories maintained by the federal government. **West Virginia University** (WVU), with some 25,000 students spread across three separate campuses, keeps what would probably be a sleepy town lively year-round.

The university also provides a cultural backdrop that is probably unrivaled among West Virginia cities. The **WVU Creative Arts Center** schedules more than 500 music, theater, and performance art shows a year as well as a host of visual art exhibits. Tours and performance schedules can be had by calling (304) 293–4841, extension 3108 or visiting www.ccarts.wvu.edu/. The center is located about a mile north of downtown off Beechurst Avenue on the Evansdale campus of the university.

Another interesting campus site is the **Core Arboretum,** run by the WVU biology department, featuring 3 miles of trails that wend through a forest of virtually every type of hardwood and pine tree native to West Virginia. Along the way you'll also see an amazing variety of wildflowers, shrubs, and decorative plants common to the state. It's located opposite the arts center on Beechurst. For special tours and bloom and foliage information, you can call the biology department at (304) 293–5201.

Probably the best place to begin your familiarization with the WVU campus is, strangely enough, in downtown Morgantown. Now at One Waterfront Plaza in the Wharf District, the **WVU Visitors Resource Center** operates out of the first floor of a multistory building next to the Morgantown Radisson Hotel. In a few minutes of maneuvering through the high-tech, interactive displays, you'll hear the marching band, learn the layout, and find out more about West Virginia's largest university than if you read five brochures. The exhibit follows the course of the university's PRT (Personal Rapid Transit), so the next thing you may want to do is hop into one of the little blue and yellow cars waiting a few blocks away. Or you may opt for a guided bus tour. Either way, if you start here you'll learn about WVU's public offerings: the library, Mountainlair student center, Cook-Hayman Pharmacy Museum, WVU Creative Arts

Touchdown Mountaineers!

In the Empire State, it's the Big Apple. In California, it's the City of Angels. Illinois boasts the Windy City. Go down the list and you'll see that every state has its version of the Big City. Yes, some West Virginians will even say they have one in Charleston, or perhaps Huntington. But in reality, the biggest city in West Virginia isn't a city at all. It's a football stadium filled to capacity on a gorgeous autumn afternoon. Of course, we're talking about the 66,000-seat Mountaineer Field on the campus of West Virginia University in Morgantown, a sporting shrine of sorts that holds at least 10,000 more people than the entire city of Charleston. While the Mountaineers may not win every time they take the field, it's always a celebration in Morgantown on a football Saturday. If you plan to go, be wise and take a pair of earplugs . . . or two pairs. Decibel levels after a Mountaineer touchdown have been known to eclipse the noise level of a runway during a jet takeoff.

Center, and the WVU Student Recreation Center with its new climbing wall ($7.00 a session).

While you're still down by the Monongahela River, you may want to stroll through a few shops, perhaps check out what's happening at the *Hazel Ruby McQuain Park Amphitheatre,* where both the Wheeling Symphony and Patty Lovelace have recently performed. You can also stop by the *Morgantown Radisson Hotel* for a Swedish massage in the spa or a session with the slot machines in the cigar bar. Or you can rent a bicycle at Wamsley or Whitetail Cycles and shoot out of town on the Caperton, Decker Creek, or Mon River Trails for miles.

Despite its skyscraping buildings and energetic downtown, Morgantown has an outdoorsy feel. Hiking boots and parkas appear on the streets as often as suits. The 330-mile *Allegheny Trail* begins at nearby Bruceton Mills and wends its way south to meet the Appalachian Trail at Peters Mountain on the Virginia–West Virginia border. Kayaking, canoeing, and rafting are popular activities on the Cheat, and it's possible to go caving in local wild caves. If you're in town in mid-April, you can catch the annual *Outdoor Film Festival,* sponsored by Adventure's Edge outfitters on 131 Pleasant Street. Call Jan Kiger at (304) 296–9007 for more information.

Scratch around in Morgantown's past and you'll find glassmaking at its core. Although most local glassmaking operations except for *Gentile Glass* in Star City (304–599–2750) have ceased, you can visit the Riverside Glass Museum at the *Seneca Center* on weekends and browse through a variety of shops in this renovated glass factory on Beechurst Avenue. You'll even find some Seneca glass for sale in the antiques shops, but some of the finest examples are not for sale—they're on display at the **Glasshouse Grille** (304–296–8460), a truly fine restaurant in the etching room of the old factory.

If it's music, indie films, and nightlife you're looking for, the club **123 Pleasant Street** has everything from rock to jazz to rockabilly. Hank Williams III plays the club frequently, doing the music of his granddad, his dad, and then his own. Check out their schedule on the Web site, www.123pleasantstreet.com. The **Blue Moose Cafe,** at 248 Walnut Street, draws connoisseurs of good coffee and good acoustic music. It serves up live music at its new music venue, the **Rosewood Theatre,** half a block up Walnut Street, several times a week, hosting local, regional, and national musicians of all genres. You may also walk in on fiction readings, poetry slams, or art receptions at this culturally conscious cybercafe. And to chill out, you can come in for a chair massage on Sunday afternoon. To check Blue Moose's schedule, call (304) 292–8999 or log on to www.theblue moosecafe.com.

If you have a hankering for sudsy sustenance, head over to the **West Virginia Brewing Company** at 1291 University Avenue. It's billed as West Virginia's first brewpub, and the collegiate types that pack the cozy bar give testimony that the house-crafted stouts, cream ales, and pilsners are fine. The Brewing Company is also outstanding in Morgantown's entertainment scene, hosting a weekly jazz night and a fiddle jam every Wednesday, as well as live bands on weekends. Call (304) 296–BREW to find out what's happening.

When you're downtown during the day, hop into a local gallery, pub, or shop. **The Appalachian Gallery** (44 High Street, 304–291–5299) is known for its rotating exhibits of works by regional artists. Another tucked-away find is **Garo-Tomlinson Collection,** 111 Walnut Street, a gallery with a surprisingly large selection of original graphic works, mostly from the late 1800s and early 1900s.

At the Old Post Office, 107 High Street, you can browse through the **Monongalia Arts Center.** Inside the neoclassical-style building, with its pronounced Doric engaged columns, is Benedum Gallery, housing touring exhibits from around the country. The adjoining Tanner Theater regularly stages plays and community events. The complex is open weekdays 9:00 A.M. to 4:00 P.M. and on weekends for special engagements. For more information, call (304) 292–3325.

Lightly populated West Virginia probably isn't the first place to come to mind when thinking of rapid-transit systems, but one of the best in the world can be found in Morgantown. It's the **Personal Rapid Transit,** or PRT, an electrically powered system that transports WVU students to classes across the three-campus university. (If you've ever ridden the People Mover at Disneyland, this is much the same concept.) The computer-automated cars, resembling small subway vehicles, whisk as many as twenty standing students per car at a time at a comfortable 30 miles per hour. Nearly 14,000 students ride the seventy-plus cars every day; the longest trips last just over ten minutes. The PRT stops on Walnut Street, Beechurst Avenue, and near the university's student housing complex, engineering department, and medical center. Studied by city planners, environmentalists, and transit officials worldwide, the thirty-two-year-old WVU system has transported more than 60 million passengers without a single injury or a single hydrocarbon released into the air. Students ride the system for free, but visitors are also encouraged to hop aboard. Adults pay a $1.00 round-trip fee, a minimal charge considering this is one of the most interesting and relaxing ways to tour Morgantown and the university. The PRT is open Monday through Friday 6:30 A.M. to 10:00 P.M. and Saturday 9:30 A.M. to 5:00 P.M. It's closed Sunday and during university breaks. For more information call (304) 293–5011.

October, as mentioned throughout this book, is a wonderful time to tour West Virginia. In Morgantown it's especially enticing given that this is when the annual ***Mountaineer Balloon Festival*** lifts off. The color in the sky nearly matches the blazing foliage as dozens of hot-air balloons ascend and exceed the height of the surrounding mountains. Hart Field, aka Morgantown Municipal Airport, is the site of this festival, which also features an array of balloon races, carnival rides, music attractions, food booths, crafts, and games for the kids. The fete is usually held in the middle of the month, a time when the leaves in the surrounding countryside have reached their peak. In a state that's brimming with festivals, this may be one of the best. For exact dates call (304) 296–8356.

Spectacular as it is, you don't have to settle on just watching the hot-air balloons from the ground. Try flying in one! It's possible through ***Fun Aviation Inc.,*** a balloon-flying service that will take you up for an hour-long champagne flight for $200. (Don't worry, the passengers are the only ones doing the drinking.) If you get really hooked, the Morgantown company will also offer flight instruction classes. Fun Aviation is located at 156 Fields Park Road. Call (304) 594–3959 for more information.

After a busy day in Morgantown, you need a place to rest those weary bones. The regal ***Clarion Hotel Morgan*** is located in the heart of downtown in an eight-story brick building. It is the place for those who like to ditch the car and walk around town, sample the Wharf District, or use the Personal Rapid Transit system. The hotel will happily store bikes overnight. The Morgan celebrated its seventy-fifth birthday in 2000 with a $3 million face-lift and restoration. The lobby is still a grand entryway of oak panels, oak pillars, crystal chandeliers, and 24-foot ceilings, but the eighty rooms have been redesigned for today's traveler. Each minisuite has an oversize desk where real work can be accomplished, dataports, refrigerators, microwaves, and king-size beds. In the morning, you can grab a fresh pastry or make your own waffle in the breakfast lounge. The eighth-floor restaurant has a working fireplace, sunken bar, and new American cuisine with scrumptious desserts. For reservations call (304) 292–8200.

When you're ready to venture farther afield, visit Anna Brown on Bull Run Road; you'll find the place easily—it's the one with all the herbs and lawn sculptures. Anna runs *Brown's Creations in Clay* from the series of out-buildings that house her gift shop, studio, kilns, commercial kitchen, and one ton of West Virginia clay.

Anna keeps a mining lamp in the corner because she doesn't want to waste time if the electricity should go out. It appears she never sleeps. While she hand-builds pottery, she is dehydrating ramps (wild leeks) for the biscuit mix she sells. She presses the herbs she grows into her clay creations as decoration. The variety of uses she dreams up for her products is almost as creative as the products themselves. Her tea-bag holders fit neatly over the tops of her tea mugs, her spoon rests fit a variety of spoons, and her hanging acorns double as wren houses. Brown's work is sold on QVC, at Tamarack, the Greenbrier, and over the phone (304–206–6656), but it's more fun to buy at her shop. This artist is sweetness personified, and if she takes a liking to you, she'll tell you five ways to use ramps in modern recipes. The shop is open Monday to Friday 9:00 A.M. to 6:00 P.M. and Saturday 11:00 A.M. to 6:00 P.M.

While you're up in that neck of the woods, you could take in a *Joe Pyle Auction* at the Clinton District Fire Hall, off US 119. (Just follow the JOE R. PYLE auction signs.) On Tuesday night and Saturday, Pyle auctions off steamer chests, boxes, and bags full of estate valuables and junk. Check the Web site (www.joerpyleauctions.com) or call (724) 324–9000 for information on upcoming auctions.

And if you find yourself in need of some quiet, contemplative time, you may visit the *Good Counsel Friary,* at 493 Tyrone Road off Route 857 (which is off US 119 after the airport). The first thing you'll notice is the twenty-three-room, arched, stone castle on the right side of Tyrone Road. Park between that building and the Franciscan chapel. The *Bible Walk* in the hardwood forest behind the friary is always open, although the life-size mannequins representing biblical characters may seem a little spooky at night, especially after a strong wind has left Abraham or Joseph prostrate across the path. Each scene is paired with a biblical passage, and the walk ends with the Stations of the Cross.

The Roman Catholic friary has opened its facilities to individuals and groups seeking a retreat experience. Meals are served daily, and recreation facilities include basketball, volleyball, and horseshoes. For more information call (304) 594–1714 between 9:00 A.M. and 4:00 P.M. Tuesday or Thursday.

For many West Virginia artisans, works that are not sold at craft shows or other irregularly scheduled events too often gather dust in the back rooms of studios and houses. ***Jackie's Gifts and Things*** in the town of Hundred, about a half-hour drive west of Morgantown, has created a market for some local artisans with perhaps underexposed talents. Jackie's shop exhibits works from about two dozen craftspeople, including folk toys, quilts, paintings, jewelry, stuffed animals, and floral arrangements. Jackie's Gifts and Things is typically open Monday, Wednesday, Friday, and Saturday 10:00 A.M. to 4:00 P.M. It's located on Main Street (US 250) in "downtown" Hundred. Call (304) 775–3326 for more information or special appointments.

While in Hundred, be sure to detour off US 250 at County Road 13 and drive over the ***Fish Creek Covered Bridge,*** a 36-foot-long structure built in 1881 and spanning the namesake creek.

Places to Stay in Mountaineer Country

AURORA

Brookside Inn
U.S. Highway 50
(304) 735–6344
(800) 588–6344
Expensive

CLARKSBURG

Holiday Inn
Interstate 79 and U.S
Highway 50E
(304) 842–5411
Moderate

Jackson Square B&B
154 East Main Street
(888) 605–7233
www.bbonline.com/wv
/jacksonsquare
Inexpensive

FAIRMONT

Comfort Inn
Interstate 79, exit 133
(304) 367–1370
Moderate

KINGWOOD

Preston County Inn
112 West Main Street
(800) 252–3271
www.prestoncountyinn.com
Moderate

MORGANTOWN

Clarion Hotel Morgantown
127 High Street
(304) 292–8200
www.clarionhotelmorgan.com
Moderate to expensive

Lakeview Golf Resort & Spa
1 Lakeview Drive
(304) 594–1111
www.lakeviewresort.com
Moderate

Radisson Hotel at Waterfront
2 Waterfront Plaza
(800) 780–5733
Moderate

SHINNSTON

The Gillum House B&B
35 Walnut Street
(304) 592–0177
(888) 592–0177
Moderate

TERRA ALTA

Alpine Lake Resort
State Route 7
(304) 789–2481
(800) 752–7179
Inexpensive

Places to Eat in Mountaineer Country

CLARKSBURG

Minard's Spaghetti Inn
813 East Pike Street
(304) 623–1711
Inexpensive

FAIRMONT

Village Bistro
1825 Locust Avenue
(304) 366–3711
Inexpensive

KINGWOOD

Heldreth and Sandy's Family Style Restaurant
State Route 26 South
(304) 329–1145
Budget

MORGANTOWN

The Restaurants of Historic Downtown Morgantown
(40 restaurants within 1-mile radius), Interstate 68, exit 1
University Avenue
(304) 292–0168
(800) 458–7373
www.tourmorgantown.com
/dining.php

Glass House Grill
Seneca Center
(304) 296–8460
Moderate

TERRA ALTA

Alpine Lake Resort
State Route 7
(304) 789–2481
Inexpensive

FOR MORE INFORMATION

Bridgeport Clarksburg Convention and Visitors Bureau
(800) 368–4324
www.greater_bridgeport.com

Greater Morgantown Convention and Visitors Bureau
(304) 292–5081 or (800) 458–7373

Grafton Taylor County Convention and Visitors Bureau
(304) 265–0164

Marion County Convention and Visitors Bureau
(800) 834–7365
www.marioncub.com

Index

About the Author

Su Clauson-Wicker is a Virginian who has been spending a month of Saturdays and Sundays in West Virginia each year since 1985. She is a regional travel writer and author of the *Inn-to-Inn Walking Guide for Virginia and West Virginia*, which won the West Virginia Best Book Award in 2001. Her work has appeared in *Blue Ridge Country, Country Living, MD News*, the *Cleveland Plain Dealer*, the *Washington Post, Recreation News*, and other publications.

Her diverse career has included a decade as editor of *Virginia Tech Magazine* as well as positions in journalism, educational television, medical public relations, child welfare, and historical interpretation as a colonial "wench." She lives in Blacksburg, Virginia, where she practices therapeutic healing touch, staffs a crisis hotline, and writes about a variety of topics.